RED MAN'S RELIGION

RED MAN'S

RELIGION

BELIEFS AND PRACTICES OF THE INDIANS
NORTH OF MEXICO

Ruth M. Underhill

THE UNIVERSITY OF CHICAGO PRESS

Chicago & London

THE UNIVERSITY OF CHICAGO PRESS, CHICAGO 60637
THE UNIVERSITY OF CHICAGO PRESS, LTD., LONDON

© 1965 by The University of Chicago
Third Impression 1974
Printed in the United States of America

Designed by Adrian Wilson
Woodcuts by Dianne Weiss

ISBN: 0—226—84166—9 (clothbound); 0—226—84167—7 (paperbound)
Library of Congress Catalog Card Number: 65—24985

FOREWORD

This study is intended as a companion to the author's *Red Man's America*. The details of social organization and material culture necessary for the understanding of religious usages must be looked for in that volume itself or in the excellent studies listed here after the appropriate chapters. Like *Red Man's America*, the book is intended primarily for those making their first acquaintance with the First Americans, as they were in history and as they are today. Therefore, it is written in non-technical language, but it is hoped that even the experts may find in it some useful suggestions.

The scope of one volume is necessarily limited so that some areas and ceremonial developments have been left for future workers. This first attempt at a continental survey must be considered as exploratory and as proposing questions of origin and relationship rather than settling them.

Warm thanks must go to my helpers, Jenny Whalen, Barbara Reed, and Miriam De Mille, who looked up references and collated material. Editha Watson and Mary Webster did invaluable editorial work. Nina Webb made unusual efforts to get the typing done when needed. Gertrude Pierce spent time and artistic talent on the maps.

DENVER, COLORADO
January 1965

# CONTENTS

ILLUSTRATIONS

MAPS

INDIANS AND THE SUPERNATURAL

The big wooden dance house near Puget Sound had been newly built in the old Indian style. That meant a ceiling so high that men could only just reach the rafters when they drummed on them with their long poles. Spaced on the earthen floor, a hundred feet long, were the four huge fires. No need for a tiny "Indian style fire" in this country of great forests! The guests around the wall sat on tiers of benches, men on one side, women on the other, while at the back sat the host tribe, wearing blankets over their ordinary clothes. One blanket was an ancient Chilkat, of white dog's wool, with decorations in yellow, turquoise, and black.

The talking ceased when we heard from that rear section a low moaning. A man was swaying forward and back, moaning louder and louder. Suddenly he rose, leaped from his place, and began running down the room, circling the fires.

Enemy come!
Enemy come!

So my companions told me that he was chanting. Companions of his own, who had been sitting behind him, were running with him now, getting between him and the fire so that he should not rush into it and burn himself.

> Enemy come!
> Enemy come!

They were taking up the song while the men with poles pounded loudly on the rafters.

"He has got the war spirit," said my Indian neighbor reverently. "It's rare. Powerful!"

"But there is no war now."

"Spirit is powerful for lots of things. His grandfather had it. Oh, this is good! We feared no one would get a spirit this year."

The neighbor who told me this was glowing with enthusiasm. A spark of hope and confidence had been lighted in him and in that whole roomful of modern Indians, puzzled and frustrated by all the new ways that custom had forced upon them. What if there was no war! The coming of a spirit meant that Indian courage and ability were not dead.

A Mohave boy had died. The ten-foot-high funeral pyre had blazed for hours while his clan marched up and down, singing the saga of their early wanderings. Now and then someone had danced slowly toward the pyre to throw in some special gift. Now his comrades from the government school came out in football clothes to play a game in his honor. The game lasted until the fire died down, while girls cheered from the sidelines.

"You see," one of his classmates explained to me, "his soul played with us. Feel happy before it goes."

"Goes where?"

But here the boy was vague. He had not been brought up with his eyes on an afterworld, as many Christians are. "Maybe under big river [the Colorado]. Maybe come back some day."

He went back to the game.

We had entered the ceremonial tipi at dusk and sat upright on the carpet of white sage while the drum, rattle, and staff passed around the circle. Each man held the staff and shook the rattle while the man beside him drummed faster than I ever heard rain-drops rattle on a roof.

> I walk the peyote road.
> It is a good road.

We had eaten four of the nauseous-tasting buttons. I found them nauseating but an Indian mentor told me later, "Peyote doesn't make you sick unless you have pride in your heart." (An impersonal investigating attitude, I think he meant.)

I had tried to eliminate such a white man's attitude, but perhaps some shreds remained, for I got no vision. I had seen the heads of others nodding in time to the drum beats. Most of them did not have a vision, I knew, for that takes more buttons than these Oklahoma Indians could afford. They were happy in the feeling that they were on the Road together, the Peyote Road, revealed especially to Indians. It is a hard road, for those who follow it should take no alcohol. They should work, they should not quarrel. Later, Indians of the five different tribes present would testify as to whether they had been able to keep on the Road.

Now midnight had come. There were no watches in the group, or, at least, none were looked at. The leader, the Road Man, had simply glanced at the stars through the smoke hole. He rose and we filed out behind him into the November night.

"I call the winds now," he told me. He lifted a birdbone whistle and blew four times, to the east, south, west, and north.

"Now we go in and I pray. For all in the world. Birds, horses, cows, people, Indians, white, Germans, Russia. All."

It should be plain from the episodes cited above that Indian religious beliefs cannot be summed up in the popular white man's formula of a Great Spirit and a Happy Hunting Ground. In former days, there were many small groups, with no autocratic chief, to whom the idea of a ruling deity, a Great Spirit, would be meaningless. They applied for help and comfort to their fellow beings on earth, the animals, the plants, even the rocks. Other groups did speak of a Being in an upper world, but this deity ranged all the way from a Great Holy Flame of Life to the California condor.

As for the Happy Hunting Ground, that was obviously a concept only for hunting people and there were many even of them who had never heard of it. Some tribes thought of the afterworld as a shadowy village, where the departed were homesick for their relatives. Fortunate dead of the Alaskan Eskimo could be seen in the aurora borealis playing their version of football. Navaho dead disappeared in the infinite, like drops of river water poured back into the stream.

Beliefs about the Supernatural sometimes form the whole subject of a book on religion but in this study they are secondary to action. The reason is twofold. For one thing, there are already compilations of mythology—or, from the Indian point of view, theology—some referring to the whole of North America, some to special regions. Few of them connect belief with the ceremonies and religious usage of the people and, in fact, this connection is often tenuous. Myth and ritual, which may be twins developed from the same ovum, can grow apart until the relationship is barely recognizable. To the thinker and seer, the belief was the religion and the ceremony simply its servant. To the Indian layman, the ceremony was the essential. From it he received security and courage, whereas the myth might be as vague as some fine points of theology are to the modern churchgoer.

Indian ceremonies, like ceremonies everywhere, were not original inventions. Some of their elements could be traced back, from source to source, as far as the Old World. But they were not copies. Each ceremony grew up within its local group, using some traditional and some borrowed elements, and adapting itself, through the generations, to local needs and knowledge. Yet according to Indian belief, the rites were on a plan established by Supernaturals long ago to avert evil, bring good fortune, and keep man's world operating as in the beginning.

Their purpose was not worship. Perhaps it can be thought of as the renewing of a partnership between man and the Supernaturals, to the benefit of both. Its proper conduct required a great deal of both officiant and layman. For the time being, they entered the sphere of the sacred and must purify themselves before stepping into it and out of the secular world. Those most concerned bathed, fasted, and sometimes underwent ordeals. Others at least observed rules and taboos. These rules had to do only with reverent treatment of the sacred, not with good behavior toward fellowmen.

Does this mean that license was permitted to mankind? By no means. Indian groups fought each other as white groups do today, but within the group, order was kept by the people themselves acting in their own interests. The groups were small. Each man needed help from his neighbor in hunting, house-building, or farming, and certainly in defense. Kindness was the best and, in fact, the only policy that he could afford to use; for if he failed in kindliness, the neighbors could fail him. In a ceremony, too, peace and unity were necessary if it was to be successful. And ceremonies, major and minor, were constantly held. There was no division between economic and religious life. The Indians' scant knowledge about the causes of sickness and weather made mysterious accidents likely at any moment so that no activity could be undertaken without a protecting ritual. Ceremonies great and small were the very fabric of life. They furnished the chief opportunities for learning, for feasting, for lovemaking. They gave courage to a lone hunter. They fused a group together in heartening ritual. They combined the functions not only of a church but of a school, clinic, theater, and law court.

All such activities will be discussed here as parts of religion. Some feel that this term should apply only to Christianity or at least to the monotheistic faiths. That would leave no word for the sincere and reverent approach, even the companionship with the Supernatural, which was the Indian way. And the word Supernatural must be used rather than any more definite term, such as *spirit* or *divinity*. Often the Indians did not think of the Powers, which they believed existed and influenced their lives, in such personal terms as does the white man.

Under religion we must include sorcery and witchcraft. With whites these imply the use of evil powers, but with Indians all power was one, and the distinction was in the way it was used. The same man, calling on the same power, could work evil or good according to his desire. Perhaps, from an Indian point of view, a white who calls on his God to harm those he hates would be practicing witchcraft.

The following pages attempt what must be considered a preliminary study of Indian religious behavior north of Mexico. The reason for not carrying it farther is simply the size of the undertaking. The beliefs and ceremonies described here are, as far as possible, those held before white settlement had changed Indian life. Some of the performances we see today have been a good deal altered since that time. My accounts of earlier rituals rely on descriptions given by the first white observers. This means the early 1660's for the East, middle 1800's for some of the West. Excellent and careful work has been done by a series of scholars, but not over the whole field.

There are gaps that cannot be filled, since the tribes they concern are gone. Sometimes we are reduced to using the accounts of early travelers, which may be brief jottings or misinterpretations, such as "They worship the Devil." Or some priestly missionary may have gone to the other extreme and translated the Indians' talk of Power as a belief in God. Even when Indians themselves gave information, the English words they must use could not carry their exact meaning. Once, at the Zuni festival of Shalako, I stood with a crowd of Zunis, looking through the window of a house where two spirit impersonators were being entertained. They had removed their masks and we could see their lips moving.

"They're prayin'," said the Zuni next to me. Later, however, when I read Dr. Bunzel's excellent translation of the ritual, it appeared that the supernatural visitors were simply recounting the incidents of their journey from the sacred lake. This is not prayer in the white man's sense of supplication, for the Zuni do not supplicate. It would take many words and much sympathy to explain their concept of friendly communion between the Supernaturals and their human hosts.

My Zuni acquaintance, at least, was describing a living ritual. It is harder to get Indian accounts of those that are past. Some old people can remember the ancient rites from childhood or from tales of those still older. And some have chosen to forget

2

RELIGION: ITS GEOGRAPHY AND HISTORY

The first Americans, anthropologists are agreed, did not originate in America. When they filtered over from Asia, perhaps fifteen or twenty thousand years ago, they already had a long history behind them. This was toward the end of the Ice Age, when, in the far northern part of the world, areas of ice had increased and areas of water had shrunk. Shallow Bering Strait had disappeared so that Asia and North America formed one continent, its two huge land masses joined by a tundra-like expanse over a thousand miles wide. Over this browsed the big game animals, the mammoth and the ancient bison, and after them came the hunters who were to become the Paleo- (or ancient) Indians.

They were probably Mongoloids. Most statements about that remote time must be informed guesses, but the few skeletal finds in eastern Asia at the end of the Ice Age indicate people of that dark-haired, dark-eyed stock which later differentiated into such well-known types as Chinese and Eskimo, as well as American Indians. Some think the Mongoloids had developed on the spot from the one another. It would seem that American Indians have not a religion but many religions.

All have in common a focus on duty toward the Supernatural, rather than toward fellowmen. In fact, the rituals described here contain nothing at all about kindness, honesty, and forgiving of trespasses. Yet Indians practiced these virtues quite as often as did any white man. (Let it be understood, of course, that this does not mean *always*.) They simply approached ethical behavior from a different angle. In addition to practical considerations, service to the Supernaturals often meant union with a group, and that involved right treatment of all. Concentrating one's thoughts on the purpose of a ceremony left no room for envy and hatred. The result has been hymned by George Catlin, our famous painter of Indians, who often said that he saw more kindly behavior among the Red Men than among his own people:

> I love a people who are honest without laws, who have no jails and no poorhouses.
> I love a people who keep the commandments without ever having read them or heard them preached from the pulpit.[2]

REFERENCES

General books on primitive religion: Eliade, 1949; Karsten, 1935; Norbeck, 1961; Pettazzoni, 1954; Radin, 1937. General articles in Publications of American Ethnological Society, 1964.

Books aiming toward some special conclusion: Durkheim, 1954; Goode, 1951; Hsu, 1952; Jensen, 1963; Radin, 1953; Yinger, 1957.

[2] Catlin, 1959, p. xxv.

final. With most groups, ideas about the Supernatural were still fluid. A new item of ritual learned from enemy or friend during trade or marriage added to the current equipment like a new weapon to an arsenal. Especially was a new art or property felt to need its own ritual so that it might be used successfully. Often its owner or priest came with it. He would naturally be jealous of his status and would guard his art from becoming public knowledge. Thus the various Hopi clans tell stories of arriving at their mesas each armed with its own particular rain-bringing ceremony. This was the clan's passport to citizenship. So, during the summer, the Hopi have ceremony after ceremony for rain, each the property of a special clan priesthood. Ceremonies have been arranged in a standard order, but there has been no attempt to place them all under one leadership as might be done in a centrally organized church. On the contrary, if a clan priesthood dies out, its ceremony is lost and its place in the calendar left vacant.

In groups less organized than the Hopi, the borrowed and inherited beliefs may contradict each other, but no one is troubled about explanation. A ceremonialist who practices some small rite for healing or divination is quite unaware of another using a very different rite. Or there may be two Supernaturals whose functions duplicate each other. Thinking of the well-ordered pantheon of the Greeks, I once inquired: "Are they relatives?"

"No-o."

"Do they know each other?"

That question seemed equally immaterial. Nor could I find if there was a difference between them. The final dictum was simply: "I don't know."

It is plain, then, that a complete picture of myths and ritual in any Indian group cannot be obtained without questioning many different individuals. And the result is no clear-cut picture, even for a single group. In fact the following survey of Indian religious usage seems like combing out a skein with threads of many sizes and colors. A strand that looks brilliant and easy to follow at one point is almost obliterated at another. Strands cross and tangle, so that beliefs acquired at different times and places contradict

them. Of these, a number have joined Christian churches, others
have no church at all, and a few have developed new churches
of their own. The material here comes from questions asked of
hundreds of Indians, during some thirty years' acquaintance with
various tribes.

Only certain individuals were even interested in my subject.
I came to agree with Radin that there are two very different
levels of religious understanding in any group.[1] One consists of
the few thinkers or seers, who inquire and meditate, and another
of the many non-thinkers or doers, who are content to carry out
the rules while intent on their daily work. They are somewhat
in the position of the modern patient who goes tractably from
one medical specialist to another without attempting to understand their prescriptions. That is to say, they go to ceremonies or
take part in them as they are bidden. To them it is the actions
that are important, and they are content to leave the reasons for
them to the ceremonialist.

The specialists among Indians are the medicine men, the priests,
or merely those with a philosophic turn of mind who think more
deeply than the average men and ask the *why* of behavior. Such
thinkers are rare among a hard-pressed, busy people, and they
become rarer the more remote their situation and the fewer their
contacts. The reason is simple. Thinkers must in the first place
be free, at least for part of the year, from the exacting routine
of food-getting. This gives time for thought, for questioning, and
perhaps for starting the framework of a theological structure.
The structures, however, cannot be built by one man alone. Remember the centuries of church councils and papal bulls that
went into deciding the details of Christian beliefs. The religious
leader must be stimulated by contact with others of his group
or of a different one. This rarely happens except when groups
can come together for protracted meetings. And opportunities
of that sort were not common in North America. But Indians
were eager for any ceremony or any part of a ceremony that
seemed to give power over life's difficulties.

Yet no Indian group considered its own religion complete and

[1] Radin, 1937, pp. 15–39.

primitive Pekin man of one hundred thousand years earlier. Whether this is so or whether they were invaders, the ancestors of our immigrants must have had a long time of living with other Mongoloids, sharing the shapes of stone tools and perhaps some simple rites for inducing good luck and averting evil. After our migrants had made their trek to the New World, other Mongoloids moved slowly south into Indonesia and the Pacific Islands. In those areas we find surprising parallels to some Indian ceremonies.

Some Indian myths and "superstitions" or beliefs about ways to avert evil are even more widely known. The fact that such occurrences are dotted all over the world may be due to separate inspiration by local thinkers. Yet it would be strange if these thinkers had waited to be inspired until the Ice Age had ended and they were established in new homes. Before that time, there had been ages when human beings of different degrees of development roamed about Eurasia. There must have been communication from group to group, since their tools were similar, sometimes identical, over huge areas. Surely they communicated something besides the usefulness of tool shapes. There was time for the ancestors of Indians to share, even if remotely, in that communication. We miss something if we study Indian customs entirely from the isolationist point of view. It is more interesting to see them as part of world history.

We cannot trace the exact route of the migrants from eastern Asia, for such camp sites as they left on the way, and perhaps on first arrival, must now be under water. Yet within the country there are sites that can be demonstrated by radiocarbon dating to have been abandoned some eleven thousand years ago, or in about 9,000 B.C. These are scattered sparsely over the country, with one site at the very southernmost tip of South America. We imagine the explorers, generation after generation, making their way south and east until they reached better hunting grounds and better climate. Finally the Ice Age, which had been waning by degrees, came to a halt about 8,000 B.C. Melting ice swelled the rivers and lakes of Alaska and flooded the Bering land bridge. The next arrivals from Asia would have to come by boat, and in the succeeding centuries some did.

For those within the country, this was a time of exploration and settlement. It may be thought of as the incubation period for Indian lifeways. This was the time when different groups established their types of subsistence and dwellings; and when dialects differentiated. Surely religious ideas were subject to stresses. There is no telling how different the migrant groups may have been and what varied concepts they may have brought. Yet the habit of learning and comparing must have gone on among them, as it has through all human history. If such a fashion as the Clovis point was common property over a wide area, it would be surprising if attitudes about birth, death, and sickness were not shared in the same way. In fact, under all Indian religions in North America there is a substratum, a layer of basic beliefs and practices, that unites them all.

Its essentials seem to be common world property, for relics of such beliefs and practices can be met almost anywhere. Yet, as the early Indian tools often developed forms unknown in the Old World, so these dealings with the Supernatural have been worked into elaborate ceremonies. In some parts of America that remained long untouched, we may find a primitive ceremony in more complete form than even in the motherland of Asia.

The simplest item in the substratum is the use of wonder-working objects such as tokens and amulets. The belief that an object which was present at a time of good luck may bring good luck again seems so instinctive that it may have been used by the earliest human beings. Spells, or magic-working by words, seem more sophisticated, but their use too is worldwide.

Another form of dealing with the Supernatural is the propitiation of animals to be killed and plants to be used. This also, it seems to me, might be of most ancient origin. We know that the most primitive hominids hunted large carnivores, and it seems likely that some muttering of apology and promise of good treatment would have stimulated their courage.

Three attitudes toward other human beings may be a later development, but they are deeply rooted in the Old World and the New. First of all, fear of the menstruating woman is widespread throughout the world. Female catamenia, related to childbearing, indicated a power impossible to males. In time, there

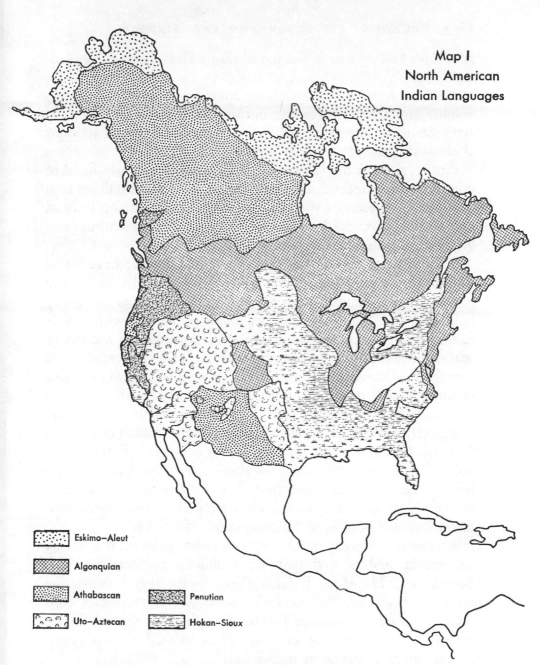

Map I
North American
Indian Languages

Eskimo–Aleut

Algonquian

Athabascan   Penutian

Uto–Aztecan   Hokan–Sioux

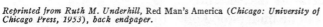

Reprinted from Ruth M. Underhill, Red Man's America *(Chicago: University of Chicago Press, 1953), back endpaper.*

grew up a feeling that it was harmful to all male activity, including ceremony.

A second form of fear-avoidance concerns the dead. Death was another mysterious power but, in this case, harmful to everyone. Attitudes toward the death fear vary from submission to attempts at eliminating it.

Finally, there is the reliance on some individual better fitted to cope with the Supernatural than the average. The medicine man or shaman also seems a worldwide phenomenon. Among Indians, he does not surrender his place to the priest until agriculture and group organization are well developed.

This substratum, inherited from the Old World, I have found to lie at the basis of most Indian religious behavior. In the simpler groups, it is seen quite uncovered, with no structure of ceremony built above it. The only rites are those connected with female functions or with death, and those are conducted by the family without assistance. All other approach to the Supernatural is through the shaman. At the other extreme are the elaborate rituals conducted by settled agriculturists, where the shaman has often been supplanted by the priest. The substratum here may seem completely covered until one meets the use of a sacred object or a formula. One may find that the warrior-farmers of the Creek federation exclude women from their annual purification ceremony "because they are dangerous." And the corn-growing Zuni, whose pageantry is the most elaborate north of Mexico, quarantine a widower because of his connection with death.

A mass of different beliefs and usages has grown up over the substratum, and at first they seem difficult to interpret. The Navaho and Hopi, for instance, have myths that concern the same Supernaturals. Yet the Hopis have hereditary priests, conducting public ceremonies for the benefit of a whole village. Navaho rites are for the cure of one individual who pays the chanter, though spectators may attend.

Such differences can be understood only by a study of the background and circumstances of different groups. Not that circumstances produce religion. We assume that all human beings are capable of that upsurge of fear and wonder that yearns toward a

Power greater than themselves. It is less in some individuals of any race, greater in others. It can lie dormant for life or be stimulated to action. The form which this religious urge will take with any individual, the mold into which it will be poured, depends very largely on his knowledge and opportunities. The same could be said for an Indian group where, generally, knowledge and opportunity were the same for all. There was little chance for separate sects and individual preachers of new doctrine. All heard the same myths. All joined in the same ceremonies, which were often the only ones they knew. This mold for religious expression was provided by tradition, by livelihood, and by contacts.

Was a group, for instance, living from hand to mouth, obliged to trudge about constantly, collecting nuts, seeds, roots, and small animals? Among such food gatherers no one had time to dream. They received little stimulating contact from elsewhere, and their myths remained at the simple stage reached thousands of years before. In my early myth-collecting days, I asked a man from such a culture: "Who do you think made the world?"

The question was out of his line but finally he ventured: "I guess it was Wolf. He's our most powerful animal."

I was reminded of the Swiss children whom Piaget tested by the same question. The children were not poor, but they had had no more opportunity for thought than had the food gatherer. They named the most powerful agent they could think of: "I guess some gentlemen at Geneva."

The children learned better in later life. The Indian and his group continued with a bounded idea of the universe. They could have few ceremonies since they could never be sure of assembling at a given time or of having food enough for a gathering. They held their simple rites for adolescence, death, and the honoring of first fruits without any special officiant. When one appeared, he was the medicine man, self-appointed through his vision and serving for pay.

The hunter of big game had no such routine. He and his family could feast sometimes—and starve sometimes. The difference is plain when we look at the seal hunter or the buffalo hunter. True, they had days or weeks of leisure, as the plant gatherers had not.

But they did not have the consolation of constantly working in a group. One or two roaring feasts during the year might be possible, but for most of the time each man worked alone. What he needed from the spirits was courage and luck for himself as an individual. So his chief contact with the Supernaturals was the solitary, personal vision.

At the other extreme of ceremonial life were the planters. They, of necessity, settled in groups with fields around them. They cooperated in breaking ground, harvesting or, later, tending irrigation works. Even if a family planted and gathered its own crops, the rain or sunshine needed must concern not it alone but the whole area. It was most practical for a group to deal with the Supernatural as one, uniting its efforts to produce ceremonies and offerings. With such a beginning, the way was open for an immense development of ritual. Ceremonies could be standardized and localized. Dates could be set in accordance with known agricultural seasons, and because of stored food, a large number of persons could congregate in one place. In time a ceremonial calendar could be developed. At the meeting place there might rise some ceremonial structure, even a temple. Here could be stored paraphernalia and this, in time, might reach magnificent proportions.

Finally, a particular officiant could be relied upon to be always present. Since he knew what he must do from year to year, he might develop a long ritual, perhaps including dancing and costumes which he supervised. As the ceremony grew more elaborate, he needed assistants, unofficial and voluntary at first, then official and permanent. They too must learn the ritual, so that at last there developed a self-perpetuating priesthood.

These are the three outstanding varieties of Indian livelihood, each with its ceremonial consequences. There are many others, and some hardly classifiable. Students of the Indian long-ago have broken up North America into culture areas which have become as familiar to them as the states of the union. Here we shall often have to refer to the Plains, the Southeast and other areas, since each has had its particular kind of livelihood, history, and contacts with people of various kinds. All that has helped to make the color and the pattern of its religion, which could not be understood otherwise. A map of culture areas, therefore, is appended, page 18.

For general discussion, we need a broader distinction. The difference between planters and hunter-gatherers will constantly crop up; the map on page 156 gives its main outlines. Hunter-gatherers is a blanket term, including the hunters of caribou and buffalo on the Plains and Barrens, the deer hunters of northern forests, acorn gatherers of California, and several more. On the map, they seem very much in the majority. In the first centuries of Paleo-Indian life they occupied the whole country, and it was only gradually that the ancient habits brought from the Old World gave way before the discovery of corn. Even then, much of the northern area was impossible for agriculture because of climate, rainfall, and the inadequacy of primitive tools.

But a map restricted to America north of Mexico gives little perspective on the usages of hunter-gatherers or of planters. The hunter-gatherer region must be extended far into Siberia, where some beliefs and practices are the same as those of Pacific Coast Indians.

The planters' area, on the contrary, looks small, crowded into the southeast corner of the map with a few dots west of the Mississippi. It looks small, that is, only if we cut the map off at the Mexican border. Actually, planting Indians in the United States were only the northern rim of a huge agricultural expanse stretching through Mexico and far down into South America. Descriptions will show that many of those in the States were only part-time planters. The lush new country around them was so full of natural foods that most of the men kept on with their hunting, leaving the farm work to women.

Such knowledge of livelihood is only one step in understanding the religious usage of any North American group. We need to know its history: How has it moved and among what people? Was it accessible to neighbors of different customs, or to travelers from foreign tribes? Miracle plays from Spain, crosses from Jesuit missionaries, have become established in some places so that they

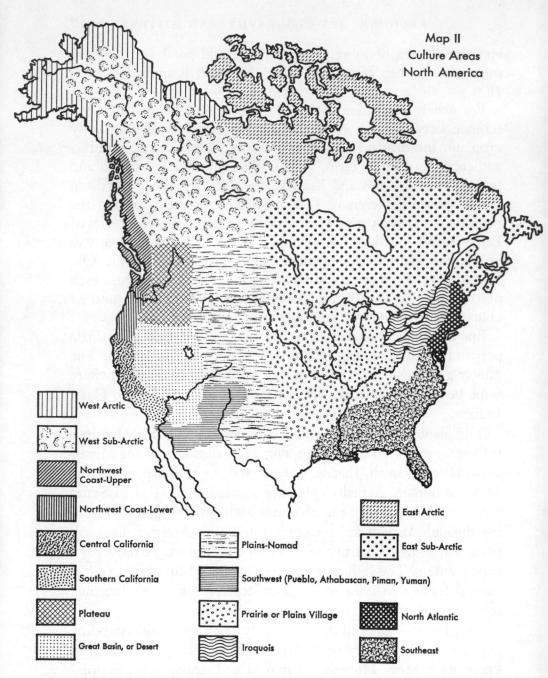

Map II
Culture Areas
North America

West Arctic

West Sub-Arctic

Northwest
Coast-Upper

Northwest Coast-Lower

Central California

Southern California

Plateau

Great Basin, or Desert

Plains-Nomad

Southwest (Pueblo, Athabascan, Piman, Yuman)

Prairie or Plains Village

Iroquois

East Arctic

East Sub-Arctic

North Atlantic

Southeast

After Harold E. Driver and William C. Massey, Comparative Studies of North American
Indians (*Philadelphia: American Philosophical Society, 1957*), *p. 170.*

too must be considered in the web of religious patterns. The next pages will follow some pattern threads, beginning with the simplest and oldest.

REFERENCES

On early migration see: Giddings, 1960; Haag, 1962; Krieger, 1964; Wormington, 1962.

Mongoloid prehistory: Coon, 1962.

Early settlement: Haynes, 1964; Mason, 1962; Martin, Quimby, and Collier, 1947.

Culture areas: Driver, 1961; Driver and Massey, 1957 (good maps); Jennings and Norbeck, 1964, pp. 117–291; Kroeber, 1939.

Distinction, hunter-gatherers, and planters: Underhill, 1948.

3

IMPERSONAL POWER

"The child is *wakan*," said the old Dakota (Sioux) as he heard his grandson recite in the government school.

The boy had computed the weight of a sack of grain, without seeing or touching it, and had announced that it would be about as heavy as that girl in the front row. This the grandfather knew to be true, but the method of finding out the facts from written figures was, to him, utterly mysterious. It meant that the boy was touched with supernatural power.

Belief in this kind of impersonal power is part of that substratum spoken of in the last chapter. It was a power unconnected with any individual spirit. Though unseen, it was present everywhere. Scholars have called it by the Melanesian name, *mana*. Codrington, the missionary bishop, who first became aware of mana in the Pacific Islands, described it as:

> . . . what works to effect everything which is beyond the ordinary power of men, outside the common processes of nature; it is present in the atmosphere of life, attaches itself to persons and to things, and is manifested by results which can only be ascribed to its operation.[1]

Since that first discovery, something like mana has been found among most primitive peoples of the world. It is never the sole

[1] Codrington, 1891, pp. 118–19.

religion. It can be seen sometimes alongside the most elaborate ceremonials, but its mystery and simplicity must have had an appeal to all peoples from very early times. It is a part of the substratum which links Indian tribes to each other and to the Old World.

There are Indian names for something like mana all the way from Vancouver to Labrador, but of course, since Indian groups have different religious patterns, the words have slightly different meanings. The Osage, an organized Prairie tribe of Siouan language, use *wakan* in a manner which seems poetic and philosophical. At least that is how an educated Indian puts it:

> All life is *wakan*. So also is everything which exhibits power, whether in action, as the winds and drifting clouds, or in passive endurance, as the boulder by the wayside. For even the commonest sticks and stones have a spiritual essence which must be reverenced as a manifestation of the all-pervading mysterious power that fills the universe.[2]

Their relatives, the Oglala Sioux, used *wakan* sometimes merely for something strange and wonderful. Thus they called their first horse the "*wakan* dog." Yet they also spoke of Wakonda, *Great Wakan*, in terms which approached the meaning of Supreme Being.

For the Iroquois, the *orenda* power was different for each plant, animal, man, or spirit, just as brains and muscles were different. In their myths the powerful being called Earth Grasper had so much that no one could hurt him, whereas the little otter, although he was a person in ancient days, had almost none. Some thought the power could come and go, focusing temporarily on its object as electricity may do. The old Sioux quoted above must have had that conception.

Like electricity, the unseen force was thought able to injure as well as to strengthen. Just as the handling of electrical equipment is left to the expert, so primitives did not lightly handle an object or approach a person who possessed mana. Some sort of preparation, like bathing or reciting a spell, might be necessary; otherwise harm would follow as surely and as impersonally as the shock from a live electric wire. This avoidance of danger from mana has been

[2] La Flesche, 1925, p. 186.

called by another Melanesian word, *tabu* (forbidden). I shall give it the English spelling, *taboo,* so as to keep it clear of other Melanesian associations.

Taboo was a constant element in Indian religious life, from the simplest rituals up to the most elaborate. No one can attend an Indian ceremony without finding some object or place that is too sacred to be approached. This kind of reverence is worldwide and has been sanctified by age. How else can we explain the reverence paid today to material objects such as flags and church paraphernalia?

Recognizing the power in the world about them, Indians, like other early people, devised ways of using the power for their own ends. Frazer, who wrote before the concept of mana was in use, thought of such handling as a kind of protoscience and called it magic. There have been many definitions of magic before and after him but, for my purposes, Frazer's simple one is very useful. He described magic as the manipulation of unseen forces by rule, without the help of any priest or ritual. Primitive thinkers, he suggested, considered that they had discovered and learned such rules, as later ones discovered the law of gravity. Their chief rule was that things that looked alike were probably permeated by the same power. So the magic-worker, instead of learning Newton's law about falling bodies, would learn: (1) Like produces like. Therefore, if a school of fish does not arrive when the fishermen want it, they put a wooden fish into the water and the fish will come, by imitative magic. (2) Things that have once been joined will go through the same experiences, even when separated. Thus burning somone's fingernail clippings will cause their owner to burn by. contagious magic.

The chief criticism against this pseudo-science is that even primitives had too much intelligence to believe in it; they must have imagined some god or spirit behind the power. To that, we might answer that the critics do not carry the idea of primitive back far enough. To picture a god or spirit with reasoned actions is the work of a full-sized brain. But there were thousands of years before the days of *Homo sapiens,* thinking man, when human brains were very small. Yet they must have been able to recognize events that were out of the usual course, and they must have had strong desires to influence those events. Witness the half-shame-faced ritual that even some moderns observe, of using special gestures in throwing dice, or carrying a rabbit's foot. I am ready to believe that like was thought to produce like because of similar mana long before a theology of gods and spirits was evolved.

In fact, there was proof of the process, as some Indians believe today. I was once walking with an old Papago Indian on the Arizona desert. It was just before the rains, when the whole land looked dry as concrete. A peculiar stone lay at the old man's feet and he picked it up. It was not one of the usual formations, which are rough and gray. This was smooth and rounded, its white surface striped with green lines. It had been washed down by torrents over a long period, from some distant hill.

"This is not a stone-stone," said the Indian. "I think it may have power. Perhaps it can bring rain."

Holding it in his right hand, he whirled it sunwise around his head. "I will take it home now and see what happens."

"And if it does not bring rain?"

"Oh, then I shall throw it away. But I always look for rain-bringers. Some day, perhaps, I shall find one."

The rains came in the course of nature; they were especially heavy and the old man was jubilant. The stone became famous through the area and villagers borrowed it when threatened with drought. To me it seemed that the old man's procedure, from hypothesis through testing to conclusion, might well rank as pro-toscience.

On this basis, magic procedures have become established with many different groups, their successes remembered and their failures forgotten. The little fur parka of an Eskimo boy was often covered with what could be called lightning conductors for imitative magic. There was a hawk's wing to give him speed, a fox's tail for cunning, the skin of a seabird for future fishing luck. His father procured these things and his mother sewed them on without spell or ceremony. A Kwakiutl mother laid a raccoon's forepaw on her baby's right hand to make him industrious, or a squirrel's if she wanted him to be a good climber. The navel cord of a

Hopi boy used to be attached to an arrow shaft for keeping and the girl's to a stirring stick. Thus the boy would become a hunter and the girl a cook by contagious magic.

All this was done with no help from priest or medicine man, even though such officiant were present in the tribe. However, such officiants sometimes produced magic-working objects by taking an effigy, or indeed any chosen object, and "breathing" their own mana into it. Such objects have come to be known as *fetishes,* from a Portuguese word used in East Africa.

Easier than searching for a magic-working object would be the uttering of a form of words—a spell—which one could have always at hand. Getting results merely by the violent expression of a wish must have seemed natural even to the earliest people. Babies do it. Children may keep on with the attitude for a good many years. Some spells seem to express this same childlike insistence. Thus the hero of a Pawnee tale exclaimed:

> I want the clouds to rise.
> I want the dark clouds to come.
> I want the snowstorm to come.
> So that it will freeze everything.[3]

If the hero's wish happened to come true on this occasion, he might follow the procedure of the old Indian with the stone. That is, he would remember the words and use them again. If they still seemed to bring luck, they might be crystallized into a formula to be cherished, bequeathed in his family, even sold. This means a kind of impersonal power different from that used through objects. The words themselves are thought to have mana because they have produced results. The user could not be sure just where the mana lay, and so in using this magic tool he would be careful to use the very same words in the same order. A change might ruin efficiency. Many an urgent wish may thus have come into circulation and achieved the status of magic. Such spells were private property of individuals or families and their wording was closely guarded, for therein lay the power. Owners of the spell generally laid its origin to some ancestor or famous man whose wish was powerful because he had mana.

[3] Dorsey, 1904, p. 42.

There is a more elaborate kind of spell, almost a poem, like the beautiful canoe spells which Malinowski found in the Pacific.[4] These, according to the people's own tradition, did not arise from an individual's wish. They were given by a Supernatural, and here we have the combination of magic, impersonal power, with the personal power of higher beings which Frazer called religion. The question of which came first in human history need not concern us here. It seems useful, however, to distinguish between two psychologically different approaches to the Supernatural. There are objects and forms of words that are tools, sure to bring the right result if handled according to regulations. Also there is personal relationship with Supernatural beings, through prayer or bargaining. Here the result is in doubt, since personal relationships can vary endlessly. The two approaches are usually combined, and it is interesting to note their proportions in different religious patterns.

One such combination occurred when a spell was dreamed by a medicine man, who then sold it to his patients. (Or the doctor might, himself, have obtained it from a predecessor.) An example is the love spell that could be bought by a Cherokee brave wishing to oust a rival from a woman's heart.

Cherokee Love Spell

Where [other] men live it is lonely.
They are very loathsome.
The common polecat has made them so like himself
That they are fit only for his company . . .
They go about clothed with mere refuse . . .
But I—I was ordained to be a white man.[5]
I stand with my face toward the Sun Land.
No one is ever lonely with me.
I am very handsome . . .
Your soul has come into the very center of my soul,
    never to turn away . . . I take your soul. Sgĕ!⁶

---

[4] See Malinowski, 1922, pp. 216–17.

[5] "White man" is not used here in its modern sense. White was the old Cherokee term for success and happiness.

[6] Mooney, 1891, pp. 376–77.

The medicine man who sold this spell very likely had a stock of such remedies, suitable for different occasions. This is the case with many examples of magic, both in the Old World and the New. The handmade product, as it were, has gone into mass production and is being handled by merchants. There were private owners, also, who passed formulas down in families. In time, the concept of magic objects and formulas blossomed out into a wealth of pageantry.

A spell might develop into a complete ceremony but it kept its essential quality. Every word and every gesture must be exactly like the original or the tool could not operate. This rule held, even though most of the words used were nonsense syllables, and it holds still. I have heard Indian spells that had been borrowed through several languages, so that they were quite incomprehensible to those who spoke them. Perhaps they were being changed by mispronunciation of the current owner, but as long as he was unaware of the fact, his belief in their power was unshaken.

A spell soon came to include some sort of action, like that of my Indian in whirling the stone around his head. Sometimes it might be symbolic, like moving toward the north to bring death or toward the east for life. Or the action might involve sympathetic magic, like using the stems of chickweed, which look like worms, to cure worms in a child. As religious ideas developed, we find an admixture of prayer or, at least, a calling upon spirits to help bring about the magical result. The belief, however, still was that if the conjuration was recited verbatim, the spirits must do as it stated. Mistakes were so dangerous that, even today, the Navahos follow every long ceremony with a special rite meant to undo them.

Other groups feel that the whole ceremony must be repeated. The Papagos frequently told me of a long-past rain ceremony when a young officiant, improperly trained, omitted some words. The two-day performance was too elaborate to repeat "so there was no rain that year." The magic formulas used by whites in ancient days had this same requirement, a very useful one for people who had no writing. Moreover, the well-known lines, heard over and over, came to seem to each devotee an inalienable possession, almost like his own limbs. Some modern religious sects that insist on new inspiration for every speech and prayer miss this emotional appeal.

With the wonder-working tools of formula, fetish, and ceremony, the rule of .taboo was in force. Just as the unprotected hand should not touch an electric wire, so magic words and objects were to be avoided by those not empowered to use them. Sacred fetishes of clan and individual should be touched only by their owners. Anyone else might be made ill or even killed by the contact. Even the owners must handle them with a prescribed ritual, or the objects would, at least, lose their power. The Creek Indian "war bundle," when taken to battle, was carried on the back of the war ceremonialist or his assistant and never allowed to touch the ground. On the Omaha buffalo hunt, the sacred white buffalo hide was carried by a specially appointed woman and every night guarded in a special tent. Failure in this would ruin the hunt.

Taboo reverence can outlast many of the ancient customs. In the 1930's, the Papago Indians wore modern clothing and many lived in wooden houses. One of these houses belonged to a medicine man of my acquaintance who died suddenly. He had never allowed me to see his magical objects but I asked his widow if this might now be possible. The bundle was usually kept in the hills where it was unlikely that anyone would touch it unintentionally and be injured. The owner had been using it, however, just before his death and had brought it to the house. There it was secreted behind lumber in the corner of a woodshed. The widow said she dared not go near the place, even to get wood. She had sent for a powerful medicine man to come and remove the dangerous object.

Misfortune happening to me, I argued, would not be her fault. Also, I promised to "feed" the sacred objects with eagle down that I had brought and to leave them just as I had found them. She consented. Then she and the whole family went into the house, shut the door, and pulled down the shades. The house remained dead while I rolled out the keg and unwrapped its treasures: two deer tails, some eagle down, an eagle claw, and four quartz crystals. When I drove away after replacing everything, the shades were still down. The family avoided me ever afterward.

Mention of the dangerous power inherent in the Supernatural brings us to witchcraft—its evil side. Mana, in the primitive view, was neither good nor evil but worked benefit or misfortune, according to how it was used. As the idea of personalized spirits developed, they too had this same quality. Only in two or three highly developed Indian groups do we find the idea of an all-good Being.

Spells can work evil as well as good. Burning or destroying some of a victim's hair, his fingernail parings, or excreta is obviously contagious magic, which seems to have occurred to the vengeful all over the world. What could an injured or jealous individual do in ancient days if he dared not show enmity, and could not move away or make a new career, but must work on day by day near the person he hated? Our stories of the Middle Ages are full of just such persons who relieved anger and frustration by evil magic. Perhaps the Paleo-Indians, in their caves and brush shelters, did the same thing. Even today in some Indian groups, the accusations of magic come quickly if a man wins too often at games (Indians always bet on games, even if they have nothing to offer but a wooden-tipped arrow) or if a baby dies after a stranger has passed. Merely looking into a neighbor's window may seem suspicious.

No wonder! The reservation Indian, unacquainted with modern opportunities, is as frustrated as the medieval villager. How is it that his neighbor's farm is prospering while he is poor? Why does one child get ahead in school when the other does not? Old-fashioned Navahos refused to be any more prosperous than their neighbors, no matter what help the government farmer offered. The fear of being accused of evil magic was a powerful leveler.

Belief in evil magic dies hard, in spite of modern teaching, for there is real comfort in it. For the magic-user, muttering a spell all alone where no one can blame or punish is a great relief to the feelings. The victim of bad luck or even of his own incompetence has equal relief. He need never ask himself, as whites so often do,

"Why must I suffer so?" He merely has to find the witch and his trouble is ended. Even if the harm is incurable, he can achieve emotional outlet by taking vengeance on the witch.

REFERENCES

Mana and magic, or the manipulation of mana, are generally taken up together. See Frazer, 1922, chaps. 3–5; Webster, 1942 (taboo), 1948 (magic).

On magic and religion: Jensen, 1963; Malinowski, 1948.

Spells: Mooney, 1891, 1932.

Witchcraft: Kluckhohn, 1944; Parsons, 1927.

The whole subject is treated in the general books on religion listed after Chapter 1. Examples can be found in studies of separate tribes.

4

WORLD ORIGINS

The Papago origin myth was being ceremonially told. The one-room adobe house was dark, crammed from wall to wall with softly breathing people. In the center, a tiny fire cast its red glow on the narrator's face, wrinkled and blotched like a neglected apple. That face changed from grim to humorous and back again, and the voice ranged from deep to shrill as he imitated the characters in the tale. He used poetic and ancient words for the heroes, bad grammar and forbidden terms for the clowns and villains. Every so often he stopped and we all breathed the syllable that showed we were attending.

The incidents were the familiar ones that seem to float like pollen from one campfire to another. They were shortened, transposed, or fitted to our particular locality to suit the audience; but that part was not important. The essential thing was the songs. These came at dramatic points, as in the minstrel lays of old Europe. They were sometimes in archaic language, which even the narrator could not translate. Still, he pronounced every word carefully; for without the songs in their ancient form, the sacred narrative had no power. For this account of past miracles was a kind of spell. It ensured that the events that had happened for the benefit of the human race would continue to happen. The seasons would follow one another and the people would increase as in the beginning.

The origin myth, in tribes that follow the old customs, is not lightly told to any who ask for it. Here I do not mean the adventurous and comic tales, mostly about animals, which may be told by anyone who knows them. Among adults, they served for entertainment and reminders of the tribal ethics. With children, they were one of the chief means of instruction. Indians, who rarely punished their children, found it useful to let the youngsters join with them in scorn for the greed and disobedience of Coyote or Mink. The tales made it plain that behavior of that sort always brought disaster.

The actual genesis story was sacred and known only to specialists, something like the chained Bible in the medieval church. In organized groups, the specialists were priests, heads of clans or societies who learned the narrative from their predecessors. In many of the Pueblos there were a number of different societies, each with its own story magnifying the society history. Thus the Hopi Snake priests, in the eight days of preparation before their ceremony, told the neophytes how their clan had once been snakes, carried in a bag at the end of a rainbow, how all snakes were their brothers, and how they would bring rain after having been entertained in a dance. Members of an Osage medicine society had the esoteric symbols that told their history tattooed on their breasts.

In less completely organized groups, the myth was often ceremonial property, passed down to the males of a family. A man might learn it by years of careful listening, teach it to his grandson and so pass down his particular version, featuring the places and details he liked best. In the Southwest, where much of my work has been done, his services must be requested four days beforehand, with a handful of cornmeal. He spent the four days in preparing himself by fasting and offering tobacco. Even so, the myth could not be told at any time. The official period, when no payment was required, was the four days of the winter solstice, "when the sun stands still." Other winter nights were allowable if the hearers would pay, but neither the myth nor any part of it should be told in summer, "when the snakes are out."

Snakes, in the Southwest of the United States, are an important part of the animal population. (No Indian would kill even the poisonous rattler or sidewinder, for they are supernatural beings connected with rain.) Perhaps, I was told, they might note some mistake in the narrative or the narrator and punish accordingly. Or they might consider the origin myth sacred material, not to be exposed to laymen. Northern peoples looked differently upon the snake, but he had sacred qualities in Mexico, in China, and especially in India.

I tried to collect versions of the local myth in any tribe I visited and found that the mere plot of the tale, such as is often given in myth collections, could be had from many people. Not so the songs. Once I failed to find the official narrator and asked his wife: "Could you not tell the story? You must have heard it often."

"Of course. All the family knows it. But not the songs."

Songs were the essential magic, and the woman was both amused and horrified to learn that I was willing to hear the myth plot without them. Once I even collected some songs from faithful listeners but was warned: "They have no power, you know. Not this way." No one could understand how the whites could be interested in this phantom food without nourishment.

The basic plots that tell of earth beginnings are very few in number. And they are world property. These dream pictures, about a time when life was not as it is now, might have been conjured up by any seer or poet at any time or place. Perhaps that did happen, over and over again. The result is that some half-dozen of these genesis stories seem to be known in every country, with emphasis now on one theme, now another.

A favored story, spread all over eastern Asia and its former appendage, North America, is that known to folklorists as the Earth Diver. It begins: "At first, there was nothing but water." So it must have been dreamed by people who lived near a body of water, who knows how long ago! In the next episode there appear some diving birds or diving animals; the poet does not explain whence they come. They dive under the water, and one at last brings up a little soil, out of which the earth is made. (Researchers would have a colorful journey, following this germ of myth through various tribes.) Soon there is a Being who commands the divers. In Asia, where many religions have rolled past, he may be God. In America this theological version does not appear. The Being may come from nowhere, like the animals. He may be sent by a higher Spirit. Sometimes there are two Beings, destined to oppose each other later.

This is a tale of the hunter-gatherers. It is especially popular around the Great Lakes, where the primeval water, Longfellow's "big sea water," is present for all to see. It goes on with many elaborations, for the flat earth must be enlarged by singing, by dancing, by running about it. It must be supported, perhaps on the back of an animal, perhaps by pillars at the corners or by spider webs sewing it to the sky. And this brings up the question of where it is in space. Often it appears that the water, with the earth floating on it, is one of a series of disks, piled above one another like plates and skewered in place by a center pole. That pole is important in the profession of the wonder-working medicine man, for by it he climbs to the next disk, which is in the sky. Most Indians seem to envisage this kind of a layered universe, generally of three layers, with the earth in the middle. The Pawnee have nine. The Chukchi of Siberia go as high as thirty-three.

There are, of course, other tales besides the Earth Diver, and sometimes they exist along with it. The Eskimo of the Arctic, however, and many Indians of the north Pacific coast cannot believe that the solid earth was ever created. Surely, it was always here and required only some shaping into mountains and valleys. Indians in parts of California and of the Southwest take the opposite view. In the beginning, there was nothing at all. A Being floated about in nothingness and finally made the world by wishing, by commanding, or by using pieces of his own body. The Zuni say that the Creator, Awonawilona, even thought himself into being. In one small area on the California coast, there is an entirely different idea. The world was born from two supernatural parents. Sometimes they found themselves within an egg. With the Luiseño they were floating in space. The female said:

". . . I am that which stretches out flat or is extended [the earth]."
The male replied: "I am that which arches over [the sky]."[1]
They united and from them were born the thoughts of all that
was to come. This strangely metaphysical picture is so like those
of Polynesia that it has caused students to wonder.

None of these Creators remains permanently to guide and
cherish the world he has produced. In the Mohave myth, the
Creator was killed. In that of the Papago, he was worsted in a
contest, but often his disappearance is unexplained. He performed
his task of world-making and then was gone, like the wind or
the rain. I have called him the Vanishing Creator.

After the flat disk of earth had been made, the incidents of its
shaping and furnishing follow much the same general course.
There must be rocks and rivers, vegetation, and finally inhabitants. Here the plot blossoms into complexity. The ancient myth-
makers did not gloss over the fact that earth and all upon it was
far from perfect. There was death, there was hard work, there
were night and cold. Primitive philosophers, like later religionists,
must have asked themselves why a kindly Creator allowed such
things. They found a very human answer. The Creator could
not do everything. He left some tasks to a helper who was a
bungler or just plain mischievous. Thus Coyote, being told to
place the stars in the sky in geometric order, dropped the sack
that contained them and they scattered every which way. The
brother of the Iroquois Creator foiled his plan to have river cur-
rents run both upstream and downstream so that canoeing would
be easier, and that is why water runs only downstream.

These two brothers or companions, the desirable and the undesirable, appear in many guises throughout America and Siberia.
Gradually their characters became sharpened until people saw
them as God and the Devil. Indian tales never quite reached that
point, although they abound in accounts of the mistakes and
mischief of early days when human life was being shaped.

After the disk of earth was in order, we might expect the next
episode to be the creation of mankind. With many hunter-

[1] DuBois, 1908, p. 139.

gatherer groups, however, that was the final event that closed the genesis story. At least it is so with the creation or the coming of the present-day man. Sometimes there were earlier, unsatisfactory populations destroyed by a flood. The inhabitants who fill the greatest part of the tale are not human, or only partly so. Nor are they animal. They may be called man-animals for they had the speech and behavior of humans, though in animal bodies. In some tales, they were not created. They simply appeared on earth, as of right. If the Creator fashioned them, he did it long before he made men. They were man's predecessors and sometimes ancestors, not servants and inferiors.

With them began the great age of myth, from which has gushed an almost endless series of tales. Some are part of the sacred story of beginnings, but most are incidents with almost the character of today's comic strip. They are colorful, comic, instructive—also obscene, in the matter-of-fact way of a child. They could be told when the sacred stories cannot, and often they formed the whole intellectual schooling of the Indian young.

In many tales, the man-animals not only shaped the world and formed its hills and valleys, they also decided on the length of the days and nights and of the seasons. (Navahos say this was done by a gambling game.) More often the transformation was left to a fantastic figure who was the very focus of the mythical age. This was the man-animal whose powers rose sometimes to the height of creation. In some tales he transformed the world from a wilderness to a fit habitation. In others, he played clownish tricks. He is known to students of myth as the Trickster-Transformer.

In size and general behavior, this Being ranges all the way from the greedy little mink of the Plateau to the noble Nanabozho of the Great Lakes who was Longfellow's model for Hiawatha. Generally, he was the most intelligent animal of his area. In the Northwest, that meant mink, raven, or bluejay; in the Plains, coyote or Old Man Spider; in the Northeast, the white arctic hare. Some tribes have humanized and ennobled him, but the enthralling figure for students of man's past is the earthy, greedy, sensual child-animal who believes everything, tries everything, finds nothing unnatural. Carl Jung compared him with man's own subconscious. Yet he has the powers of a Supernatural. He goes about the world making rivers and hills, inventing artifacts, even stealing the sun; but all at his own whim, for he knows nothing of good or evil. When he does something particularly stupid, it results in his death, but he immediately comes to life again as witless as before. Whether the human race profits from his actions or whether it suffers is a matter of chance.

This all-too-human figure must have been cherished by many primitive peoples. We know of Tricksters in southern Asia, in India and Indonesia, and in Africa, with moralized echoes in Aesop and La Fontaine. Even the later European Till Eulenspiegel and Merry Andrew may belong to the Trickster family. But these latter clowns always get their deserts. They have been smoothed and dimmed out of the primeval state where no right or wrong existed. Perhaps in the American Trickster we have one of the most vivid remaining examples of early thinking.

His place in the myth varied. Sometimes he was one of the man-animals who kept his place long after the Creator had vanished. Sometimes he slid into the place of helper and brother to the Creator. Then he may not have been simply careless or mischievous: he had his own plans for the world and became a genuine precursor of the Devil, though with more humor and less grandeur. In a Maidu myth, the world was created from nothing by Earth Initiate whose plan was to make life pleasant and comfortable for the future human race. Food he made easy to get. The women simply put out their baskets at night and in the morning they were filled with cooked food. Coyote told the people, "That's no way to do"; so it was stopped, and now women work to fill their baskets. Earth Initiate had wanted no sickness or death, but Coyote said it was better for people to get sick and die. Then there could be big funeral ceremonies which he would arrange. So it was decided that way and the first person to die was Coyote's own son. Coyote was sorry now, for he is not portrayed as wicked, only thoughtless and impulsive like human beings themselves. He tried to get things changed but it was too late. "Coyote began to cry. And," say the Maidu, "these were the first tears."[2]

This may look like an early picture of good and evil, God and the Devil, and so some early missionaries tried to interpret it. It is a subdued and humanized picture, however, and Coyote's arguments on the desirability of work might be approved by modern thinkers. In these hunter-gatherer myths, the incompetent partner is never wholly bad. Sometimes he is merely careless or victimized, as human beings may be. In any case, the whole affair happened in the mythical era, before the advent of humankind. So death and the other misfortunes of life are not man's fault. Indians who accepted these myths did not believe in original sin nor in a fallen race needing redemption. Their requests to the spirits were for long life and plenty, not for pardon.

Mankind finally enters the scene. He may be a second creation, after the first has been destroyed for misbehavior. In that case, we have the Earth Diver all over again, perhaps with a man commanding the divers. As for the man-animals, they give up their position as masters of the earth and retire to the woods and streams. In some tales, a few of the more important turn into human beings. Others resume their fur, scales, or feathers, to be laid aside only occasionally when they appear in visions to favored human beings.

Human beings, in their early days, are pictured as almost helpless. They had to be taught how to make dwellings and pots, spears, arrows, or fishtraps. Sometimes even their bodies were incomplete. Fingers had to be cut apart and mouths opened. The protagonist of this period was the Culture Hero. Perhaps he came from nowhere, like the other Supernaturals. Perhaps he was born of a human and an animal. He carried out the work of teaching and cherishing left undone by the Vanishing Creator, and it is on him that stories center, rather than the mysterious First Cause.

In fact, the First Cause is vague and shadowy in all the hunter-gatherer myths. He is given strange names like Earth Initiate or Earth Magician, but he is rarely described. Episodes, comic and otherwise, gather about the more human characters of the tale,

[2] Dixon, 1902, p. 44.

the bungling helper, the Trickster and the Culture Hero. It would be interesting if we could trace a progression from destructive helper through the Trickster, who may do either good or evil, to the Culture Hero, who is generally benevolent but may have human fits of bad temper. Indians did not see such a progression. As we look over different myths, the characters slip and slide about; so the Helper is sometimes also the Trickster or the Culture Hero. Any one of them may take a hand at the work of creation.

All this appears mostly in hunter-gatherer tales. Those of the planters may have one or more of the same elements but they are overlaid by others connected with the ceremony. Here the Creator is envisaged not indeed as a person, but as a Power in the sky to be treated with continual reverence. Some Southeastern tribes called him the Great Holy Flame of Life. Some on the Mississippi River and its tributaries seem really to have used the term Great Spirit. Human origins, also, have a different slant from that given by the hunter-gatherers. In many planter myths, humankind, or at least one ancestor, descended from the sky. Some animals also were sent down, but as helpers and messengers for men, not their superiors. In the Southwest appears a story well known in the Old World but rare in America. Human beings were begotten upon Mother Earth by Father Sun, and they climbed out of her lowest womb as seeds send up shoots. The rich detail of these beliefs will be explored further in connection with the ceremonies.

Ceremonies, it has been mentioned, may grow far apart from the myths supposed to explain them. There has been much discussion as to which of the two came first, and perhaps I may add my bit of what I consider proof on the subject. I hold with those who consider that, in human development, action came before thinking. So with primitive man, even perhaps with apes, there might have been some dance or game after which good luck often followed. So it became institutionalized as a good luck ceremony, and only later did the thinkers begin to consider who brought the good luck and how. That, however, was only the beginning. Thinkers, of course, took pleasure in elaborating their story. Then the ceremony was elaborated to accord with it and so the two influenced each other reciprocally. At any point after the beginning, one could not tell which came first.

Neither can Indians tell. Their answer to any inquiry is: "It has always been so." Perhaps the ceremony has blossomed so elaborately that it touches the myth at few points. To the performers, and even to the ceremonialist, that is not important. Somehow the whole affair was ordained by the spirits. Somehow it represents the original condition, when the behavior of the sun, the seasons, and the game animals was set in order. If the ceremony is re-enacted, point for point, that order will continue.

REFERENCES

Collections of American Indian myths: Alexander, 1916; Thompson, 1929, has an excellent bibliography.

Old World myths to which American ones have similarities: Kramer, 1961 (Eurasia); Holmberg, 1964 (Siberia, Finland).

Examples of American myths: Bunzel, 1932c (Zuni); Michelson, 1930 (Fox); Radin, 1948 (Winnebago); Swanton, 1905 (Haida). Publications of American Ethnological Society, American Folklore Society, University of California, University of Washington, Columbia University; Museum, City of Milwaukee. Some myth material is generally included in all tribal studies.

Discussion of myth: Kluckhohn, 1942; Reichard, 1921; Sebeok 1955; Tylor, 1889.

Trickster: Radin, 1956, comments by Jung and Kerényi.

Songs in myths: McAllester, 1954; Nettl, 1956, Chap. 8; Mandelbaum, 1949, pp. 463–67.

5

THE SPIRITS

For the old-time Indian, the world did not consist of inanimate materials to be used and of animals to be butchered and eaten. It was alive, and everything in it could help or harm him.

The Sioux, in his sweat bath, prayed to the rocks on which he was pouring water:

> Oh Rocks . . . by receiving your sacred breath
> Our people will be long-winded as they walk
> The path of life; your breath [the steam]
> Is the very breath of life.[1]

The priest at Zuni pueblo, making offerings for his altar, talked of

> My mother . . .
> Cotton woman [and] the flesh of our two mothers,
> Black paint woman,
> Clay woman.[2]

The questions immediately asked about all these "nature persons" are: Were they all alive and powerful in their own right? Were only some of them powerful? Or was the power from some

[1] Brown, 1953, p. 37.
[2] Bunzel, 1932d, pp. 660, 695.

indwelling spirit which might come and go? This sounds clear and simple, but there is no clear and simple answer. Perhaps the thinkers in each group had one, although it might be different in different areas. For the average Indian layman, it was enough to know that the "nature persons" were all around him and that he must follow the rules for gaining their co-operation.

These rules were much the same as he used for getting on with human beings. This meant treating them with courtesy, not exploiting them, and when he asked a favor, giving a favor in return. As Spider said to a hunter who gave him the feathers he liked: "We *have* to help you, because you never forget us; because you always take feathers out for us, we help you."[3] This attitude of give and take was universal with most tribes and most spirits, although we shall come to exceptions. The spirits, however, were differently imagined in different parts of the country. Here we must make the usual distinction between hunters and planters.

For the hunter, the all-important spirits were those of animals. The glamour of being earth's first inhabitants clung to them, and man still regarded them as his superiors in power. Such an idea was common in the Old World also, dating perhaps from the time when the beasts, with their claws and wings, were better able to get on in life than primitive man with his crude tools. In Egypt and India the Powers worshiped were these animals before they slowly took on human form. Even the imposing Greek divinities seem to have had a similar history.

The animal spirits of North America did not go through this change. They had always had a dual form, human and animal. When mankind arrived and the animals retired to the forests and waters, they kept the ability to put on human guise when they chose. In their own homes they always did so. Hidden away where no mortal could find them, they had camps or villages with clans or moieties (the division of a group into ceremonial halves) just as the local Indians did. Here, favored people might visit them and be taught some of the wisdom and the magic powers that the man-animals retained (see Chap. 10).

[3] Parsons, 1939, Vol. I, p. 207.

Every hunter needed this help from the animals and could hardly live successfully without it. Yet he had to kill animals for food. This should have meant war between beasts and humans, but tradition said the matter had been settled long ago, when the humans first came. The Indians believed, as did many Old World peoples also, that the animals did not really die. They simply sloughed off fur or feathers and went back to their original home. Here was a practical reason for belief in immortality, one that might well form the basis for a similar belief about the human race. In fact, many of the hunting tribes did believe in rebirth, at least for infants who had not had a real life.

The fact that animals were really indestructible did not mean that a hunter could waste and use them as he chose. Before abdicating their world rule, the animals had made conditions about giving their bodies for food. So the hunter practiced a form of conservation that was part religious and part practical. On the religious side, he took care of the bones or other remains, keeping them away from marauding dogs or that horror of the hunter, the menstruating woman. Tales speak of a fisherman who lost one salmon bone, so that Salmon Boy was lame forever after. On the practical side, the hunter, fisher, or gatherer killed no more than he needed and did it without undue pain to his quarry.

Sometimes the animals made this contract themselves, not liking their new company. At other times, they were commanded by the Culture Hero or even the Creator. Generally the contract was not with the animals en masse but with their Owner. Each species had such a leader or Elder Brother who still kept charge of them. Usually he was an animal larger than the rest but with peculiar markings. The Salish of the Northwest Coast could always recognize the leader of the salmon run by his crooked mouth. This fish must be cooked and eaten in a special ceremony. More often the Owner was a spirit animal and could not be killed. He was sometimes seen shutting his people into a cave so that an ill-behaved hunter could not get them. Or he might drive them directly toward a hunter who carried out the proper rites and observed the taboos.

All these beings could take human form if they wished, but

there were some who never appeared as animals. Such was the Mother of Game in the eastern Pueblos. At the winter dances she led the deer, the mountain goats, the buffalo, and hares into the plaza as a forecast of successful hunts. A grimmer kind of Owner was Sedna of the eastern Eskimo. This undersea woman, the "Great Food Dish," is the Owner of the sea mammals on which the Eskimos live. She is no animal herself as are the other Owners. Tradition says that she was a woman who married one of the man-animals, first a dog, then a stormy petrel. Her father rescued her from the latter and was taking her away in his kayak when the bird followed them and raised a terrible storm. The father threw the girl out to lighten the boat but she clung to the gunwale. To loosen her grip, the old man cut off her finger joints, one by one. These became the seals, walruses and whales who live in her house under the sea. When the people on earth break a taboo, such as cooking sea and land animals together or failing to confess an abortion, the "Old Mother" becomes angry and shuts the animals away from the hunters. The way to pacify her is to comb the long hair which gets in her eyes and which she cannot handle without fingers. So the Eskimo shaman must journey down and do it for her. Among the western Eskimo the sea-animal Owner was the moon, a male. To get his favor, the shaman must travel into the sky. This idea of the Owner must be an ancient one among hunting people, for it was shared with tribes in Siberia and as far west as Lapland and Finland. Could it have been brought to America by the first immigrants and retained here in purer form than anywhere else?

Usually the Owner was favorable to hunters who observed taboos and went through the proper rites. One exception to this kindly agreement was the attitude of the Cherokee in South Carolina. According to their myth, the animals were at first friendly to the human race; then men increased too rapidly and invented new weapons so that they became a menace. The animals met to decide what was to be done. Finally the most persecuted, the deer, hit on the expedient of giving rheumatism to the human race. After that, other animals selected diseases that they would impose. The plants, say the Cherokees, then took pity on the human race and each variety of herbs and grasses agreed to provide a remedy for some particular disease.

This sophisticated idea seems unique. Usually, the hunting groups looked upon animals with a kindliness, a reverence, a brotherhood that civilized man finds hard to imagine. Families or groups were proud to be called by animal names and to boast that in the mythical days some ancestor had married an animal Owner, or at least had been helped by him.

Sedna was not the only human being of mythology who married an animal. Usually this was the Owner of his species, appearing temporarily in human form. Probably that was the case with Sedna's dog and petrel husbands, for the dog-husband story is popular throughout the North. In other areas, human males or females often married bears. In each instance, the animal spouse appeared to be human and revealed himself or herself only in some crisis. The offspring generally had the gift of turning into animals or at least of exercising animal powers.

This brings us to totemism, a subject of learned debate for more than half a century. Since the word is still used in a mystic and religious sense, perhaps we should pause over it. *Totem* is a version of an Algonkian Indian word meaning something like brother or sister. It has been used in connection with organized primitive groups who distinguish themselves by an animal or plant name. Usually they forbid marriage within the group, as in a family. An outstanding example is one that has usurped the totemistic stage of the Arunta of Australia. Their totemic groups regard themselves as descended from some mythic plant or animal that they will not kill but whose numbers they increase by sacred ceremonies so that others may kill and use it.

Thanks largely to the Arunta, totemism came to be regarded by some as the mystic impetus that pushed primitive people into organization and exogamy. Further facts about clans and other groupings with animal and plant names have shown that this is putting the cart before the horse. Incest taboos and family exogamy often developed before clan organization. Clans organized as their economic situation made organization desirable. People working as a unit needed a name to distinguish them from other units, and what was more natural than to take a plant or animal name with which they felt a connection? This connection varied from actual spirit ancestry to temporary dealings with a spirit.

The Hopi Snake clan claims a male ancestor who married the daughter of a snake chieftain. Since the Hopis count descent through the mother, the snake woman became the ancestress of the clan. Her human descendants recognize their kinship with all snakes whom they ask for rain and never kill. The snakes, in their turn, can supposedly be carried in a snake priest's mouth without his being bitten. The Elk clan of the Osage, on the Prairies, was the only one authorized to make elkskin coverings for sacred objects. They, however, must not kill the elk who offered himself for that purpose. The killing must be done by some other man with a different taboo. This kind of arrangement is more or less common. The Iroquois clans with animal names, however, kill the animals at will and have no duties connected with them. And plenty of organized clans, like the Navaho Folded Arms, have no totems at all.

Today the word is used often in connection with the famous totem poles of Alaska, which do not belong to clans and have no religious significance. They are the equivalent of a crest or a coat-of-arms that refers to some great event in the owner's past. Thus a Kwakiutl chief, on Vancouver Island, has a huge Thunderbird on his totem pole. The story is that the Thunderbird appeared when the first house of the Gilikum family was being built. These houses are huge plank structures, and the chief and his men were trying to raise the crosspiece that would support the roof. Even all the men together could not lift it, and they appealed to the Thunderbird for help.

"This is why I have come from above," said the bird. Then he took the immense log in his claws and laid it on the two upright posts. Before he left, he said: "You will always have a friend in me to watch over you; when any of you die, I shall weep with you."[4]

Sometimes the mythical animal on the pole was an enemy

[4] Barbeau, Vol. I, p. 150.

whom the pole-owner killed, as he might kill any of the creatures represented. Or some other event may be pictured, like the visit of Secretary Seward when the United States bought Alaska. Seward, in his frock coat, stands atop an empty pole, as a reminder that, although the Russians received money for Alaska, the Indians got nothing.

Spirit powers beside the man-animals were the Sun, Moon, Winds, and other natural phenomena. The sun, in the Far North, was sometimes not a divinity at all. It may be one of the man-animals who volunteered for the task of carrying a light across the sky. (Since these myths date from before the days of horses, there could be no sun chariot.) It might be an object that was thrown upward by the man-animals themselves or that was stolen from its possessor.

The Thunderbird was an important spirit not only in the Northwest but through most of the country. On the Plains his great voice meant the beginning of spring and, in the Great Lakes country, he was a great bird with flashing eyes and wings that made a roaring sound. This Thunderbird was constantly at war with the Water Monster, the evil-minded one who killed the Transformer's brother. With the Fox and their neighbors around the Great Lakes, the Winds were manitous sitting at each of the four directions, and they were appealed to for long life. There was a long list of other invisible beings, but the most important was the Spirit of Fire who hung head-down in the smoke hole and reported to the Great Manitou everything done in the house. In the Desert area, where there were few large animals, the spirits might be Mist, Fog, or Mountain, or even ghosts. Among the wealthy salmon fishers of the Pacific Coast, imagination made a flight and conceived of such invisible spirits as Wealth and War.

The range of "nature persons," from the animals to the thunder, the winds, and the heavenly bodies, can be found everywhere. The emphasis, however, is very different. With some of the hunter-gatherers in the Desert area, the animals seem to be almost the only Powers present in man's thought. In the wide open Plains, the animals bring visions, but ceremonial reverence is offered to the directions—to the earth, the sky, and the four quarters of the world or the winds which personate them. Sometimes the sky power is focused in the sun, as one who is able to see all and can be a witness to behavior. Each of these has mana in its own sphere. The world is full of distributed power so that man lives constantly among potential companions and helpers.

With many tribes, the personalizing of power goes no further than this. Yet, occasionally, the sense of pervasive mana flowers, in some thinker's mind, into the picture of an all-powerful Being, who is not only a creator but a protector and guardian of both men and spirits. Such a conception would be difficult for wandering hunter-gatherers since they knew nothing of organized states or powerful leaders. Their mobile bands were dependent on the earth and its products, and to these they gave their reverence. The sun sometimes shared this reverence, which came from friendly respect, rather than worship. Some Pacific Coast fishermen spoke of the One Sitting Above or the Lord of the Shining Heavens, but these Beings are not mentioned in the origin myth and do not appear in ceremonies. They and some other mentions of a sky god seem to belong to a level apart from the ancient myth. Perhaps they echo some teaching from outside. Perhaps, as Radin has suggested, they are the sort of ideas which have occurred to thinkers all over the world but have not been taken up and used by others unless those were ready.

The planting Indians were ready. Most of them lived in organized groups, even federations, so that the idea of a single powerful leader was not foreign to them. Their different concepts of such a being must be separately described, since they varied with the situation and contacts even, perhaps, contacts with early Christian missionaries. Subordinate to the great Being were the winds and sometimes the stars. Mother Earth, too, had her place. There were no special ceremonies for her but she constantly was revered as people walked or danced on her bosom. She is not the outstanding mother-goddess who blossomed in the Old World when agriculture took the place of hunting. There, Ceres, Isis, Astarte, and various other names were fused into one great symbol of fertility, connected with yearly death and rebirth of vegetation and with human sacrifice. North America had almost no sacrifice, even of animals. Mother Earth did not demand it. This kindly producer of food is sometimes the soil itself, sometimes the vegetation. In one Winnebago tale, she takes corn from her body. Estsan Atlehi of the Navahos is young, mature, and old every year according to the changing seasons.

These were ever-present Powers, dealt with in ceremony and in individual prayer. They were kindly when kindly treated. When offended, they simply withdrew their help and protection. But the hunter's life was always full of danger, and he sometimes conceived of really evil spirits who must be responsible for his bad luck. These gruesome beings loom up principally in the Far North, where the forest and tundra pose a menace unknown on the sunny Plains.

Ojibwa hunters, who often face starvation in the snowy wastes, have nightmares of a cannibal spirit called Windigo. Perhaps he represents a temptation they have often faced or even succumbed to. Their legend is that Windigo devours a man, then spews him out as a cannibal. Men have come back from the woods in a state of frenzy which made people believe they had actually eaten human flesh or thought of it. All men fear this Windigo disease, which is thought incurable, and some who could not face the danger have become psychotic.

It is most interesting to see what has happened to the cannibal spirit on the Northwest Coast. That is an opulent fishing country where the huge runs of salmon would allow the Indians, if they wished, to live comfortably without any hunting. But there are dark forests stretching back from the coasts where a little hunting is done; these are populated with a number of gruesome spirits, among them a cannibal. No one is afraid of this being, however —in fact, he is courted. True, he is said to devour people and spew them out as cannibals, but these people must be the sons of chiefs with an inherited right to such treatment. At puberty they are secluded in the forest and, supposedly, devoured. They come back in simulated frenzy and are thus constituted members of a very select secret society.

These Kwakiutl conceive of other gruesome spirits such as

he-who-shouts-in-the-wood, who pursues lost travelers with his horrible yells until they go insane. There is a cannibal woman here, too, black and gigantic, with large hanging breasts, who is able to tear down huge trees. The Tanaina, hunters of western Canada, speak of a Bush Indian, half man and half animal, who attacks solitary hunters and eats their fat. And the Eskimo, out alone in the snowfields, may see the half man gliding without legs over the white expanse to hypnotize him into death. The half man, the cannibal, and the giant-who-shouts-in-the-woods inhabit the forests of Siberia, Lapland, and Finland also. Obviously the tales go back to the ancient life of many hunting peoples.

The contrast of these frightful beings with the gaily costumed rain-bringers of the Southwest is striking. Dark forests and deadly cold must have influenced the imagination of the northern people until they feel, like the Ingalik of Alaska, that "there is six times more bad in the world than good."

These bugaboos of the hunters, it will be noticed, are mostly female, whereas the benevolent spirits are male. This emphasizes the great rift felt in the hunting country between women and game animals, for the mana of the two are felt to be in a hopeless opposition. Women in hunting groups, as later chapters will show, are under far more disabilities than they are among the planters.

The spirits mentioned here by no means complete the roster. Each tribe also had its legends of giants, little people, and strange monsters, some ancient, some borrowed from European or African fairy tales. Except in the Far North, most of the spirits were kindly. It is true that witches and evil medicine men could get their help in doing evil, but that was not by the spirit's wish. The spirits, of their own free will, did no harm so long as their taboos were observed and the balance of nature maintained. That meant that man must not exploit the children of Mother Earth unduly. He must take no more than he needed from animal or plant and must give back thanks and respect. The white man's wholesale exploitation of natural resources seemed to them shocking. Smohalla, leader of a hunter-gatherer group on the Columbia River, told an official: ". . . the work of the white man hardens soul and body. Nor is it right to tear up and mutilate the earth as white men do. . . . We simply take the gifts that are freely offered. We no more harm the earth than would an infant's fingers harm its mother's breast.[5]

REFERENCES

Idea of spirits: Karsten, 1935; Teicher, 1960; Tylor, 1889.

See also General Books listed after Chap. 1.

Animal Owner: Hultkrantz, 1961; Paulson, 1961, 1964.

Totemism: Kroeber, 1952, Part IV; Levi-Strauss, 1962; Linton, 1936, pp. 206–7, 425–26; Lowie, 1947, Chap. 6.

Explanations not accepted by modern ethnologists: Frazer, 1910; Freud, 1950.

Description of some totemic clans and moieties: Gifford, 1916 (Miwok); Fletcher and La Flesche, 1911 (Omaha); La Flesche, 1921 (Osage).

Description of totem poles: Barbeau, *Totem Poles*, no date; Garfield and Forrest, 1948.

[5] Mooney, 1896, p. 724.

6

WOMAN POWER

Some distance outside the Papago village and facing away from it were the small huts where women of the different families went to spend their menstrual periods. No man would go anywhere near these little structures and those happening to come in sight of them turned their faces away.

"Not used any more," an old woman told me. "Bad. Lots of trouble come because we Bean People forget that."

She meant the ancient belief that woman, at her periods, is the vessel of a supernatural Power, the power that allows her to give birth. This power is so different from man's power to hunt and kill that the two must be kept apart. Indians can tell of occasions when a mere glance from a menstruating woman has taken away a man's hunting ability for life. If such a woman crosses a deer trail, the deer may leave the country forever. If she goes where people are gathered, if she attends a ritual—and most rituals are conducted by men—it will lose its efficacy. Even for her to move about in public is dangerous.

No wonder then that many groups, especially the hunting people, demand that she segregate herself until the fateful period is over. Many have special huts, as the Papago did. Others demand that, at least, she stay in her own home. She must not touch hunting weapons or they would become useless. She must not cook for men or eat from the dishes they used. She had special dishes which might be kept from month to month. Or they might be destroyed after each use.

"Did some spirit make these rules?" I asked my Papago informants. They shook their heads.

"No spirit. Just got to do. Like you come in when it rains."

"And if you did not come in? I mean, go to your special hut?"

"Maybe flood. Fire. People die."

The penalty, it appeared, might fall upon the whole village, in the form of a flood or an epidemic, any catastrophe usual in the area. Fear of such consequences was the reason why women were so often excluded from ceremonies, a blanket prohibition being the safest rule. It was why so many Indians feared white schoolteachers and hospital nurses. It was why, in many areas, women could not become shamans, at least until after the menopause. A specially brave man, however, could gain power by defying the danger, after taking magical precautions. Thus a bold whaler on the Northwest Coast might carry some cloth contaminated by a menstruant in his canoe.

This dread and exclusion seems not to have impressed the women of olden times with any sense of inferiority. "Do you mind being sent out of the house?" I once asked a Papago woman undergoing her days of separation. She laughed at me.

"Mind! Why, it's a holiday for us women. No work to do, no matter how the men may want it."

"You don't mind—er—people knowing?"

Now she was amazed. "Why should we? That is the time when we are powerful and the men are afraid. We like to see them slinking past with their backs turned." Then she chuckled. "No matter what my husband wants me to do in these days, he can't make me do it."

In fact, stories told by the women often deal with the way in which the men have been routed and frustrated by this power unattainable to them. Women did not mind letting the men conduct ceremonies and have visions while they, the females, attended to the essentials of propagating the race and providing it with food and shelter.

History cannot tell us when this attitude changed, but there is proof that it did change even as far back as the Old Testament. If a woman bears a male child, says Leviticus, "she shall be unclean seven days . . . she shall touch no hallowed thing, nor come into the sanctuary, until the day of her purifying be fulfilled."[1] There were further restrictions and sacrifices connected with male or female babies and all because of uncleanness. At a woman's monthly periods, also, she was judged to be "in impurity" for seven days. Anyone who touched her or touched her bed was unclean until evening and must be purified.

The practical directions here are not too far from those of the Papago. The divergence is in the term "unclean." This change of a tabooed person or thing from the status of powerful or sacred to that of unclean is a well-known historical process. Frazer, long ago, showed that objects and persons once untouchable because they were sacred continued to be untouchable after the reason for their sacredness was forgotten. The explanation then accepted was that they were unclean.

This happened to the pig, once sacred in Egypt, Greece, and Syria, and it would be interesting to follow the process by which a like fate befell women. The idea of their power at physical crises must have held on among simple folk in Europe, just as pagan festivals did. Rabelais has a tale about a farmer's wife subduing the Devil at such a time.[2]

Restrictions for woman during her reproductive life are known —or they once were known—throughout the world. In fact, comments Webster: "The wide diffusion of these taboos . . . points to their great antiquity. The ideas back of them must be deeply implanted in the human mind."[3] Even today, there are rural areas where a menstruating woman must not handle cream because her touch will sour it.

Seclusion of woman and her avoidance of all hunting gear were for the benefit of the community. Other precautions were neces-

[1] 12:2–4.

[2] *The Works of Rabelais*, reprinted from the translation of Urquhart and Motteux (London, 1708), Book IV, pp. 321–23.

[3] Webster, 1942, p. 93.

sary so that she herself might not suffer from the Power possessing her. This was especially necessary for girls just attaining maiden-hood. Boys, at this time, went through severe fasting in the hope of attaining Power. The girl, on whom Power had come without her volition, must see that the Power was tamed. To that end she did not touch her head, the most important part of her body. She used a scratching stick of wood or shell.

"I kept it tied around my neck," one woman told me. "So it would always be ready."

"What would happen if you forgot to use it?"

"Hair fall out, maybe. Or get gray right away."

The nameless, impersonal force would have exacted a penalty. In some places, the girl must not touch water to her lips but must drink through a tube. She must fast, at least from special foods. Often she had no fire, even in winter, but this was not a punish-ment. Fire was the representative of the sun on earth, and a person in seclusion must keep out of the sun. So much was done by many other people under supernatural influence. But this was a climax in the girl's life, when her character as a woman was being set. She must practice in miniature all the virtues that would be expected of her later. Each area had its own ideas about this and its own re-quirements.

In the Great Basin, where families trudged about constantly on the food quest, a grass hut might be built for the pubescent girl. Otherwise, she sat in a corner of the house, face to the wall, thus keeping away from sun and fire. She fasted from their best food, which was often fish since big game was rare. She was bidden to sleep little, talk little, and never laugh. Thus she would avoid being a chatterbox in later life. Also, with these hard-working people, the rule of inactivity was set aside. The girl was required to run daily, as women did when getting firewood. The Walapai had her run up a mountain. When in the hut, she must be at work weaving baskets. A bath ended the ordeal with no further cere-mony.

Further north, in western Canada, the people lived by hunting; so the powers of man, the provider, must be kept up to the mark at all costs. He could not risk contact with dangerous woman

magic, and inconvenience to the woman was of secondary importance. The Kaska of that area placed their maidens far from camp,
within a hedge of spruce boughs high enough to keep out the sun.
Here a girl sat for a month, undergoing the usual restrictions and
wearing a long leather robe which was pegged to the ground.
Talking and laughing were obviously no temptation but still she
must keep busy. So she industriously picked needles off the spruce
boughs of her shelter. Perhaps, to her, this was as great a public
service as rolling bandages in an army hut might seem in another
culture.

If she were of the Dené tribe, in the same general area, she
might stay in seclusion for three or four years. During this time
she worked and carried wood but she and the sun never saw each
other. She wore a headdress of tanned skin with fringe that hung
over her face and breast. Men never came near her, and if while
gathering wood she came to the trail of a hunter, she waited some
time before crossing it, lest her influence reach him.

The prosperous fishing people of the Pacific Coast had very different needs. This area stands out among Indians as one where
wealth and status were guiding motives. The huge wooden houses
with their wealth of stored food, the household heads with their
pride of name and ancestry, and the extravagant feasts will appear
often in these chapters as influencing ceremonial life. Here the
prominent men had magic of their own, so that fear of woman
power did not loom important. The bold ones even used menstrual
material as whaling charms. What they wanted for their daughters
was not industry and humility, but the good looks and health that
would attract an important suitor.

Still they felt that the rules for maiden seclusion should not be
ignored. Therefore, a coastal girl at her first menstruation "went
into the corner" of the huge, barn-shaped house, where she sat on
the shelf-like bed that went along the wall and was screened off
with cedarbark mats. Here she lived on dried fish and cold water,
perhaps for the usual four days, perhaps longer. Among the
Makah of northern Washington, the girl sat with her knees up
against her abdomen to make it flat and her back against the wall to
make it straight. After four days of this, she still spent most of her

time in the corner, washing her hair, anointing her face and body. Makah houses were walled with horizontal planks hung from upright posts like slats. An ambitious suitor could raise one of these slats and poke in gifts of furs. If the parents approved, this might release the girl and bring about marriage. Otherwise, the father, as soon as he could, would give a feast at which suitors might contest for the girl's hand. Such a feast, with or without marriage arrangements, became a feature of the end of the puberty ceremony among tribes further south. In fact, the ribald songs in order at such a time were a standard form of amusement with a number of Indian groups.

As we move away from the stark North, we find more attention to the girl's comfort. The Gosiute of southern Utah, for instance, had a device that should have been used oftener. These poor people, in a desert area, had almost no hunting. They were food-gatherers, with whom the woman's contribution to subsistence was at least as great as the man's. Perhaps this was why the secluded girls were allowed the same warm bed that the men used when traveling in winter. This "hot bed" is a most efficient device for people who have little clothing or blankets. It means making a fire in a pit as for baking, then scraping out the embers and lying on the warm sand. Or heated stones may be placed in the pit with leaves or grass over them. Gosiute girls worked during seclusion, according to the Basin habit. Still, they and some of their neighbors could keep warm while they rested.

In southern California, the hot bed was an institution. Here the people were linguistic relatives of the Basin groups and, like them, were hunter-gatherers. Their food, however, augmented by fish, was more plentiful. They were organized into clans and the clans into groups called phratries or moieties. They had ceremonial houses, ceremonial leaders, and a good deal of formal reciprocity between groups. All this was brought into their treatment of maidens.

With the Luiseño, who have been best described, the hot beds were made in the public square, sometimes within the ceremonial enclosure itself. They were of heated stone, carpeted with grass and reheated once a day when the girls got up for a short time.

The girls lay on their backs, with stones on their abdomens, doubtless to flatten them. Baskets were put over their faces, "to keep off the flies," say the Indians, but more likely to prevent them from looking at people or the sun. This was necessary since, far from being secluded, they had relays of dancers and singers from other clans around them—men at night, women in the day. The songs were often clan songs, satirizing and threatening enemy clans, and these the girls learned.

The girls did not work during this period, but they had intensive instruction afterward from the clan leader himself. It was similar to that given to the boys, a system not usual in Indian life. Also, as we shall see, it had a southwestern atmosphere, different from the family affairs of the north. Each girl held in the mouth a ball of sage seed mixed with salt—the first salt she had had for four days. Resisting temptation to swallow it, she watched the leader mark a circular design on the ground. It was crude compared with the sand paintings now famous among the Navahos, but it was the girl's first picture of the world where she must now take her part. The old man instructing her said, in substance:

> This is the earth. The white outside it is the Milky Way and the black inside is our spirit. This pile of sand is the sea, which gives the breath of life. Others are the bear, the rattlesnake and sickness. All these will harm you if you do not lead a good life.[4]

He described the good life, which consisted principally in always having food ready for her husband and for guests, and in being peaceful and courteous to everyone. Then the girl spit her ball of sage seed into the center of the figure, thus becoming part of the world. As a finale, there might be a race by the girls, a painting of their faces by the leader's wife, and a design put on a rock to commemorate the occasion.

Among the Yuma and Mohave on the Colorado River we find the hot bed again. A horrified Jesuit father thought at first the girls were being buried alive.

In the uplands of New Mexico are the Chiricahua Apache, part of a group that once filtered down from the Canadian North.

4 Kroeber, 1925, p. 685.

Although they roamed within reach of farming people—Navaho, Pueblo and, later, Spanish—these Apache remained hunters and raiders. They had few ceremonies compared with these neighbors, but one of the most important was that for the maiden. Instead of being a private matter, this was an occasion of happiness and blessing for all the people. It took place not at puberty, but on some fine summer day that could be appointed beforehand so that hundreds might attend. At present, the date of this "coming out party" is usually the fourth of July.

The essentials of partial fast, scratcher, and drinking tube were present. So was avoidance of the sun, for the girl spent four days in a special tipi. But this was ceremonially built and known as "the home of White Painted Woman," the divine mother of the Apache Culture Hero. The girl herself was White Painted Woman for four days and able to give blessing like her namesake. She was painted and dressed by a woman who must be industrious and good and had perhaps had a vision from the White Painted Woman. A male singer "cared for her" daily with sacred songs.

At the end of this seclusion, the girl scattered pollen over the people, especially children, who were brought for her blessing. At night, there was an imposing dance of masked men, representing the spirits of the four directions, come to bring blessing as they did on all crucial occasions. Then there was feasting and dancing. No wonder a girl who was maturing was known to these Apache as "she through whom we shall all have a good time."

This genial ceremony is perhaps the high point of girls' rites of a beneficent kind, whereas the Kaska treatment exhibits the extreme of fear and rigor. These ceremonies and the others which mark the end of a woman's seclusion have been spoken of as "rites of passage" moving the individual from one social state to another. This seems to me a more desirable term than purification. We shall find similar rites marking the end of seclusion for other individuals under supernatural influence.

After her strenuous initiation the maiden, now a woman, was expected to attend for herself to the duty of avoiding men and their gear. Most of the hunting people had special huts, but the planters simply asked her to keep away from men and gatherings and not to cook.

Childbirth followed much the same pattern as adolescence and menstruation, but Indian common sense did not require the mother to fast. Instead, she ate foods whose shape and color should work good magic for the child and avoided those that might have unlucky properties. In the North, where fear of woman power seems to have been strongest, she was often sent to a separate hut even in the winter. This flimsy, fireless shelter, just large enough for a crouching individual, has shocked white observers. However, it kept out the sun and admitted less wind than a larger shanty. Also, since birth was given in a kneeling position, the occupant did not need to lie down.

A new feature connected with childbirth was the husband's share in at least some of the restrictions. This behavior was first noticed by students among the Basques in Europe and called by the French name *couvade*. The Basques were an extreme case, for the report is that among them the wife went about her duties soon after childbirth while the husband lay in bed as though recovering. One South American tribe, the Tupinamba, follows the same custom, with the husband lying in a hammock and receiving visits, while his wife is up and working. This has been interpreted by some psychologists as jealousy on the husband's part because he cannot give birth.

The "semi-couvade" in California throws more light on the subject, for here the new father and mother share much the same restrictions before and after birth, with those for the father being somewhat lighter. The reasoning seems to be that the two parents are physically one, so that the man, instead of being injured by the woman's mana, actually partakes of it. Therefore, he must keep away from others and guard his own safety just as she does.

He rarely stays in the birth hut with her, for most Indians have the conviction that a male presence (except occasionally that of a medicine man) is unlucky at birth. However, he sometimes uses the partial fast, the special dishes, and the scratching stick. He avoids ceremonies because of the danger to others. Often too he gives up the male activities of hunting, fishing, and gambling: the female power upon him is too great and he would not be successful. In the California version of the couvade, however, he does not sit still. In accordance with the local idea of keeping busy, he performs the woman's tasks, such as running to fetch firewood. He may bathe every day and have an old man to attend him, as his wife has a woman. All this is for the good of the child, as understood in much of California and, to some extent, further north.

Far from being an abnormal custom, these restrictions for the father may once have been quite usual. We hear of them at certain points—for instance, among the Ainu of Japan, in south India, and in Melanesia. With one Papuan tribe, indeed, restrictions are so many that the poor father is practically a pariah.

East of the Rockies and, certainly, east of the Mississippi, information about seclusion of women is scanty. Perhaps this is because the women's ceremonies were obscured by more elaborate ones. Or perhaps it is because the eastern tribes were visited earlier and began earlier to give up their old ways. We hear occasionally of seclusion or avoidance of men's gear and can imagine that once the whole roster of restrictions may have been common.

Those restrictions were placed upon others besides women. The next chapters will show them used for mourners and sometimes for anyone having contact with the dead. One or more of them might be used for priests or for those officiating at a ceremony. Some tribes used them for a warrior who had killed an enemy, some for a murderer. Van Gennep has pictured this silence, seclusion, and fasting, with other magical precautions as a rite of passage. The person under supernatural influence goes through a mimic death before emerging with new powers. That is how an observer can sum it up, but we cannot suppose that the first people to practice such a retreat saw it so clearly. Perhaps the practice spread as they saw—or thought they saw—that it was efficacious.

The Power demanding it was not always impersonal. When the widowed and the mourners retreated, it was because they feared the soul of the dead. So did the enemy-slayer and the murderer. We can imagine that these retreats, with their theological explanations, were worked out by people who had begun to have theories about the Supernatural. It seems possible to me that the fear of woman power may have been one of the first beliefs of early men giving rise to some of their first rites.

REFERENCES

Discussion of taboos for women at puberty, menstruation, and childbirth: Van Gennep, 1960; Webster, 1942, Chaps. 2–4.

Documentation of girls' puberty ceremonies west of the Rockies: Driver, 1941.

Description of special ceremonies: Kroeber, 1925, pp. 661–65, 673–85 (Southern California); Opler, 1941, pp. 82–134 (Chiricahua Apache).

Documentation of taboos for women at menstruation and childbirth west of the Rockies: Series of Anthropological Records, University of California.

For all above usages east of the Rockies, see tribal monographs from museums and universities.

7

ATTITUDE TOWARD THE DEAD: FEAR AND AVOIDANCE

In a bark house of the Sinkyone of northern California, the family sits on the earthen floor for the evening meal. One man, however, sits alone. While the others eat fresh fish, his must be dried and eaten from a separate basket. He does not look around, and occasionally he scratches his head with a special stick. For ten days he will stay away from his wife and will not hunt or gamble, nor will he smoke for five days. Finally he will be purified by chewing the roots of special plants, rubbing them on his body and then bathing.[1] This is a case of retreat in the presence of supernatural power, of the sort we have seen used for maidens and menstruants. In this instance, however, the power to be feared is not birth but death. The man is a gravedigger who has handled a corpse.

Fear of the supernatural power connected with death is part of that substratum of Indian religions that has its roots far back in the Old World. In parts of Africa, Australia, and the Pacific Islands, corpse-handlers are under the same sort of restriction as the

[1] Driver, 1939, p. 355.

Sinkyone and for the same reason. Among the African Nandi such people may not touch food with their hands, but must scrape it up with bits of gourd or pottery. In Samoa, they have to be fed by others, like babies.

Corpse-handlers are not the only people in danger at the time of a death. In both the Old World and the New, some form of retreat is necessary for the bereaved family, sometimes for all present at the funeral, and occasionally for the dead man's whole village. Throughout North America, this was the attitude toward the dead, no matter how beloved they had been in life. It was not that they turned into evil ghosts. They were thought to feel kindly and to be still bound by those family ties that mean so much in Indian life. They did not want to give up those ties. From many different afterworlds, they tried to return and take their loved ones with them. To understand this belief, we must know something about the soul and its destiny.

To moderns, the soul is a single entity and the very word carries with it the adjective "immortal." Most Indians thought that each individual had at least two souls and neither might live forever. One was the life or breath soul that died with the body. That might mean when breath was gone or when the body finally decayed, so that soul might linger long around a grave and perhaps have continual needs. The other was the free soul. That was the one that wandered about in dreams or which left a person when he was ill and had to be sought by a shaman. The different tribes had varied descriptions of these two souls, and some thought there were more than two. The shadow and the name were sometimes thought to have separate existences. Some Eskimo and some Siberians thought there was a soul in every joint, else how could the joints feel pain separately? The primitive thinkers were working at problems of psychology, and their interpreters often found no words to explain their meaning. If Indians had been supplied with such terms as subconscious and ego, perhaps they would not have had to use the word soul in so many senses.

Name and shadow souls generally disappeared when the body died, although, as we shall see, the name could be given new life by adoption. The free soul went to the Land of the Dead. The various tribes pictured this afterworld in different ways, according to their own surroundings and experience. The element of fear usually showed, even where the afterworld was thought of as happy. And the groups dealt with their fears in different ways, some showing it openly, some hiding it, some transmuting it.

The area where fear was shown openly was that of the hunter-gatherers in the Desert area, the Arctic, and the Subarctic. The destiny of the soul in this area was no Happy Hunting Ground. As a rule, it was a shadowy place very like the soul's home on earth, except that night and day, summer and winter might be reversed. The dead lived in families as on earth and spent their time dancing. (They might dance on their heads or with their feet crossed.) Or they might play games. The aurora borealis gave a vision of some Eskimo dead at their version of football. These were the fortunate who had died by violence. When there were two afterworlds, they were not for the bad and the good but for those who died peacefully or by violence. The latter had the advantage.

No games or dancing could make up to the soul for separation from its loved ones. Indian families have always been closely united and an individual's whole life took place within the circle of his relatives, real or symbolic. People with whom he had no ties were looked upon with apprehension, as possible sorcerers. Even up to recent times, the Indian coming to a city has been appalled to realize that he must make advances to strangers. If the same feeling applied to life in the afterworld, we can imagine a ghost eagerly returning to seek his kin. He might even try to take one of them back for company. This meant death. So the loved ones, even while they wailed, adjured the free soul: "Your home is no longer with us. Go and do not return!" Yokuts corpse-handlers pushed the body into the grave with the admonition: "You are gone now. Go!"

Burial with most of the hunter-gatherers was a purely practical affair. Their digging sticks would not penetrate deeply into the desert gravel, so they thrust bodies into rock crevices and covered them with stones to keep out wild animals. Tribes further north dragged them out on the snow or abandoned them in igloos or bark tipis. Those who died by violence, such as witches and victims of an epidemic (thought to be caused by witchcraft), were cremated. Was this to make sure they were gone and could not return to finish the life that had been cut off?

Even the peaceful dead had better be buried by someone less subject to harm than the family. This might mean old people, who had little life left to lose. Or it could be non-relatives, members of the opposite moiety, or the berdaches, those males who led a woman's life. The corpse-handlers were purified afterward, and sometimes they were paid. As they carried out the body, they took all precautions against the soul's return. One device was not to use the house door, which the dead would remember. Instead, a hole was cut in the rear wall, the body taken through it, and the hole closed. The returning soul would find only a blank wall. A Navaho burial party, when its work was done, returned by a roundabout way, perhaps zigzagging or walking backward to confuse the trail. Later, Navahos were glad enough to let the government or the missionaries attend to the dangerous business of burial.

Still, families did what they could to assure comfort for their dead. Food and water, sufficient for the journey to the other world, were left beside the body. The Papago reckoned the time as four days, though some groups made it five or even twenty. The soul on arrival would need only spirit food, with tidbits thrown into the fire now and then as remembrance. Richer people, living toward the margin of the area of the hunter-gatherers, gave the dead full equipment, and might even kill a horse or dog for company.

All property of the dead not left at the grave had to be destroyed, given to non-relatives or, in later times, sold. This left the family practically destitute, but it was the price of their safety. Even the house must be destroyed or abandoned: that is, unless the family or the dying person himself had seen that his dangerous presence was removed before death. I once made a long search for an ancient Navaho woman who might give me some information. I found her in a flimsy shelter, scarcely larger than a dog kennel, but she was smiling and calm. Her end was coming, she knew, and the last favor she could do for her family was to save their house for them by not dying in it.

Above all, the family must never mention the name of the deceased, and many, in this hunting and gathering area, could not even hear it spoken. This is a stumbling block for census takers and students of history. Among the Salish-speaking people of Puget Sound, it can even interfere with the learning of language. For instance, if a man called Brown Elk died, the words "brown" and "elk" would go temporarily out of use, to be replaced by such roundabout expressions as "the tall animal" and "the color of dead leaves."

In spite of all precautions there were generally some dissatisfied free souls, without family connections, perhaps, or improperly buried. They wandered about, causing bad dreams or illness. A bad medicine man could use their power in witchcraft, and a good one could foil them by his spells. All this was a constant source of apprehension, but it would have been worse if the dead kept their identity longer. In this region and in many others, the soul was not thought immortal. It lived in the other world until there was no one left in this world who remembered the dead person. "If it were not so," an old Maidu explained to me, "the afterworld would be too crowded. Just as this one would be if Coyote had not brought death."

With such beliefs in mind, the hunter-gatherers could not hold a creed of work and self-denial in this life as preparation for eternal reward. They had no word for eternity. Their ideal was a long life in this world, and one man was overjoyed at seeing a vision of himself so old that he must crawl instead of walk. Few of them could hope for such an age and they did not plan for it. They did not even plan for several years ahead as farmers can do. Some of that attitude carried over into modern life, for early teachers and agents were constantly complaining: "These Indians feel no urge to look ahead and *save*."

Hunter-gatherers of the Desert area did not suffer unduly from the loss of house and property. Possessions were at a minimum and dwellings were easily replaced. Perhaps that is why some of them retained the custom almost up to modern days. People who had a more settled life and more substantial homes gradually turned to other ideas of death less onerous for the living. Before looking at these other groups, we may pause to note one group of settled people who burned their big houses at huge expense and sometimes despite protest from the heirs. These were the Yuman-speaking tribes of the Colorado River Valley, the Mohave, Yuma, and Cocopa. Tribes planted fields, whose boundaries they defended violently, and built large wooden houses that sheltered three generations. Yet they burned these houses after a death. They even destroyed model cottages built by the government until loans were refused to any who followed the practice. Were they newcomers to the fertile valley who had not yet become farm-minded? What they said was that a large scale destruction with frantic dancing and wailing "made them feel better."[2]

The dead were cremated in their part of California and, in fact, in the whole southern third of the state. Cremation was unusual with historic Indians, though known in earlier times. The River Tribes followed this practice, giving as the reason the command of their Creator, who was cremated after being killed by one of his own people. I shall never forget the funeral pyre of a Mohave youth, towering into the sunshine, while his clan danced—or rather marched—up and down, chanting their migration myth. Afterward came a football game that honored this school hero as Greek games once honored Achilles. His soul, said some of his clanmates, had gone to the Creator. Others spoke of a land of the dead under the Colorado River. There he would have a second death and be reborn as an insect.

This short period of life in the other world troubled some Mohave relatives. They felt, says one investigator, that their own deaths might come too late to enjoy the dead man's company. A shaman, however, did not have this difficulty. He could manage to put the souls away in some kind of storage where they would not grow older but would be available to spend with him all the afterlife due them. The same could be done with people he had killed by witchcraft and wished to use as slaves. This concept of slave souls is one that has received very little notice. More of it later!

[2] Forde, 1931, p. 209.

Every few years the Yuma, Cocopa, and their inland relatives the Diegueno held what has been called a Mourning Anniversary. An even better term might be Dismissal Ceremony, for it quieted the claims of all who had died since the last occasion. This was the time of orgiastic grief, when immense amounts of labor and goods were expended. Our best description of it, written in the 1920's, comes from the Yuma.

Long before the date of the ceremony, families began making images of their dead. They were almost life-size, made of rods draped in skin or canvas, with painted faces and eyes of mica. The proper way to honor them in this warlike tribe was with a mock battle. For this the whole community joined in making leather shields and feathered standards, every move punctuated with ceremonial speeches and singing.

> Over in the western heavens
> They are making the circle [the shield]
> To remind the people for all time.
> Over in the eastern heavens
> They are making the circle
> To remind the people for all time.[3]

Guests came from other tribes, even hostile ones, and all luxuriated in wailing together.

The battle took place with all the panoply of Yuman war, with the images as spectators. Meantime, a "house of crying" had been constructed. All marched toward it, singing a dirge.

> The house will have to be burnt at dawn
> And light will stream from it . . .
> Night bird and then night-hawk sing.
> It is getting toward dawn and
> A feeling like death comes over the house.[4]

At dawn, as threatened, the house and all paraphernalia were destroyed in a grand holocaust. Wailing grew frantic. Mourners threw their possessions into the fire and sometimes tried to throw in themselves. But, said the funeral orator: "We shall all be better people, stronger to whip the enemy, living long in good health."[5]

[3] Forde, 1931, p. 245.
[4] Ibid., pp. 249, 251.   [5] Ibid., p. 229.

Psychologists might make an interesting study out of this gigantic emotional outlet. The Cocopa, at least, refused for a time to give it up despite government urging, but some young Mohaves felt differently. They have been known to curse the dead for all the trouble and expense they caused. In fact, the custom favored the old rather than the young. No junior could fail to resent having to care for aged relatives when he knew what destitution their deaths would bring.

The Yuman holocaust is our most exaggerated example of destruction to counteract the death-evil. Throughout the southern third of California, there were groups that held Dismissal Ceremonies, but not on this scale. Some burned gifts but not dwellings. Some made the occasion one for intergroup rapprochement and exchange of shell money. Here, on the margin of the Desert area, the rule of destroy-and-forget was losing its force. Indians were persuading themselves that supernatural danger was a lesser calamity than loss of property.

One group that could ill afford the destruction of property and removal from profitable land was that of the fishing Indians of the Pacific Northwest. From the Indian point of view, which defined wealth as plenty of food and shelter, these coastal groups all the way from southern Alaska to northern California were some of the richest tribes in America. They had no fields, but the fishing sites on coast and rivers were an equally permanent source of wealth. Here prominent men with their relatives lived in huge wooden houses not so easily replaced as a straw wickiup. After a death in the family, the reaction of a Kwakiutl often was, "Why should we grieve alone! Let us make someone else grieve!" Then he would organize a headhunting expedition against either friend or foe. It did not matter so long as emotion had an outlet.

Death was an insult that had to be wiped out, not by avoidance of the dead but by glorifying them. As soon as possible there was a potlatch, the great giveaway feast by which these coastal people signalized every event in the life cycle. Up to that time, perhaps, the name of the dead had not been spoken, but at the feast mourning songs were sung and lavish donations of oil, food, and skins given in that name. Then his successor assumed the name, which was really a title, and proceeded to make it famous by war and feasting.

There was no hiding away of the body. Usually there was a cemetery near the village where coffins were placed on posts or in trees away from marauding animals. "Coffin" is a fitting term, for these woodworkers made cubical boxes into which they squeezed the corpses. Or they placed them aloft in dugout canoes, always with a wooden grave post nearby to show the family crest. A shaman's body was so dangerous that it might be hidden in a cave and crudely mummified. It was a feat of ghastly daring to steal parts of these bodies for use as whaling magic. A few groups like the Tlingit used cremation, but only for ordinary people. These needed to be near the fire in "the great house of the dead" but the brave man did not feel the cold.

This house of the dead was like the huge structures built by the Indians themselves. It was usually on an island or at least across water, although members of the Wolf Society went to the wolves in the forest and harpooners to the killer whales undersea. They lived out their lives in these afterworlds, and then usually were reborn as infants. Rebirth was an accepted dogma on the Northwest Coast. True, it occurred here and there all over the country but not so consistently as among these tribes with close relationships to Asia (see Chap. 2). In the regions on both sides of the Bering Sea, the free soul was thought to be very easily separated from the body. As future chapters will show, the soul could be easily lost and recovered, possessed by spirits, or reincarnated.

The last idea was especially appealing in the case of infants who died before they had really lived. The Quileute and others on the coast of Washington thought of a special babyland where the unfledged souls waited together for their next chance. The Tungus of Siberia pictured a tree on which the little souls perched like birds. There were various ideas about where the reborn souls went. In some groups, the dead person's name would be given to the next child born in his clan, and that would be sufficient to call the soul. In others, relatives stood over a newborn infant, pronouncing different names until the baby smiled and they knew what dead ancestor had arrived. They called the child by the right term of relationship, even though it might be grandfather. This meant, with some, that the child must be treated like a grand-father. That custom was found as far north as the area of the Central Eskimo, and Stefansson has told of his uncomfortable experience with a child who had the soul of such an aged relative and therefore could not be disciplined or asked to work. Besides this reborn soul, the youngster had a new free soul of its own, although it was very feeble at first and needed the older soul to act for it. By the age of twelve—maturity in Indian terms—guardianship was no longer necessary. Then the child could be disciplined while the reincarnated soul left, its fate unknown.

The Tlingit of British Columbia gave a wider scope to the returning soul. After a death, it would enter the next child born into the dead person's clan or family and would, of course, receive the appropriate name. If two children were born, perhaps of different sexes and at quite different times, each would have the soul, or part of it. Meantime another part was still in the realm of the dead, receiving gifts and hearing songs of mourning.

All this could be interpreted as a belief in several souls. It could also mean that Indian thinkers were fumbling with the idea of inherited characteristics. If they had had such words as gene and chromosome they would not have needed to describe the family likenesses they saw in terms of soul. And they might have separated the facts of heredity from the folklore and wishful thinking which said that a dying person might arrange his next birth with his future mother. Or she might choose him for her child. The proof that the right soul had come would be a birthmark or perhaps only a facial resemblance. The fact that such a resemblance might occur with children who were related but not in the clan was ignored.

The Eskimo of Alaska were neighbors to the Tlingit. They had no clans but they gave the name of one who died to the next child born in the village. Perhaps there were several boys and girls with the same name, but they may not have been related and nothing was said about a resemblance. The existence of namesakes was a comfort to the bereaved, who used them as a means of communication with the dead. Every few years, or every year if they could afford it, they summoned souls of the recently departed to an Inviting-in Feast. Perhaps it was on the same order as the Bladder

Feast, given for all the seals killed that season and whose souls, if properly treated, would take new bodies and be killed again. The souls of the dead entered, at least momentarily, into their name-sakes to be feasted and honored. Then, apparently, they went away content.

In winter, when the hunt was over, men at Norton Sound gathered in the underground clubhouse and notified the guests by singing, drumming, and pounding on the earthen floor. Lamps were kept burning night and day to guide the progress of the souls, and dancers imitated paddling canoes or walking on snow-shoes to speed them from their distant burial places. The souls would arrive under the firepit, where they could feel the dancing and listen to the songs in their praise. Each bereaved person sang a mournful song to his own departed:

> Oh, my brother, come back to me,
> Come back, my brother, I am lonely,
> My brother come back and we
> Will give you a small present.[6]

The present was huge and meant years of work and saving, but this Chinese-like depreciation was Eskimo etiquette. The gift was not destroyed but went to some living person who bore the name of the dead. If there were no such person, one was named. It is hard to say whether the Eskimo ceremony meant reincarnation or adoption. For adoption of a living person is the next way we meet to negate death.

REFERENCES

Avoidance of the dead: Frazer, 1936; Webster, 1942, Chap. 5.

Documentary account of treatment of the dead west of the Rockies in series of Anthropological Records, University of California. Also mono-graphs on tribes by museums and universities.

Special descriptions: Devereux, 1937 (Mohave); Opler, 1945 (Apache); Strong, 1929 (southern California); Wyman, Hill, Osanai, 1942 (Navaho).

Ideas of the soul: Gayton, 1935; Hultkrantz, 1953; Tylor, 1889.

[6] Nelson, 1899, p. 374.

8

ATTITUDE TOWARD THE DEAD: ADOPTION OF A SUBSTITUTE OR "DELAYED BURIAL"

The fear of death could be transmuted by adopting someone in place of the departed. Thus the love once given to the deceased and the services expected from him could still go on. Whether the name-soul of the dead was transferred to the adoptee is not made clear. Certainly the presence of someone who would fill the vacant place in the group was a consolation to relatives and a help to family pride.

Many tribes in the Mississippi Valley practiced adoption when any member of a family died—man, woman, or child. These were people who had large wooden houses and extensive cornfields. They could ill afford to destroy and forget, so they adopted a person of the appropriate age and sex and handed over to the adoptee not only the name of the dead person but also his or her functions. It would appear that the free soul could not leave for the after-world until this had been done.

This afterworld was not the shadowy replica of the present one described for the hunter-gatherers. It was part of the story of the Culture Hero Nanabozho who was venerated all the way to the Northeast. Nanabozho, the Great Hare, had a younger brother Tcibiabos, whom he loved and protected; but the Water Monsters sucked Tcibiabos to his death under Lake Michigan. After four days, the boy returned as a spirit and knocked at his brother's door. Nanabozho would not let him in but sent him to rule the Land of the Dead. "It is a land of plenty and of dancing," the Fox dead are told. "You will dwell more pleasantly there."

The funeral ceremony in this country of cornfields was completely different from the furtive disposal of the dead practiced by Desert people across the Rockies. As a Fox Indian described it: The dead was dressed in all his finery and all night his clan sang and wept around him. He was buried in a shallow grave roofed over with wood or stones, and a respected man gave directions for the journey to the Land of the Dead:

> You must go and live with our nephew [as Hare and his brother were always called by mortals] . . . When you start to leave them [relatives] this day you must not think backwards of them with vain [regret] . . . And do not feel badly because you have lost sight of this daylight . . . Bless [the people] so that they may not be sick . . . You must merely bless them so that they may live as mortals here.[1]

The relatives were then bidden to bring tobacco so that the dead man might carry it to Hare's brother when he asked for a blessing. As each relative threw tobacco on the corpse, he said: "This day I give you this tobacco as message for you to take to our nephew." Then he asked for blankets, for success in war, and for long life "that I may continue to see this earth of the manitou as it changes [with the seasons]."[2] A dog might be strangled and hung on a post as a guide to the dead. The Fox were among the few tribes that sacrificed living creatures.

It took time to collect wealth for the adoption feast; but no more than four years were allowed to complete the task. After that the free soul, which had been kept waiting, would turn into an

[1] Michelson, 1925, p. 417.
[2] Ibid., p. 419.

owl. The feast had to provide more food than could be eaten, for, although living people consumed it, the real guests were ghosts. After the feast, the favorite game of the dead person was played—bowl dice for a woman, lacrosse for a man. "It is as if they were playing with him [the dead] for the last time, so it is said."[3]

The adoptee was loaded with gifts which he or she would repay later on. He kept his own clan but had all the privileges and duties of the deceased. If the deceased had been married, this resurrection set the widow or widower free for remarriage, although not necessarily with the substitute.

Here it seems plain that the soul of the dead person did not enter the adoptee but somehow enjoyed the gifts the adoptee received. There were also ways of sending gifts directly to the soul to be enjoyed in the afterworld. It may be that Fox souls were lonely there, as were those of the hunter-gatherers farther west. The funeral plea that they should "not think of their relatives with vain regret" would seem to indicate it. The relatives perhaps felt safe enough with their adoptee, but they sent others to the dead as slaves. At the grave of a Fox warrior a post was erected and painted with red crosses to denote the number of men, women, and children he had killed during his lifetime. He would claim these victims as his slaves now that he had gone to the other world.[4] Slaves might even be donated to the deceased by other warriors who felt they had plenty at their disposal.

At a warrior's funeral, it was the custom for men to strike the post and go through the recital of their exploits as they did at all ceremonies. At a Fox funeral, a warrior might proclaim: "At such a place I killed an enemy, I give his spirit to our departed friend."[5] An Omaha father who had lost a small child would ease his grief in the usual Plains manner by going on the warpath. He would carry one of the baby's moccasins with him and lay it beside the first man he killed. The dead warrior would protect the little one on the perilous journey to the other world.

Farther south, among the Natchez, we find almost the only

[3] *Ibid.*, p. 385.
[4] Blair, 1912, II, 173 (quoting Morrell Marston).
[5] *Ibid.*

example in America of living people killed to accompany the dead. The Natchez of the lower Mississippi Valley stand out in any description of Indian life because of their remarkable class system, presided over by a glorified ruler that was more like some systems in Nuclear America or even the Old World than in the tribes around them. Small as the now-vanished tribe was, it requires special mention if the roster of Indian customs is to be complete.

When a great man of the Natchez died, a score of people, both wives and servants, were killed to accompany him to the next world. Parents killed their young infants because the mother and father themselves then rose in the social scale. Other adults volunteered to die and go with the ruler. We can hardly believe that this meant a personal devotion such as no other Indians showed. More likely this action allowed the volunteer to go to a special heaven with the potentate. At least, the people who served him in this way were buried near him and not with the other commoners.

Adoption, if a group was adjusted to it, must have gone a long way to assuage grief. Another relief for sorrow was secondary burial or what I might call delayed death. This ritual was based on the belief that, although the body was inactive, the soul remained until sent away. The bereaved could sit by the body, talk to it, and show their affection. They could assume that the free soul, hovering near, could be present at feasts and could know all that was done.

An impressive example of this attitude was reported by the early Jesuits from the Hurons on Lake Ontario. In this tribe, the dead were placed in a shallow grave near the village. In fact, they were still considered residents of the village and present at all its ceremonies. Relatives regularly sat by their graves, telling them the news and expressing their affection. It was an excellent way to assuage grief and to do away with fear.

Every twelve years or so, "the fire was stirred up under the Big Kettle." In other words, the remains were finally interred and the souls released at a Feast of the Dead. Each family had its appointed corpse-handler who picked the bones clean. Brébeuf remarked how loving relatives often performed this office, cleaning and caressing even the recent dead without a sign of revulsion.[6] The remains were wrapped in valuable skins and placed in bags decorated "very artistically" with skins and wampum. Processions of men and women carrying such bags moved toward the head village and wherever they stopped, the souls were feasted. In one house, where they were thus entertained, "there were fully a hundred souls hung to and fixed upon the poles." At the head village a wide pit was dug, lined with furs, and surrounded by scaffolding. Here the bags of souls were hung, to watch games and dancing and to see gifts given in their names. Finally all were placed in the pit with skins and mats over them, along with three kettles and some corn. Then there was the dancing and merriment that ended most funeral feasts. One Indian explained that "people from different villages should all be friendly now, knowing that the souls of our relatives are all here together."

As usual, details about the souls and their destiny are none too clear. One thinker told the missionary that there were two souls, both of which remained with the bones until the Big Kettle. Then one flew to the village of souls in the west, bearing the gifts it had received, while the other remained with the bones "unless reborn." Some thought that one soul became a bird. But at least the kinfolk were relieved of all obligation.

Secondary burial is mentioned by early writers all the way from Virginia to Florida, and the Choctaw carried it on until recently. Scattered throughout most of the eastern woodland are hundreds of "burial mounds," many of which covered pits of bones like those left by the Hurons. They are of various styles and shapes that range all the way from the simple ones dated 1000 B.C. through the magnificent structures of the Hopewell culture in the Ohio Valley. Some were produced in Wisconsin as late as A.D. 1300.

There has been much discussion about why these elaborate burial mounds stand alone, with no sign of dwellings nearby. That arrangement can be understood if we picture the dwellings or even villages scattered at various distances. In such villages, relatives of the dead might work at carving and pottery, and at the accumulat-

[6] Kinietz, 1940, pp. 105–17 (quoting Brébeuf).

ing of trade goods such as are found in the tombs. Then at stated periods, we can imagine processions carrying "souls" to those tombs. Some tombs contain only one individual surrounded with gifts, whereas others, without gifts, lie massed nearby. So an important chief or priest might lie with his retainers at hand and we may guess at elaborate organization. The above is conjecture, however, for the builders of mounds or barrows moved away long ago and changed their customs. This particular area of Indian history still offers vistas for study.

Preservation of bones was a habit practiced in some tribes along the Atlantic coast when they were visited by the early whites, but it was a preservation of a peculiar kind. This was a region of autocratic chiefs, often called kings in the reports, and their caste system seems to have been continued among the dead. The bones of these "kings" were preserved in temples and guarded by sacred images. Among the Natchez on the Mississippi, the bones and skin themselves were made into a sort of mummy stuffed with sand. Natchez rulers came to "worship" these images, but worship is not an Indian custom. We wonder if they were not talking to these ancestors as the Hurons talked with souls at the graves. The Canadian Iroquois, who now include the Hurons, still hold rites some time after a death, with games and gift-giving, to honor the deceased and "to send the soul away." The Iroquois of New York State have a feast of the Big Kettle that they celebrate together in the presence of the dead, although the deceased have long been buried.

On the Plains, where groups had migrated from the East and the West, there was a medley of ideas on death and the soul. It is from this area that we have the tradition of a Happy Hunting Ground where all men were brave, all women beautiful and good tempered. Some investigators have found no trace of such a belief, although I know a few Indians who maintain it today.

The Sioux are one of the most famous of the Plains tribes, yet their traditions are from the East. They kept company with their dead somewhat as the Iroquois did, although there was no secondary burial. They seem to have been one of the few groups who did not fear the dead. Was this because the Happy Hunting Ground kept the souls from having any desire to return? The Sioux believed in four souls, three of which died with the body. The fourth could be kept for a while by a loving family in the form of a "spirit bundle." Black Elk, one of their religious thinkers, has feelingly described how parents cut a lock of hair from a lost child, wrapped it in valuable skins, and kept the bundle off the ground on a tripod. By such close contact with the dead, the bereaved father became a holy man who must continuously pray for the good of his people. All the camp brought gifts to the soul, which were stored up toward the day of its final release.

When that day came, smoke was offered on behalf of "the two-leggeds, the four-leggeds and the wingeds" to the Great Mystery, Wakan Tanka, to the Four Winds, and to Mother Earth. The soul was given its last meal of buffalo meat and wild cherry juice, the food and drink given to the Indians by Wakan Tanka. Four virgins were selected to eat of this food after the soul had been satisfied. This communion would assure to them some of the soul's power so that, when they became mothers, the tribe would have four blessed families. Then the bundle was carried out of the tipi and the soul released with the adjuration: "Always look back upon your people that they may walk the sacred path with firm steps."[7]

The spirit bundle could well be a form of secondary burial worked out by a nomadic people who could not afford to keep the bodies of their dead always near them. The consecrating of the four virgins seems similar to an adoption, so we have here a mixture of customs in the usual Plains manner.

Even when they did not "keep the ghost" in this way, the Sioux, untouched by fear, maintained a kind of companionship with their dead. True, Sioux mourners proclaimed their grief by passionate wailing, by lacerating their arms and legs, and even by cutting off a finger joint. Is this a sacrifice to the dead, who might otherwise take the whole body? If this is so, then the fear that first dictated the sacrifice has been forgotten. The Sioux caressed the bones of their dead and kept them where they could be visited. Because it is impossible to dig in the tough prairie sod, the corpses were laid on platforms under which kin might sit for days, the

7 Brown, 1953, p. 29.

women wailing, the men silently brooding. Later, the relatives might remove the skulls and lay them in a circle, with a buffalo skull as guard. There women have been seen to sit by the hour, talking to their lost ones "in pleasant and endearing language."[8]

The town-dwelling Pueblo Indians came nearest to having what we might think of as a modern point of view toward death. In their theology, the abode of the dead was a blessed place and the dead themselves bringers of blessing. Thus they were buried just outside the pueblo, where the rubbish heap made digging possible. Babies were placed under the hearth in the hope of a rebirth. The funeral ceremony allayed not the fear of the survivors, but their grief.

The gorgeously costumed katchinas are the ancestral dead who come to dance in the plaza, bringing promise of rain and fertility. These spirits themselves do not come; they did so once but the result of each visit was that someone went away with them, that is, someone died. Now the spirits are represented by reverent maskers who temporarily have the katchinas' power.

This is the first note reminiscent of the fear that surrounds death in the Desert area. The ancestors of the Pueblos were food-gatherers in that area some two thousand years ago and most of their languages are related to those of the present-day Desert people. Archaeology reveals a history of gradually moving southward, of acquiring planting knowledge, of building solid, permanent homes. Destruction of property and fear of things touched by the dead would be impossible in such a culture.

Yet a close scrutiny will show many traces of the fear and avoidance in the case of death which was felt by the food-gatherers. The Hopi speak of death as a "bad thing" and avoid all talk about it. On the night in November when the dead are in the street, women shut themselves away in fear. Individuals of an Isleta group, after buying food and toilet articles for the dead man, come running back from the grave and "close the trail" by a mark on the house door so he cannot follow. The widowed undergo as severe a seclusion as that imposed in the Great Lakes region where such people are believed to kill grass by sitting on it.

[8] Catlin, quoted in Bushnell, 1927, p. 68.

These are stark reminiscences of a more savage life, but the Pueblo people have put them under. Their method did not involve keeping bones, or adopting a substitute, or even believing in rebirth, except for infants who practically had no life. Their method was that institutionalized ceremony that regulated all their lives. Before a corpse was buried, the priest made a smudge from its hair which the mourners breathed. The purpose of this is phrased not as purification but as a way to make them forget their grief.

The dead themselves they do not forget. Prayer sticks are planted for them at certain times as they are for various gods and spirits. Bits of food are placed in the fire for them at meals but not accompanied by the irate plea of a Plateau mourner: "Take it and go away!" The offering is more in the modern spirit of placing flowers on a grave. Earnest seekers for wisdom have even prayed to a revered ancestor and have received help. These organized people have moved a long way from the primitive concept of death-avoidance once shared by Indians with the Old World.

REFERENCES

Burial customs east of the Rockies: Bushnell, 1920, 1927.

Secondary burial: Bushnell, 1909 (Choctaw); Kinietz, 1940, pp. 99–120 (Huron); Tooker, 1964, pp. 128–43 (Huron).

Discussion of secondary burial adoption: Hertz, 1960 (Indonesia); Michelson, 1925 (Fox).

Descriptions of death usage: Brown, 1953 (Sioux); Shimony, 1961 (Canadian Iroquois); chapters on death in Grinnell, 1923 (Cheyenne); Voegelin, 1944 (Shawnee and others).

Also see monographs on tribes from museums and universities.

MEDICINE MAN, SHAMAN, AND PRIEST

9

In every hunting and gathering group there is at least one specialist who receives some pay for his service. Although his profession may supply only part-time work, still he is in a different class from the other men and is not dependent for his status on hunting and fishing. This is the medicine man or shaman. American anthropologists use the terms interchangeably but, as will become apparent, they should really have different meanings. The two kinds of practitioner are alike, however, in that both get their powers direct from the Supernatural through visions and trances.

Thus they differ from the priest who is trained for ceremonial duties and can perform them without a special vision. The contrast is something like that, in modern days, between an ordained clergyman and a self-appointed revivalist. Medicine man and shaman function most often among hunter-gatherers, the priest among organized planters. Let it be understood, of course, that there are exceptions and combinations.

The medicine man (from the French word *médecin*, meaning doctor) is the term used by Indians for a special type of healer. He works on the theory that disease is caused by some foreign object like a stick or worm that has got into the body either through chance or witchcraft. It can be removed only by one who has special power from his spirits, and most often the method is to suck it out. The sucking cure appears in every Indian group, sometimes as the sole form of "doctoring," sometimes in combination with other methods. It was widely known in the Old World also. The theory behind this cure is so peculiar that it seems unlikely that it was thought out more than once. The same is true for a frequently used part of their equipment—the rock crystal used to "see" the disease. It seems possible that this very simple kind of curing was brought over with some of the early immigrants. It is not pure magic like the seclusion of girls, for the doctor got his abilities from communion with spirits. This means a certain background of theology different in the various areas.

In America the doctor was usually a male, since females had their own unsought power. However, after menopause, a woman might dream as an adolescent boy did. Thus she could attain some minor powers, particularly for child therapy. The doctor obtained his power occasionally by an unsought dream, but more often after a quest with prayer and starvation. The spirits were usually animals, chiefly the bear and the badger, for badger digs roots and bear knows the herbs. They did not take possession of the devotee. They appeared, as other animals did, to the hunter and warrior, only more often. They gave the seeker a song, perhaps told him how to find some magical tokens, and laid down some taboos. After that, he was ready to cure.

Once I questioned a medicine man about his preparation, after he had given me a very vivid and convincing account of his visions. "I know that your power came entirely from visions. But suppose there was some young man not so gifted as you who wished to learn from an older medicine man. How much might he have to pay?"

Without hesitation came the answer: "Twenty-five head of cattle."

In spite of such probable coaching, modern psychology has taught us that self-induced visions may be very real. The medicine men whom I knew believed in their powers, although they were quite aware that sucking out the disease object was a matter of sleight of hand. "We could cure without that," another told me, "just by singing and remembering the vision. But people need something to see."

The medicine man's first act was to diagnose the disease. If his common sense told him it was beyond curing, he ascribed it to witchcraft or a broken taboo which he could not handle. Or he might find it necessary to call in a special kind of wonder-worker with power from the rattlesnake or the bear. If he handled the cure himself, his procedure was to sing, perhaps with help from the bystanders who were always permitted around the sickbed. His accompaniment was a rattle—with hunters a bunch of deer-hoofs on rawhide, with farmers a gourd containing pebbles. He might require an interpreter to translate his mumbled words. As a preliminary to the sucking, he blew on the patient, rubbed him, perhaps waved feathers, then smoked tobacco from a pipe or a cane cigarette. This might go on for several nights. Finally he extracted the fatal object by sucking or cupping. It was shown to the onlookers, then destroyed or thrown away.

When I had seen the earnest faces of the onlookers and the calm of the patient, I realized that the psychological part of therapy was receiving full attention. If this was the kind of complaint for which time and the will to live could bring recovery, then recovery was almost certain. Even without recovery, patients in the last stages of cancer and tuberculosis have felt a calm and a respite from pain which the hospital could not give to Indians. Sometimes the treatment must fail. Then the doctor's only recourse was to blame some other medicine man whose witchcraft was too powerful for him.

Witchcraft is the concomitant of the disease-object belief. It took me some time to realize that the person called "doctor" by the Indians is not trained simply to cure. He owns the disease and can inject a harmful object as easily as remove it. Without any medical association to keep them in order, it is a wonder that more medicine men do not produce a conviction of disease so they might be paid. If they lose too many patients, they are likely to be accused of that very thing. A Papago, interpreting to me his history stick, would put his finger on a certain mark that occurred at regular intervals of almost four years. "This year we lynched a medicine man. He had been killing people."

Poor medicine man! He may have been up against an epidemic of measles. If he was trusted, however, he might be sent out with a sticky kind of branch to sweep the sickness from the village. For this public service he was not paid.

The sucking doctor is most prominent among the simpler groups of hunter-gatherers like those in the Desert area. With others, he may be one of several practitioners, each with power from a different source. Or he may have powers other than sucking. These powers might be for giving luck in war, love, or the hunt; and here the process was a combination of vision and magic. The tutelary spirit had taught a song, as was done for sucking, and he had also recommended a token. This might be a weapon, an animal skin, a little image which the doctor must carve. Used with the song, the token would bring good luck. For prophesying and the like, the doctor must dream or go into a trance. Here we encounter the second kind of practitioner I have mentioned: the shaman.

The word *shaman* comes from the Tungus in Siberia and the practitioner it designates there does not often suck. He is a diviner and prophet and, more than that, an actual miracle-worker. He gets his power not by dreaming about a spirit but by being possessed by one. In the most typical cases, the spirit chooses the future shaman by causing a mysterious illness. No cure is possible unless the patient vows to take up shamanism. There are variations in which older shamans choose a promising youth or the youth himself asks for training. In any case he must go through a real or imagined illness that gives him the conviction of having died and been reborn. Thus prepared, he has the power to go into a trance. During the trance state the supernatural being enters his body and speaks through his mouth. More than this his free soul, at such a time, can be guided on long journeys to the sky or the underworld. This magic flight is the distinguishing characteristic of the Siberian shaman. Eliade, a well-known writer on the subject, considers it essential.

We can see, in this kind of practitioner, a really different phenomenon from that of the sucking doctor; it is more elaborate, demands more complex theology and, it seems to me, might possibly have developed later. The phenomenon is rampant in Siberia and extends from there all the way to central Asia,[1] and perhaps even to India and Mesopotamia. Our concern is the fact that a type of wonder-worker, well known in much of Asia, appears in North America mostly in the Northwest and the Arctic.[2] One example in South America is still a case for puzzlement and speculation.

The Eskimo shaman is very like the Siberian. He felt a spirit call which perhaps took the form of illness. Then he went through a long training when he fasted alone and in silence. "When I chose to be a shaman, I chose suffering," said a Caribou Eskimo. He told how he sat in a tiny hut, without moving, thinking of one single thing, all day long. After he had practiced this concentration, perhaps for years, a number of spirits appeared to him, generally animals. They served him by going on errands, bringing information, entering other bodies, and even killing at his direction. If no spirit came after all his labor, he might buy one from an older shaman. Whether it chose to serve him after the purchase was another matter.

Besides this practice in concentration and mental alertness, the neophyte paid for instruction by older shamans. He learned to produce wonders, some of which have not yet been fully explained. All shamans, for instance, could handle fire. They could walk on and swallow hot coals, and plunge an arm into boiling water without injury. Other tricks were more familiar. Some shamans could swallow a spear and could stab themselves or someone else without doing harm or leaving a wound. Eskimo shamans used the strange language known to most of them throughout the Arctic. It has been analyzed as part archaic Eskimo and part gibberish.

[1] Weyer, 1932, pp. 444–47. Even Siberia is probably not the original home of the shaman; the spirit flight was an old practice in Central Asia. See Eliade, 1951, Chaps. 7, 10, 12, and the summary in Weyer, pp. 444–47.

[2] He appears in full force in certain areas of South America, where Eliade thinks this kind of shamanism is ancient (pp. 292–303). From our present knowledge, no explanation can be given for this very specialized behavior in two widely separated areas.

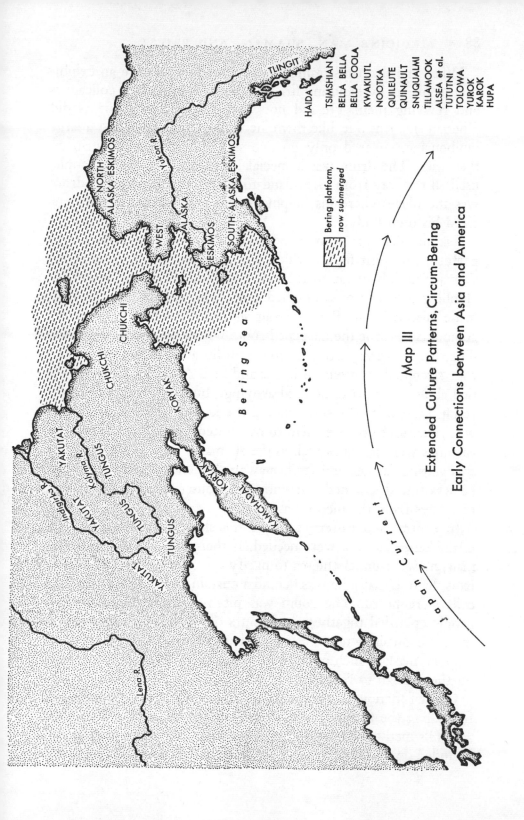

TLINGIT

HAIDA
TSIMSHIAN
BELLA BELLA
BELLA COOLA
KWAKIUTL
NOOTKA
QUILEUTE
QUINAULT
SNUQUALMI
TILLAMOOK
ALSEA et al.
TUTUTNI
TOLOWA
YUROK
KAROK
HUPA

NORTH
ALASKA ESKIMOS

Yukon R.

WEST
ALASKA
ESKIMOS

SOUTH ALASKA ESKIMOS

CHUKCHI

CHUKCHI

KORYAK

KORYAK

YAKUTAT

Kolyma R.

TUNGUS

YAKUT

TUNGUS

TUNGUS

YAKUT

Indigirka R.

KAMCHADAL

Lena R.

Bering Sea

Japan Current

Bering platform,
now submerged

Map III

Extended Culture Patterns, Circum-Bering

Early Connections between Asia and America

When the shaman's training was complete, he gave an exhibition of his art by handling fire, and perhaps by killing colleagues and reviving them. He did not wear a special costume as did Siberian shamans but, like them, he used a drum, or rather a large tambourine, covered only on one side and with a handgrip on the other. The drum was a special instrument of Arctic people, used all the way from Greenland to Finland. The shaman's drum was the place where his helping spirits entered unless they entered his own body.

Eskimo shamans were almost the only ones in America to perform the spirit flight, which was so important in Asia. Asian shamans usually went to the sky and symbolized the action by climbing a ladder or a notched pole. The Eskimo on the Diomede Islands in the Bering Strait supposedly flew to the moon. Accounts describe the darkened room where the people gathered. The shaman was securely bound with his arms behind him and a rope stretched between his hands and feet. A pair of trousers was tied above his head to be used as wings, but they were out of his reach. He was to go to the moon, the keeper of sea animals, and persuade him to release them to be hunted. In the dark, cries and rustlings were heard as well as the shaman's voice telling how he was getting farther and farther away. When the lights went up, he was found still tied but with the trouser-wings on his arms. His news from the moon was good.

In central and eastern Canada, the shaman or *angakok* flew inland when caribou were needed. If there was a lack of sea animals, he went under the sea to pacify the angry Sedna who controls them. Usually he was behind a curtain and only his cries and calls were heard. The room was pitch dark, with the excited people crowded together after hours of hypnotic drumming on the same outsized tambourine used in Siberia. The vacant-eyed wooden masks which come from Alaska were sometimes donned by the shaman to represent his spirits.

Other functions of the shaman-seer were finding lost souls and foretelling the future; these he still carried on until a short time ago. His method was to go into a trance. Sometimes he sang and pounded on his tambourine-drum until he fell unconscious; sometimes he sat motionless while the audience sang. An Alaskan song of great power refers to one of the deities:

> My whole body is covered with eyes:
> Behold it! be without fear!
> I see all around.[3]

Groans and quivers announced the fact that a spirit had entered the shaman's body. Then others might come, rustling and howling in the dark. The shaman babbled in his secret language with perhaps only a few words that could be understood. The spirits might even quarrel inside him until at last, with a shriek, he felt them go. Then he announced that the illness of so-and-so was because of breaking a particular taboo. Or perhaps the bad weather was due to such a transgression, but he did not know who was guilty. Then all who remembered something of the sort began to confess.

The wholesale confession was a regular feature of Central Eskimo life. The culprit was often a woman who had used skins or meat from sea and land animals at the same time. Worse still, she might have concealed an abortion, a frequent happening in a land where infants were so difficult to rear.

On the northern Pacific Coast, the shaman's chief function was to cure illness. Illness was generally diagnosed not as the intrusion of a foreign body into the patient but as the loss of his free soul. Souls, as mentioned, could be kidnapped by the dead. They could be stolen by a hostile shaman or lost in a fit of carelessness. The souls of children were particularly likely to wander and might sometimes be found caught on berry bushes. The resulting symptom was a feeling of discouragement and lack of energy. Perhaps soul-loss and its healer could be thought of as being in the department of mental health, while the intrusive object and the sucking shaman were in that of physical therapy. The wonder-working shaman did sometimes suck or he called in a sucking doctor, but it is surprising how many ailments he could diagnose as soul-loss.

Especially among the whaling tribes, the Nootka and Haida, the shaman was powerful and feared. Sometimes he was killed on

[3] Weyer, 1932, p. 401.

suspicion of sorcery. At his death, he was interred in a special box, and placed in a cave far from the village. This was woodworking country whose products were not only handsome wooden boxes but totem poles, huge plank houses, wooden dishes, and masks. The masks of the shaman represented his spirits, of which he usually had several. They appeared to be fantastic heads of animals but were so cleverly contrived that the shaman, by pulling a string, could open the huge jaws to show a more human spirit-face inside. This mask was his substitute for the gown decorated with iron spirit figures worn by the Siberian shaman.

In winter, the proper time for spirit visitations, the shaman might give a public performance. An early visitor to the Tlingit describes the great wooden house crowded with people, with a fire burning on the earthen floor.[4] Singers who had prepared themselves by fasting sang the shaman's songs to the sound of a drum pounded with the feet. The shaman, in the mask, dancing blanket, and the cedarbark fringe that were spirit regalia, dashed in and ran around the fire in an animal imitation. This might be done three or four times by way of calling different spirits. Finally he gave a shriek and the noise stopped. The spirit had come and he would prophesy. His prophecies might tell about the run of fish for the next summer or about the coming deaths. Sometimes he could prevent these by going to the land of the dead and bringing back a lost soul.

Lost souls were also retrieved by Salish shamans who lived on the coast of Washington. In unimportant cases the shaman worked alone, sitting by the patient and going into a trance which took his soul to the land of the dead. For important ones, there was a version of the spirit flight befitting a seafaring people. Here the loss of a soul required four or even six shamans to paddle a canoe to the Land of the Dead and snatch the soul from the ghosts. The shamans stood in the center of the room, two by two in file, each armed with a long pole. They used these like paddles, and it was understood that meantime their souls were paddling a spirit canoe. As they plied the poles, they called back news of their journey and of their tussle with the dead. Usually they were

4 See Krause, 1956, trans. by Gunther, pp. 198–99.

victorious (unless, we gather, the sick person was beyond hope). Then they faced about and paddled home. The recovered soul was put back into the loser's body through the top of his head. Sometimes other souls had been picked up on the way, whose owners did not even know they were gone.

The idea of spirit possession fades away as one moves down the Pacific coast, but there is an example in California which seems unique. This is the case of the Shasta shaman, or shamaness, for most of the practitioners were women. The future shamaness fell sick in the usual manner. The cause was not a spirit but a living object that looked like a crystal and was called a *pain*. Crystals, as we have mentioned, are an important shamanistic property in many parts of the world but with varying uses. The shamaness learned to vomit up her *pain*, then swallow it again. (This swallowing and ejecting, we shall note, is a common shamanistic ability.) Finally, she was "danced" for three nights by her sister shamans; then she could suck out diseases with the aid of her *pain*, or perhaps several of them.

Farther south and east, the idea of soul-loss and the spirit flight which it entails gradually gave way before that of disease objects and the sucking shaman. This latter retains shreds of spirit possession and wonder-working, at least in California and the Basin, where contests with knife-swallowing and, that shaman miracle, fire-handling, were held among the various specialists who could sometimes control the weather, handle rattlesnakes, and even turn into a bear. I heard of this terrifying magic from a Paiute boy, whom I questioned eagerly: "You actually saw it happen? Before your eyes?"

"Oh no. They never let you see that. It's their secret. But the medicine man turned away, and when he turned back he was a bear."

"You mean, with fur?"

"No. He didn't turn all the way. That takes time, I guess. But two big bear teeth were sticking out of his mouth."

If we go east through the Subarctic and even as far south as the Great Lakes and New England, we still find the wonder-worker paramount. Here, where the Indians were forest hunters, living in birch-bark tipis, he must have filled a need with hunters who are alone so much and have so many uncertainties to face. Reports tell of an anxious crowd waiting outside one of these tipis while, within, the shaman called his spirits which arrived whistling, howling, and shaking the tent. He sent them to find news and they reported in animal voices which had to be interpreted. Among the Menomini, on Lake Superior, the shaman was tightly bound and placed inside a cylinder of birch bark, just large enough to hold him. From here he made magic flights, astounding white officials with his correct information.

The wonder-working shamans of this whole region sometimes staged exhibitions during which they set their spirits on to kill their opponents, turned into animals before people's eyes, or at least handled hot iron or coals, the regular shaman specialty. It goes without saying that such people were feared. Most diseases and bad luck were thought to be caused by some spirit sent by an offended shaman. The sufferer could hire another shaman to take vengeance or even kill the tormentor himself. The act would be regarded by all as justifiable homicide.

The Great Lakes was the locus of the Midewiwin, or Grand Medicine Society. This was an organization of wonder-workers, known especially among the Ojibwa, the Menomini, and Winnebago. The members considered that it had been started by their culture hero, Nanabozho, the Great Hare, by order of the Great Spirit. To join it, a man must have a vision and one or more helping spirits who recommended such a career. Then he was instructed by a chosen member in herbal lore and in the traditions of the Society.

All these were recorded in symbolic form on sheets of birch bark. This was one of the few examples of writing done by Indians north of Mexico, the others being mostly rock engravings.

With each grade the candidate received more teaching and paid a more lavish entrance fee in food and skins. He was then endowed with more power by being shot in the breast by the sacred white shell, the fetish of the society. This shell was similar to one that had appeared to the Ojibwa out of the eastern sea and led them west. It was kept in the skin of an otter (the otter had been the first society initiate), and when the skin, so loaded, was pointed at anyone, he would fall dead. At the society meetings, the members shot each other with these shells, then vomited them and came to life. When a man had reached the fourth grade and had been shot four times, he was almost supernaturally potent. He could make the magic flight, turn into an animal, prophesy, find the lost, handle fire, and make love charms. He could also suck out disease and give herbal remedies.

We do not know how old this organization was, for the first reports of it date from the 1880's. It bespeaks a good deal of sophistication among the leaders and also the kind of leisure and stimulus not available to a lonely shaman in the Arctic. We know that the Ojibwa and others around the Great Lakes had moved from farther east after the coming of the French. Perhaps the increase in population and also in competition forced the wonderworkers to this move to hold their supremacy. The Winnebago had not moved, but they had been in contact with tribes to the south who had a more lofty idea of the spirit world than had the northern hunters. They made of their society a priestly organization designed to teach The Road of Life and Death, or the fact that there was life in the afterworld.

South of the Great Lakes was prosperous and populated country where neither shaman nor medicine man could hold an all-important place. Throughout this country there were ceremonies conducted by men of more or less priestly status, which means that they were proprietors of a memorized ritual passed down by inheritance and not received directly by vision. The purpose of these ceremonies was fertility and general welfare, yet often they had curing powers.

Among organized planters, the curing function was also organized. So-called medicine societies ranged all the way from the shell society of the Omaha, which was a faint reflection of the Midewiwin, to the medicine societies of the Pueblos, with their altars and their priestly ritual. Only once a year did these dignified bodies show their wonder-working heritage, when they swallowed swords or turned into bears. The Iroquois False Faces, in another planting tribe, merely acted like wild spirits, making no claim to be possessed. Besides the organized groups there were individuals having various specialties, such as divining or making fetishes for love or hunting. Sometimes there were so many that one specialty was that of diagnostician.

From this description it might appear that the trance—in psychological terms a dissociational mental state—was experienced only by the shaman and was limited to the Northwest and the Arctic, with extensions into Asia. Actually such mental states have been known to all peoples throughout history, their nature and frequency being largely a matter of the way they are regarded in different cultures.

In some instances the person "possessed" is a woman, who functions as a medium. Other women who feel a tendency to trance encourage it, whereas men are likely to discourage or conceal it. In the Northwest, men were encouraged to enter the trance state, perhaps influenced by the Siberians. Women were discouraged except among the Shasta. The men who became shamans might be imaginative and suggestible, especially those who "became ill" from spirit possession without being first chosen and instructed. When "in trance," however, their actions were standardized and all performed in about the same way. Their prophecies, which came after the trance exhibition, were largely the result of acute observation. For their miracles, they needed skill and quickness and, probably, a trained helper. None of this detracted from the belief that their own talents and training were actually guided by a spirit.

The medicine man boasted of having experienced a trance or vision perhaps several times, but it did not recur while he was curing. At that time, he must notice the patient's symptoms, perhaps perform some simple therapy and, finally, present the drama of removing the disease object. The medicine men I knew appeared to me not highly emotional types but able thinkers and executives. If they were inclined to dissociational states, they concealed and dominated them. Other individuals in the environment of both medicine man and shaman may also have experienced trances but the communities paid little attention to them, except in the instance of the vision, discussed in the next chapter.

REFERENCES

General studies of shamanism: Eliade, 1951; Jensen, 1963, Part III; Webster, 1948, Chaps. 7–15.

Shamanism in America: Clements, 1932.

Special groups: Bourke, 1892 (Apache); Devereux, 1961 (Mohave); Flannery, 1939 (Northeast); Gayton, 1930 (eastern California); Kelly, 1939 (southern Paiute); Laski, 1959 (Pueblo); Loeb, 1932 and Barrett, 1917 (central California); Park, 1938 (western North America); Waterman, 1930 (Salish); Whiting, 1950 (Paiute).

For data on shamanism west of the Rockies, see Anthropological Records, University of California. See also monographs on tribes from museums and universities.

Shaman societies: Fenton, 1940 (Iroquois); Hoffman, 1891 (Ojibwa); Linton, 1923 (Pawnee); Loeb, 1932 (Pomo); Radin, 1950 (Winnebago).

THE VISION

Said the Winnebago father to his boy at the age of puberty:

> My son, you should try to be of some benefit to your fellow men.
> There is only one way in which this can be done and that is to fast.
> If you thirst yourself to death, the spirits who are in control of wars
> will bless you. . . . If you do not obtain a spirit to strengthen you,
> you will amount to nothing in the estimation of your fellow men.[1]

The Ponka war chief told his men: "Oho! Do exert yourself!
Be sure to make yourself the possessor of superhuman power by
the aid of the animal that you have seen in your vision after fasting."[2]

A Crow Indian, eager for booty and glory, hacked off a finger
joint and prayed to the sun: "Father's clansman, you see me. I
am pitiable. This is a part of my body, I give it to you. Eat it!
Whatever easy things there are, let me secure them by good
luck."[3]

Among the hunter-gatherers, the vision and the aid of spirits
were given not only to the shaman and medicine man. Even the
average man prepared for the business of life by gaining the aid
of some supernatural being who would be guardian and luck-

[1] Radin, 1914, pp. 343–44.

[2] Dorsey, 1894, p. 390.　　　　[3] See Lowie, 1935, p. 240.

bringer throughout the individual's career. Such help was to be had only through strenuous effort, which might mean fasting, thirsting, purification or even self-mutilation and torture. The result would be a trance or a vivid dream in which the visionary made contact with his future guardian spirit and perhaps even received some visible token to prove the fact.

The Algonkians began this process in childhood. Around the Great Lakes, each family sent its son out alone, "hounded them" says Dr. Benedict, to get spirit help as a modern family might urge a good report card.

Parents began to prepare their children for this ordeal by having them go without food for a day, even at the age of seven or eight. "Because I am always fond of you," said a Fox father, "this is verily the only way. If anyone really would truly know about himself, then he should contrive to nearly starve himself."[4]

Then the father presented his girls and boys with "fasting sticks" that they were to burn to charcoal and then use to paint their faces, which was the usual sign of their being in a sacred condition. The sooner a child's stick was used up, the prouder his parents could be.

As the children grew older, the length of their fasting periods was increased. During this time the children might even receive some preparatory visions. Algonkians and Salish believed that girls as well as boys were eligible for this sign of favor from the spirits, but girls dropped the quest after puberty when a different kind of power came to them. Most Indians believed that a man who truly wanted a vision must not have recently been with a woman. Male and female powers were incompatible.

The boy continued his efforts. The Fox tell of his wandering from place to place wailing and offering tobacco to all the spirits. The Ojibwa father built his son a hut some distance from home, perhaps in a tree to insure the child's safety from wild beasts. For a boy of ten or so, this must have been a frightening experience as well as a strenuous preparation for life as a hunter.

The spirit visit was expected in a dream but the nature of this experience was not left to chance. By talks with his father and

4 See Michelson, 1930, pp. 63–65.

grandfather, the boy's mind was kept constantly on the sort of power needed. Left alone, he spent his day calling on the Great Spirit for ability in hunting, war, gambling (an acknowledged Indian road to success), or, perhaps, medicine power. The prayers were almost wordless, the cries of an unformed boy: "Great Spirit, help me. I am poor."

Undoubtedly these forest hunters, with their precarious livelihood, did feel poor. In the Fox myth just quoted, the Great Spirit said that he had made the people's lives too short and recommended that his subordinates take pity on them. The Winnebago, once neighbors of the Fox, had Earthmaker feel compunction that he had made mankind the last and least of all beings on earth. He really must send help.

Ultimately, at the orders of the Supreme Being, a visitant came to the boy in a dream and promised the desired power. The visitant appeared to be a man; he sometimes took the suppliant to a village where many men performed a ceremony and taught him songs. On leaving, the suppliant discovered that the men were wolves, eagles, or some other powerful spirit. Was this visitant the species Owner described in Chapter 2? Or did these tribes feel that every beast still had the powers of a man-animal and could work magic at will? The Lakes people have never spoken clearly on this point and perhaps they do not care to think in such philosophic terms.

Occasionally the spirit was an undesirable one, such as a Water Monster. Then the boy might tell some older man, or at least hint of the fact, and he would be advised to refuse the power. His tongue might be scraped to take away its memory. If the power were accepted, the spirit might give him some token, not as a charm but as a remembrance of the event. It might also give him food taboos or directions about ornaments. These orders must be religiously obeyed on penalty of illness or of the spirits deserting him.

After his dream, the boy labored at his career with an unshakable conviction of success. There could be no more efficient way of ensuring a youngster's interest and concentration. When Indian boys in government schools were given no opportunity for a vision quest and were, instead, made to feel inadequate in their new tasks, their energy and ambition went down to zero and generations have been needed to bring it up. It has always seemed to me that white teachers in Indian schools missed a chance here. The Indian vision was not too different from that of medieval Christians. Could it not have been encouraged and the Indians made to feel a part of a larger unit by praying for greater and more altruistic goals?

This spirit quest by the average man was a New World practice almost unknown on the other side of the globe. In the Old World, it is true, schools for adolescent boys often existed. The boys might go through ordeals and be told the tribal legends, but they rarely tried for supernatural power. Among some tribes children might have had, from the time of birth, an animal companion whose life was entwined with theirs. When one died, so did the other, but there was little mention of supernatural help from the connection. Although seeking visions through ordeals was a well-known custom, in the Old World, it was not adopted by the average man needing help in his daily work. The man who thus sought help from the spirits was a future shaman or other religious specialist. Was the quest carried on by the American Indian an innovation on the part of the first immigrants? Had they such a lack of medicine men that they felt the layman must perform some approach to the Supernatural himself?

Throughout the Great Lakes area, in the Mississippi Valley, and in scattered groups nearby, the vision was a necessary part of a boy's growing up. On the Plains, the youth often did not try for supernatural help until he was ready for mens' activities. Charles Eastman, the educated Santee Sioux, has poetically described the procedure:

The first *hambeday*, or religious retreat, marked an epoch in the life of the youth, which may be compared to that of confirmation or conversion in Christian experience. Having first prepared himself by means of the purifying vapor bath, and cast off as far as possible all human or fleshly influences, the young man sought out the noblest height, the most commanding summit in all the surrounding region. Knowing that God sets no value upon material things, he took with him no offerings or sacrifices other than symbolic objects, such as paints and tobacco. Wishing to appear before Him in all humility, he wore no clothing save his moccasins and breech-clout. At the solemn hour of sunrise or sunset he took up his position, overlooking the glories of earth and facing the 'Great Mystery,' and there he remained, naked, erect, silent, and motionless, exposed to the elements and forces of His arming, for a night and day to two days and nights, but rarely longer. Sometimes he would chant a hymn, without words, or offer the ceremonial 'filled pipe.' In this holy trance or ecstasy the Indian mystic found his highest happiness and the motive power of his existence.[5]

Most young men of the Plains tribes went through the same procedure but, naturally, they did not all have the same spiritual attitude. The prayer of a Crow to the sun has been translated:

Hallo, old Old Man, I am poor, me you see, something good give me. Me make old, a horse may I have, gun may I take, a coup may I strike. I a chief, I without help may I become a person [make a living] plenty may I have.[6]

The prayer might be crude, but before making it the suppliant cut off strips of his flesh and laid them on a buffalo chip. His flesh was the only possession he had to give. All through his life, when any extra effort was before him, the Plains Indian might make a prayer of this sort.

Prayer was usually addressed to the sun, but the sun did not answer it in person. The visitant who appeared seemed to be a human being, perhaps a beautiful woman; but sometimes there were a number of warriors on horseback. The fasting person was given a promise, and as the visitant turned away the suppliant saw a buffalo, an eagle, or a pack of wolves. Like the Algonkian boy he was told to get some sort of token—buffalo hair, eagle's wing or the like—that was to be kept as a sacred possession and given frequent offerings of tobacco smoke. He was also given a song that served to call up his spirit power. Such songs and the carefully wrapped token that went with them were a man's cherished property. However, the Blackfoot felt that they could be sold if the

[5] Eastman, 1911, pp. 6–8.
[6] Lowie, 1922, p. 333.

transfer were made almost physical; the purchaser becoming for one night the husband of the seller's wife.

Even after the most strenuous fasting, the quest was not always a success. Then the suppliant would try to wrest pity from the Supernatural by hacking off a finger joint, as in the incident noted above. This sacrifice of a part of one's own body (but a part that could be spared) may have been an old and widespread way of appealing to the Supernatural. We have noted that a number of tribes practiced it, after a death. There are rocks in New Mexico that have pictographs of mutilated hands. In what have been called the "cave temples" of the Pyrenees, there are handprints on the walls showing missing joints.

The Sioux carried their appeal for pity to dramatic heights that reached a climax in the Sun Dance. This was a yearly festival held by most of the Plains tribes after a summer of hunting when there was plenty of buffalo meat and all the people could congregate (see Chap. 14). Here, among other rituals, fasting men danced with eagle-bone whistles in their mouths, looking constantly at the sun to force a blessing. Most tribes required no more of an ordeal than this, but the Oglala Sioux had thongs put through the flesh of their breasts, and by these they were hung from the center pole of the lodge, or they dragged one or more buffalo skulls around the camp. Catlin's painting of the similar Mandan ceremony is gruesome. The United States government forbade this kind of ordeal in the nineteenth century. Yet this experience inflicted no permanent injury and perhaps was not as harmful as the flagellation practiced by monks of the Middle Ages. Indians have been known to regret its passing, since they have not found another means to produce the same exaltation and conviction of rightness.

Among the planters, it was not necessary for each man to have a vision. The elaborate ceremonies, in which most persons participated in various ways, took care of the needs of all. War, however, was a different matter. Many village tribes on the Prairie combined planting with buffalo hunting. The Osage demanded that the man in charge, at least, should have a vision and they sent their ceremonially appointed war priest to perform a six-night vigil. He was given a sacred pipe and told:

> Go thou, and pass through the period of anguish,
> To return, mayhap, on the first night.[7]

And thus six nights were enumerated, for Indians never mind repetition. He was not to return until he had received a vision, so the final verse directed:

> Go thou, and pass through the period of anguish,
> To return, mayhap, when the number of days is completed.[8]

Among the Osage, even warriors in the ranks were sometimes directed to try for a vision. They were told to blacken their faces with earth, as the crawfish had once instructed the tribe while holding a pinch of dark soil in its claws. " 'By the use of this sign, my younger brothers,' he said to them, 'we shall with ease secure the fulfillment of our desires.' "[9] If victory did not result, it was felt that someone had broken a taboo.

West of the Rockies, the vision idea had not so firm a hold. The life of food-gatherers in the Desert area and California was hard, but not hazardous. Few persons besides the medicine man needed special help to deal with it and even when they did they rarely sought a vision. If one came, it was hardly distinguishable from a dream. An exception was found in southern California, where there was a boys' initiation school. Amid other ceremonies, the boys were given a narcotic that made dreaming a certainty.

Further north, in British Columbia and on the Plateau, there were whalers and hunters whose lives were precarious enough. Here, however, we are in the domain of spirit possession and the whole procedure was different. There was no appeal to the sun or hacking off of finger joints. The way to spirit favor, in this land of streams and pools, was fanatic cleanliness. The visionary would plunge repeatedly into a deep pool, sometimes tying a stone to his feet so that he would stay down longer. Then he would rub himself with thorny branches until he bled. All this time, he fasted and remained continent. Tlingit men sometimes avoided their wives for a year, feeling that they were accumulating invincible energy.

[7] La Flesche, 1930, p. 588.
[8] *Ibid.*   [9] La Flesche, 1939, p. 6.

After these exertions, a spirit might appear briefly and sing a song which would belong to the applicant. If he were young, the spirit would then disappear, not to return until he was fully grown.

These spirits were not the powerful animals of mythology. They were the desired helpers of a rich and warlike people who were anxious for fame and possessions. So the spirits were Canoe People, Property Woman, or the War Spirit. They were not available to everyone. On the coast, important spirits came only to chiefs, and lesser ones to common people; slaves (war captives and their descendants) could have no visions at all. The procedure of spirit possession was the same as with the shaman, only the spirits were different. They arrived only in winter when the people had leisure from hunting and fishing. Then everyone expected to exhibit his spirit power and the great houses were made ready for feasting.

At this time the new vision-seeker, like the prospective shaman, might be taken with an illness that no one could understand until it was diagnosed as the return of his spirit. The visionary then might begin to mumble a song that the medicine man and helpers then took up. By questioning the spirit, they found out what sort of ornaments it wanted the visionary to wear in the dancing and how he must be painted. Fits of illness would come on him until he could finally "dance" his spirit as described on page 1.

Difficulties arose when class consciousness intruded into the spiritual area of vision beliefs. The Kwakiutl of Vancouver Island were particularly firm in maintaining status. In their opinion certain important spirits would appear only to the chiefs who were the rich men. Yet there was a problem when rich mens' sons seemed psychologically unsuited to a vision experience. The difficulty was got around by coaching the boys to act like vision recipients. Among the Kwakiutl, for instance, there was an extremely select society of those who had met the fearsome Cannibal Spirit mentioned in Chapter 5. A boy who probably would have died of fright at seeing such a creature was taken into the woods, supposedly abducted by that Cannibal, and taught his act. When the proper amount of time had elapsed, he came leaping down through the smoke hole of the house, bit the nearest slave, and went racing about like a wild man, apparently unable to speak words or to understand them. Several relatives had to tie a rope to him and hold it lest he jump into the sea. After he had finally been calmed down, the boy, of course, had extreme power.

A number of associations like the Cannibal Society had a selected membership that was usually hereditary. One had a right to receive a certain spirit through inheritance, marriage, or the killing of the spirit's power. These conditions having been fulfilled, one must be able to have the vision and to give the feast validating it. The mental drill necessary for all this sounds formidable, but evidently custom made it natural. Among the Kwakiutl, all high born persons had visions. They showed their extreme respect for this aspect of life by seating guests at their winter feasts not according to family or clan but according to what visions they had had. It is obvious that these experiences were not kept secret. For instance, a man with power for whaling sang about his huge helper:

Darkness as of approaching night
on the water.[10]

A man in an eagle mask sang:

I am dancing in the air
and dancing round and round.[11]

Many Northwestern Indians are now members of modern churches, but I am told that they think and speak of Christianity in terms of Power.

This sketch of vision experience, of course, is not complete. Specially gifted individuals in all areas sometimes had visions, even into modern times. From a bird's-eye view of vision customs in early days, we might say that, in the region of the Great Lakes and the Mississippi Valley, the vision was used as a training school for boys. On the Plains it was used by men throughout life, when they needed special encouragement. On the Pacific Coast, it took the form of spirit possession and was sometimes used to enhance social status.

[10] Densmore, 1939, p. 95.   [11] *Ibid.*, p. 101.

REFERENCES

General statements on vision and fasting in North America: Benedict, 1922, 1923; Blumensohn, 1933.

Descriptions of vision experience: Brown, 1953 (Sioux); Michelson, 1930 (Fox).

Spirit possession: Boas, 1930 (Kwakiutl); Stewart, 1946.

Data on vision experience west of the Rockies in Anthropological Records, University of California. For the country in general, see monographs on tribes issued by museums and universities.

INDIAN CEREMONIALISM

In the distance, the beat of a drum—that ancient, hypnotic thudding that must have been the grandfather of all music! As you come closer, you see no banners or flashing colors. The background is blue sky and brown earth against which the naked figures stand out no more than a flock of moving brown birds.

Such might have been a hunter-gatherer ceremony in pre-white days. Its appeal was neither in gorgeous color nor dramatic speeches. It moved the participants by a form of communication older than words—gesture. And gesture became dear through a process as old as any ritual—repetition.

There are modern artists who try to put brilliance into their depictions of ancient Indian scenes by means of scarlet headbands or brightly painted pots. But there was no scarlet cloth in pre-white days and pots had the yellow-brown or red-brown colors supplied by the flesh of Earth Mother. So had costumes, such as they were. Present-day Indians have shown a love of color but the hunter-gatherers of ancient days wore skins of gray and brown or, perhaps, mere strings of grass and bark. Feathers, which make such a striking show in modern paintings, were also gray-brown and only occasionally did the tiny scalps of wood-peckers give a touch of scarlet or yellow. The most effective decoration was perhaps the paint on brown face and breast. This, too, was mostly in the subdued colors supplied by earth and rocks—the white of chalk, the yellow-brown and red-brown of ochre, the blue-green of copper sulphate (when it could be had) and the black of charcoal. One bit of precious color must have been as valuable to an Indian woman as jewelry to a white. This was cinnabar, the bright red crystals of sulphide of mercury sometimes found embedded in rocks. Men made dangerous climbs to get it or they traded for it at a high price.

Such were the trappings of the hunter-gatherers. The more settled people, whether fishermen or planters, were equally re-stricted in color if not in form. The kilts, *mantas*, and masks of the Pueblos had no brilliant hues until the Spaniards brought baize and indigo from Mexico and later the Americans brought yarn and dye. The same was true of the garish masks used by the wonderworking shamans of the Northwest. In fact, the appeal of Indian ceremonies was not in their color but in movement. Here, again, no dance or procession is to be judged primarily from the point of view of the artist.

The ceremony was a means of making contact with the spirits and the motions were such as the spirits had dictated in that particular locality. Thus a long line of Pueblo dancers, in what we might almost call a uniform, trod the earth in a stately parade. They represented the rain spirits who had always danced in that way. The eagle dancers represented the mating eagles, and the more beautifully they did it, the more the eagles approved. It was the eagles who had to be pleased, not the spectators.

In the Plains, the jostling herd of men in buffalo skins was pro-viding a model which the buffalo must surely follow. In the Northwest the shaman, in mask and cedar bark fringe, ran around the fire like a mad thing. He need not invent the motions of an exotic dancer. He was possessed by a spirit and could not help himself. There were, too, dances of a more secular kind, for dances were one of the chief Indian ways of expressing emotion. So a crowd of people might have leaped and shouted or joined hands in a ring. Or warriors might have re-enacted their scouting for an enemy and the final kill. Here there was more chance for invention, but the emphasis was always on the idea to be conveyed, not on the beauty of the motions. I have seen trained dancers among the whites who perform Indian dances "better than the Indians." That is true only in the judgment of the whites, for their movements are more finished and better designed to impress spectators. One can tell on sight, however, that they are not Indian.

Moderns who are masters of so much material equipment hardly realize how much meaning can be given to a ceremony simply by movement. Almost all ceremonial movements go by fours. That number, representing the four directions, must have been embedded in the Indian mind from very early days. Watch in imagination as the candidate for war leader among the ancient Osage walked with his sponsor to the sacred lodge. They emerged from the sponsor's home, took four steps, stopped and went back. Three times this false move was made before they marched forward. This was in remembrance of the previous moves of the Osage after they came from the sky; it was acting out a journey tremendous in tribal history. Every onlooker, in watching these deliberate steps, remembered how the culture hero once walked over the earth, making it habitable. No Bible reading was necessary here. A simple act surcharged with meaning elicited the sacred story in every mind.

At a Plains Sun Dance, the priest is to lay a rabbit skin at the center pole in memory of a vow. It is a flimsy, grayish, little skin but he holds it in both hands as reverently as a different priest might hold a golden chalice. Three times he gestures toward the center pole and withdraws. The uninstructed visitor grows impatient, for there is no pageantry to mark the importance of this act. But the Indian spectators know the number four symbolizes perfection. Those apparently inept movements convey a whole sermon regarding the intensity of the vow.

The nomadic Sioux, who carried so little ·equipment, used movement as one of their chief means of symbolism. Since their only walls were the horizon, they paid particular attention to the directions, the homes of the four winds. Every object and every movement in a ceremony was oriented either toward the West, home of the buffalo; or the North, that of the purifying cold wind; or the East, whence wisdom comes; or the South, the warm country "towards which we always face."

In making a sweat lodge, for instance, even the most trivial movement of everyone concerned had to be properly oriented. The sweat lodge was the tiny, airtight hut used for steam baths in areas where there were no streams for bathing. It was made by planting willow branches in the ground, tying them together at the top, then covering the little dome thickly with brush, skins, or old blankets. For the Sioux, who had no church buildings and no vestments, even cutting and placing branches for this rude structure was a ceremony. Black Elk, the priest-thinker, thus interpreted it:[1]

> The willows . . . are set up in such a way that they mark the four quarters of the universe . . . the whole lodge is the universe in an image, and the two-legged, four-legged and winged peoples, and all things of the world are contained within it . . . its door [is] to the east, for . . . from this direction . . . wisdom comes.

The bather crouched inside the lodge where a pot of water stood, while outside, a helper heated stones on a little fire and passed them in to him with wooden tongs. The bather dribbled water on the stones until the steam rose up in clouds, surrounding him with "the very breath of life" (see Chap. 5).

The outside fire was laid as any camper would lay it. Yet let not the wood be piled up without reverence, for Black Elk stated that four sticks, pointing east and west, must be laid down first, then four more, pointing north and south. Then larger sticks were leaned against them, beginning at the west and going around to the south.[2]

This circuit, which sometimes began at different points, was used by most Plains tribes. It is the "sunwise" circuit, better understood by moderns as clockwise, or turning to the right. It is the direction used in passing a pipe around or in entering a tipi. Many

[1] Brown, 1953, p. 32.   [2] *Ibid.*

a time in my early days with the Indians, I was stopped, even on walking into an outdoor gathering, because one does not simply march in and occupy any vacant place. Perhaps there is a circuit to be made. Perhaps certain people should sit at the east and others at the west.

Sometimes there were six or seven directions to be considered. When the sacred pipe was being smoked as an offering of incense to the Supernaturals, the smoker puffed reverently toward the four directions in turn, then to the below and the above and perhaps the center. The Pueblo Indians of the Southwest always spoke of these six directions and, moreover, gave them colors. So did several other tribes in the Southwest and the East as did the Maya of Yucatan, the Aztecs of Mexico, and several Asiatic people. This wedding of color and direction must be an ancient human trait that would be fascinating to track down, had we the information.

The colors used were not always the same, although North was usually black, the color of evil. That was the direction from which the cold wind came and toward which witches were chased and diseased objects thrown away. East could be the white of dawn, but then the red and yellow of sunrise or sunset and the blue of the clear sky were variously distributed. I have heard of a spell used by witches in which East was black. When there are six directions, the nadir, the underground is black, and the zenith is pink or variegated.

Ceremonies always included some material equipment, simple though it might be. Fetishes seen and touched must have had their place in ritual long before complete ceremonies were developed. Even yet, the mere exhibition of some sacred object calls forth more memories and aspirations than any one poem can express. Such were the sacred arrows of the Cheyenne, the "flat pipe" of the Arapaho, or the "bundles" bestowed by Supernaturals on clans, societies, or even individuals. Would that a more sympathetic word had been established for these magic-working treasures! Spread on a museum table, the contents of a medicine bundle do seem insignificant. The first visitors who named them saw only a few shriveled skins, some bunches of herbs, perhaps a feather, a claw, or an arrow-point. Yet when the bundle was opened on special occasions, every motion of the officiant's hand in untying, unrolling, or lifting was accompanied with song and the recitation of the promises given in primeval days. Saints' relics of the Middle Ages did not receive more reverence.

I have wondered why flowers were not used for color in rituals like these. The prairies, where many ceremonies took place, were riotously abloom with color, far more brilliant than that of feathers. Early Greeks, at a time when they had little more equipment than the Plains Indians, made the use of wreaths of flowers a main point in their ceremonies. The Greeks, however, unlike the Indians, did not look on flowers as fellow citizens having as much right on Mother Earth as they had themselves. I know of no Indians who picked flowers except for special symbols or for medicine. The wholesale destruction that would have been necessary to decorate a pageant would, perhaps, have horrified them. The Pueblos, however, did use spruce, partly as a practical measure to conceal the place where a mask joined the dancer's body, and partly as a symbol of undying life.

All the movements were accompanied with sound. Indian songs, which lacked regular rhythm, melody, or parts were more distressing to listeners of the last century than they would be to moderns. Even the latter, however, would probably find them monotonous, for the same few notes seem to go on endlessly without dramatic change. The Indian would be surprised at the songs being judged from an artistic point of view. They were given by spirits, either to the [present] singers or to someone who had handed them down. The songs, like every act in the ceremony, were part of the spell.

So is the instrumental accompaniment. The drum and the rattle surely come down to us from the beginnings of human music. On me, those constant beats, especially in the night, have a hypnotic effect that no orchestra can equal. The drum might be a hollow tree trunk or a pot half filled with water with a deerskin lashed across the open end. It might be a folded buffalo hide, lustily beaten with sticks by four squatting men. In the great wooden houses of the Northwest, it might be a plank in the floor beaten with the feet. Or men might hammer on the ceiling with long poles. The hypnotic rhythm prepares the audience for any miracle.

It would seem that, with so many appeals directed to the senses, words might be unnecessary. Indeed, words were sometimes very few. A Dakota war song composed during World War II takes five minutes of chanting and furious drumbeats, but it says only:

> Wise eagle, take care!
> Over there, danger!

Why say more? The very image of an eagle, the great predator, the Thunderbird, carries memories and promises, uplifts feelings that spread out in all directions. So does "over there," the terrible war country overseas about which one can imagine anything. As for danger, it was at the very heart of Sioux life for a century, with all its connotations of glory, heartbreak, and hope. Robert Graves has said that the poet, like the child, thinks in images that can have a thousand connotations, whereas the carefully written description pins the reader down to a few. And the more beautiful and exact are the adjectives chosen, the more is the meaning concentrated at one point.

In this respect the Dakota are poets, and so are most other Indians. I have translated pages of Indian poetry and have found songs containing perhaps only two or three words and those were not in sentence form. When Gertrude Stein broke from convention by chanting: "A rose is a rose is a rose" she had the Indian feeling. If one's heart can call up the perfume and the glow and the petal-feel of a thousand roses, then adjectives from the author would only be an encumbrance.

There must have been a similar attitude among many hunter-gatherers, whose songs are so laconic. The corn-raising Indians, with their priests and their memorized rituals, could have songs containing actual sentences and they did so. This is a Papago song, in growing time:

> It moves in different directions,
> It moves in different directions,

And then it alights
From the south, on the blue water—
The dragonfly.

It moves in different directions,
It moves in different directions,
And then it stands still
From the south, on the yellow water—
The dragonfly.[3]

Of course, the dragonfly goes to the red water and even to the black. The Pueblos, Navahos, and Apache have songs with this same magic—brief, thrilling sentences whose impact lies almost entirely in nouns and verbs so that the picture strikes like a camera flash.

All the southwestern Indians mentioned had much longer, formal recitations of the kind that had to be spoken without error, even though some words were old and unfamiliar. In writing these down, a learner like me is comforted by repetition. Repetition was a well-established habit with people who had no writing. How could a young officiant learn a set piece that went on from one impressive sentence to another with scarcely a clue to their order? Actually he had only to learn a few paragraphs, a few striking epithets, and these might be repeated for different colors, different directions, different Supernaturals. The modern reader may be disappointed, at first, to find that, beautiful as the epithets are, they are few. Finally he becomes attuned to the soothing rhythm and waits for their arrival like that of an old friend. So I feel about Homer's "wine dark sea" and so also about the Zuni's oft-invoked

striped cloud wings
and massed cloud tails
of all the birds of summer.[4]

These beautiful recitatives were often spoken in a tone so low that no one could hear them except the Supernaturals for whom they were meant. Occasionally an impromptu speech was ad-

[3] Underhill, 1938, pp. 46–47.   [4] Bunzel, 1932*d*, p. 644.

dressed to the audience by a leader who reminded the listeners of their duties. The important, untraditional speeches meant to be heard were those of the clowns. The use of clowns to punctuate one of these lengthy and traditional spells seems admirably judicious and sophisticated. Audience emotions might be raised to the point of exaltation and awe, or perhaps of fright or tears. Suddenly the traditional spell would be interrupted. Uncouth creatures would take the stage, perhaps as in the Pueblo ceremony, running in front of the dancers. They would proceed to do forbidden things, such as eating filth and deriding the ceremony.

We all know the sort of relief such an interval gives and, after it, the ceremonial spell must have continued with doubled power. But relief was only the medium within which the clowns' work was done. It was understood that they were holy people, often supernatural, and that they took liberties because they were above the law. Granted this freedom, they might proceed to lampoon the local transgressors and fools as no neighbor would dare to do. Even religious leaders might be castigated, and I have seen representatives of the Catholic church and of the United States Government stand smiling while they heard about their faults.

The Pueblos have clown associations—the Mudheads, the Kossa, the Koshare. The Navaho and Apache had clowns in their groups of singing Supernaturals. The Iroquois False Faces, evil beings constrained to cure, performed their functions by crawling into a house and throwing ashes about. The Plains Indians, many of whom were displaced eastern groups, had a number of societies that indulged in backward talk and strange ethics, all dictated by dreams. It would seem that the most highly organized people with organized ceremonies had most need of this emotional outlet. I do not know of official clowning in the ceremonies of the Desert food-gatherers.

Connected with religious ceremony in many cultures was the idea of payment or sacrifice to the Supernaturals. Here a marked difference existed between most North American cultures and those of Mexico and the Old World. In these latter cultures, sacrifice was usual in every ceremony. Particularly with the planters, the death and burial of a human being was thought necessary magic to make seeds grow. North of the border, however, there were only a few reflections of this belief. Perhaps the greatest amount of bloody sacrifice came from the Sioux who were not planters. They wanted warlike renown and booty and to persuade the spirits of their earnestness, they tortured themselves or offered small pieces of their own flesh "all that they had which was truly their own."

Offerings by the planters generally could not be called gifts. Rather, they were reminders of a contract between friends and equals, for the spirits long ago had made it known that, on presentation of the proper token, their favors would be granted. In the East, the token was tobacco smoke, ordained by the Great Spirit himself. With the Pueblos and Navahos in the West, the "prayer-sticks" placed near spirit haunts before a ceremony were invitations, rather than offerings. Each bore the feather symbols of the spirit for whom it was intended—a substitute for calling the name. The principal gifts of a material kind which the Pueblos made to the Supernaturals were pinches of cornmeal or pollen placed on dancers, masks or any sacred object. This was thought of as "feeding" their sacred power, to keep it alive.

In general the Supernaturals of the Red Man's world were reasonable and approachable. The general belief was that, long ago, they had set the life of men and animals moving in the right way. To keep it moving thus, man had only to re-enact the events of "the beginning," thus keeping them as real and powerful as ever.

REFERENCES

Descriptions of sacred objects with illustrations: Fletcher, 1904 (Pawnee); Fletcher and La Flesche, 1911 (Omaha); Michelson, 1927 (Fox); Stevenson, 1904 (Zuni).
Some items on ceremony are included in most monographs on tribes.

 # HUNTING AND GATHERING RITUALS

"Hunting is a holy occupation," said the Naskapi. So was the gathering of plants, the cutting of trees, even the digging of clay. For these Nature Persons had long ago offered their "flesh" for Indian use—but on certain conditions. Every step in obtaining the flesh must be taken with care and ceremony, or the gift would be withdrawn. The Papago woman of southern Arizona, in digging materials for pots, told the clay: "I take only what I need. It is to cook for my children." If possible, she left a small gift. A Fox Indian, in the wooded country of the Mississippi Valley said:

> We do not like to harm the trees. Whenever we can, we always make an offering of tobacco to the trees before we cut them down. We never waste the wood, but use all that we cut down. If we did not think of their feelings, and did not offer them tobacco before cutting them down, all the other trees in the forest would weep, and that would make our hearts sad, too.[1]

A mere apology before taking the earth's products was not enough. It was still dangerous to eat or use them without some

[1] Jones, 1939, p. 21.

special ceremony. The honor paid to "firstfruits" of a season, animal or vegetable, may well be one of the ancient practices brought from the Old World. Often this important food must be eaten by someone with supernatural power of his own sufficient to withstand the danger. This person might be a chief, a priest, or at least the possessor of a formula. Firstfruits ceremonies of this sort were held in the Pacific Northwest not only for the all-important salmon, but also for deer, eels, candlefish, berries, and acorns. Other areas celebrated at least their most important food. Among farming people, where this was a vegetable crop, the ceremonies reached such complexity that the discussion of them must be deferred to later chapters.

Gathering of other things was done ceremonially, whether the object to be gathered was salt, red ochre, or catlinite to make pipes. Indians disturbing nature in this way went through the usual ceremony of apology, perhaps singing magical songs in the process, and treating the product reverently.

The most important Nature Persons, of course, were the animals. We find far more rituals for them than for the humble rocks and plants, perhaps because hunting was more precarious and more help was needed. Every hunting group, for instance, must carry on ceremonies to please the animals and to see that their "people" increased. One of my most dramatic memories is that of standing in the plaza of a Pueblo, in the dark of a January morning, to watch the Mother of Game bring in the deer. It was almost dawn when we heard the hunter's call from the hillside. Then shadowy forms came bounding down through the piñon trees. At first we could barely see the shaking horns and dappled hides. Then the sun's rays picked out men on all fours, with deerskins over their backs and painted staves in their hands to simulate forelegs. They leaped and gamboled before the people while around them pranced little boys who seemed actually to have the spirit of fawns.

In their midst was a beautiful Pueblo woman with long black hair, in all the regalia of white boots and embroidered *manta*. She was their Owner, the Mother of Game. But she was also Earth Mother, the source of all live things including men. She led the animals where they would be good targets for the hunters, and, one by one, they were symbolically killed.

Other tribes danced for the buffalo, the eagle, the prairie chicken, perhaps any or all game that they needed to hunt. The dances, with their skilled imitations, were a delight both for the spectators and the actors. Yet they were not performed for the sake of art, drama, or pleasure although they provided plenty of all three. They were imitative magic drawing the animals to come and do just what men were doing. The dances, too, were complimenting those great beings by showing them how well men observed their ways. Spectacles of this kind were a high point in the Indian year. They combined the pleasure of a theatrical performance, the stimulus of group reunion, the expectation of plenty, with the deep satisfaction of communion with the spirits who were being gratified.

The Naskapi of Labrador, too scattered to manage such performances, had their hunting clothes painted or embroidered with designs "pleasing" to the animals. An Eskimo of central Canada had parts of his dog harness and weapons made of little ivory figures representing seals and other game. This art has been much admired and is now being spread commercially. However, its first purpose was imitative magic in the life-and-death pursuit of the hunt.

Dramatic spectacles and the painting and carving of talismans were the responsibility of the whole group, hunters or not. The men who were to do the actual hunting went through a training in what we might call animal etiquette, beginning almost in babyhood. And here, for once, the spirits entered the domain of ethics. The young boy learning hunting methods was taught that he must not eat of his first kill, even if it were only a rabbit. It must be given to the old or needy. In some groups even mature men sometimes gave away the first game of every species or of every season, believing that otherwise they would never kill again. Perhaps this was akin to a firstfruits ceremony. Also, such taxing of the strong to help the weak was an excellent means to group survival.

Another rule, equally strict, demanded the separation of game animals and women. The seclusion of women at their physical crises was much stricter among the hunters than among the planters. Perhaps that was because, with the hunters, men were the providers and their success was vital to the group. So every magical expedient had to be used, as well as every practical one. Among the planters, where much of the food was produced by women, the danger from them did not weigh so heavily.

Nevertheless, almost everywhere, the hunter remained away from his wife just before the hunt. Alaskan whale hunters practiced this abstinence for the whole whaling season. Navahos communally hunting deer felt that any man who had been incontinent would spoil their success. The greatest danger, of course, was from the menstruant, who was thought to fill animals with horror. Therefore, she was forbidden to touch a man's weapons or to cook the food that gave him strength. Papago hunters had a song they used, when safely out of the village, to cleanse their bows and arrows from chance contact of this sort.

Still, women had their uses if they stayed at a distance. While the hunters were absent they might be told to move slowly or even lie still so that the deer or whale would give no trouble to the hunters.

Preparations for the hunt were very like those for war. In fact, in some tribes, the killing of important prey like a mountain lion or an eagle rated the same honor as did killing an enemy. Very likely the hunter had already obtained a vision assuring him of the animal's love. If he talked about his project, he was careful not to boast but to say very humbly, "Perhaps I will kill." Often he did not use the words deer, elk, or caribou but used some roundabout term, as was often done with the enemy in war. Of course he never made fun of the animals; that would have offended them deeply. This reminds one of the careful circumlocution used by the ancient Irish about the "good people," the fairies whom they feared.

On the night before the hunt, the hunter, of course, kept away from women. If he owned some sacred object, he perhaps gave it tobacco and prayed for good luck. A Menomini hunter spread

a white buckskin on the floor, with his hunting talismans and a
dish of food upon it. Remembering not to call the deer by name,
he sang:

> When hunting I want to see
> The slender legged animals.[2]

What would the Indian have done without songs! Singing was
the prelude to every activity, the way to hearten oneself for what
must be done, to make contact with the spirits, and perhaps to
work magic. Songs for hunting success were of every sort, from
a straightforward wish like that of the Menomini, to alluring
descriptions that would invite the game. The Papago even used
humor, feeling that what gave pleasure to man should be welcome
to the animal spirits also. The grandfather of one of my friends
was said to have gotten many deer after singing the following song
that he had dreamed:

> I, very eager,
> Grabbed the deer's foreleg,
> Thinking it my bow.

> I, over-brave,
> Grabbed the deer's tail,
> Thinking it my feathered arrow.[3]

The Navaho, having prayed and sweated, sometimes traveled in
a group several days' journey from home. Every act at camp—
stacking weapons, cooking, eating, sleeping—was subject to rule
according to the particular hunting method they were following.
The owner of the deer was sometimes thought to be Talking God.
A long hymn to him was sung by the Wolf Way men around
their campfire. This is an extract:

> He [the deer] searches for me . . .
> I being the Talking God . . .
> On top of the dark mountain
> He searches for me
> Among the flowers

[2] Densmore, 1932, p. 66.   [3] Underhill, 1938, p. 59.

He searches for me
The finest of bucks
He searches for me . . .
With his death blood red in color he obeys me.[4]

Once started on the hunt, each man relied on his own skill in stalking or running down the animal. When it came to the kill, others might be called to help him with the ritual. Southwestern Indians apologized to the wounded deer before clubbing him. If the hide was to be used for ceremonial purposes, they ran the animal down without shooting an arrow. Then they filled its nostrils with pollen and smothered it. At home, the Pueblos treated the dead deer like an honored guest. Before it was skinned, the deer was laid out in the house, decorated with beads and sprinkled with pollen, the usual offering to ceremonial objects.

Northern hunters treated their quarry in a similar way. Whales were given a drink of fresh water, which was supposed to be especially delightful to ocean creatures. Then they were cut up according to rule, sometimes with their eyes sewed shut so they could not see the process. Seals and caribou were not so spectacular, but their Owners sometimes made stern demands. The Central Eskimo woman shuddered at the idea of sewing on caribou skin and cooking seal meat at the same time. Perhaps her people had once been land hunters and were apprehensive about the sea. However, they translated the feeling into a conviction that if land and sea creatures were mixed, the human beings responsible would be tragically punished.

Finally, the parts not used must be taken care of in a ritual as stipulated long ago. Fish bones or seal bladders were thrown into the sea; deer antlers were placed aloft on house or tree; bear skulls might be hung on a pole; and buffalo skulls were set in a ceremonial circle.

The most important of all animals was the bear. It was hunted with high ceremony in all the northern regions from Labrador to Lapland. No wonder primitive people were awed when they saw this huge animal tower up on its hind legs and when they found its

[4] Hill, 1938, p. 106.

skeleton to be very like that of a man. Its ability to hibernate without food for months seemed supernatural. The bear was always spoken of respectfully in some such term as "the black food" or the poetic Finnish "golden friend of fen and forest."

Even the Cherokee down in the Tennessee mountains had a bear song taught, it is said, by the animals themselves before they assumed human form. It mentions the four mountains where the bears had their villages.

> In Rabbit Place you were conceived, Yoho!
> In Mulberry Place you were conceived, Yoho!
> In Uya ye you were conceived. Yoho!
> In the Great Swamp you were conceived. Yoho!
> And now surely we and the good black things,
>   the best of all,
>   shall see each other.[5]

In front of the den, the hunter called respectfully: "Come out grandfather! I don't want to hurt you." After the animal had been prodded or smoked out, it took several men to dispatch it; but this was done with apologies and with as little blood as possible. The skinning and butchering were under special ceremonial rules and so was the subsequent feast on the meat. Everywhere, this was a solemn ceremonial. As with firstfruits, it was generally old men or ceremonialists who had the first portions. Women could eat only certain parts of the meat if they were allowed any at all. Sometimes the skin was stuffed, decorated, and set up to be honored. Afterward, the skull might be hung up and kept.

It may be that the same sort of ceremony went on in the Stone Age in the Old World. At Drachenloch, in northern Europe, excavators have found two caves with bear skulls that they think were treated ceremonially. The Ainu of Sakhalin Island north of Japan, who retain many primitive customs, even rear bear cubs in the house, and their women nurse them. Finally, the bears are killed with ceremony and sent home to the Lord of the Forest to tell of their good treatment and ask for much more game. Are the Indian apologies and ceremonies perhaps only a faint echo of

[5] Mooney, 1891, pp. 373–74.

primitive man's normal attitude toward the powerful Beings he had to kill?

The above examples refer to single hunters or small groups of hunters. When animals were to be killed in quantity, the energies of a whole tribe were mobilized. Small animals could be driven into a net or a ring of men; large ones could be surrounded or stampeded over a cliff or into some kind of makeshift pen. Still, all the care and ingenuity used in these devices did not mean that the sacred nature of the hunt was forgotten. The animals would show themselves only if all taboos had been observed and the spirits were pleased. Hunt fetishes or dreams were desirable for every man taking part, but in important hunts there had to be a leader who was sure of supernatural power. The Pueblo and Papago had appointed Hunt Chiefs, who were actually priests. In the Plains, where religion was more individualistic, a man with the right dream volunteered, and if his hunt was successful he gained great prestige. The Creeks of Alabama took a medicine man with them and anointed themselves with herbs under his direction. The Paviotso of Nevada drove antelope into a corral for slaughtering, but their belief was that they would never find the herd nor drive it in without the dreams and songs of a medicine man.

The great buffalo herds of the Plains, each animal able to trample a man to death, must have seemed an insuperable problem to the Indians before they had horses. However, men on foot did drive the animals over a cliff or into a closed canyon, as piles of bones in the area can prove. Modern Sioux relate traditions of how this was done. There must be a buffalo caller, a man who had had a dream. Perhaps he called a migrating herd toward a chosen cliff, using a primitive megaphone made of bark. Or perhaps he draped himself in a buffalo robe, went on all fours among the herd, and led them straight to the cliff's edge where he must have skill and "power" enough to dodge away before the buffalo went over.

After the Indians had acquired horses, several thousand men could be deployed to surround a whole buffalo herd. This was a tribal undertaking, with scouts to locate the herd, a leader to direct the tribal march to the hunting grounds, and police to keep individual hunters from racing off alone and frightening the animals. A few tribes at the edge of the buffalo country, like the Comanche at the far west and the Blackfoot at the north, relied only upon this practical organization. Those nearer the east and south, the seat of ceremony, made of the buffalo hunt—at least the first one of the season—something like a religious pilgrimage. It was a mass contact with the Powers that kept them alive.

The hunt by the Omaha of Nebraska has been magnificently described. They were a prairie tribe who combined hunting with agriculture—planting their fields in spring, hunting buffalo in the Plains all summer, then returning in the fall to harvest. Their movement to the Plains for the first hunt of the summer was a magnificent ceremonial progress. It must have been like the march of an army in organized contingents, each behind its different banner, with the leaders and the oriflamme in front.

The contingents were different father-clans, each with its ceremonial duties and consequent taboos. They would camp in a circle every night, with the Sky (War or Thunder) clans at the north and the Earth or Peace clans at the south. Ahead of them, abreast, walked the seven permanent chiefs of the nation whom no one must precede. Then came the volunteer leader of the hunt who had dreamed and prayed for months before daring to assume such a responsibility. After the procession started, he spent a night in prayer and fasting; then, walking barefooted, he caught up with it. Near the leader were carried the sacred objects he had supplied: a staff covered with swansdown and tufts of symbolic bird feathers, and the special pipe smoked only at the buffalo hunt.

These were the leader's badges of office, his own particular banners. They were brought to the forefront every night to receive reports from the scouts who had been racing over the plains hoping to sight buffalo. But since the whole nation was on this march, the national talismans must be present to give their blessings. One of these was a decorated pole made from a tree shown to an Omaha dreamer long ago by the Thunderbirds. This must be kept in the special tent of the War People. The other talisman was the hide of a white buffalo that had a tent of its own and was in the charge of a particular subclan. At night, this tent might be opened and the hide spread out so that its influence could radiate through the camp. People who wished to acquire merit could come and make gifts to the hide.

If these sacred objects were properly sheltered and cared for; if the leader was continent and had only the minimum of food and sleep; and if the people moved quietly and did not quarrel the hunt was sure to be a success. Nevertheless, when the buffalo were finally sighted, the move toward them was made according to ceremony with three stops before the final charge. (Once an eager hunter prevailed upon the group to omit these three stops, lest the herd escape meanwhile. He was trampled to death by the buffalo the next day.)

The surround was made by two lines of men galloping on fast horses. The leaders must carry the two insignia—the feathered staff and the buffalo pipe.

The actual slaughter was a practical affair, done by skilled men on trained buffalo ponies. It was hardly practicable to take care of the bones of a huge herd, but the seven chiefs and the leaders made a meal of the tongues that had been ceremonially cut out through the throat and that had to be eaten without either bowl or knife. This feast took place in the tent of the white buffalo hide. The chiefs wore buffalo robes with the fur sides out; they sat crouching with the robes over their heads while the buffalo pipe was smoked and the white buffalo songs sung. Most of these were solemn musical phrases with only a few syllables to start a train of thought. One introductory song has been translated:

> The holy pipe!
> Holy, I say.
> Now it appears before you.
> The holy pipe, behold ye![6]

Apparently, it means that the pipe should not be thought of as a mere object contrived by man. It has come of its own accord to give a means of communication with the spirit world.

After everyone had feasted and the extra meat was dried, the sacred pole was anointed with red paint and gifts were offered to

[6] Fletcher, 1911, p. 288.

it. Then the whole tribe danced around it to songs about the buffalo and the corn.

The dance was wild, a glorious exercise by people who had feasted well. It was also a gesture of triumph, an assurance that the pole, symbol of communication with the spirits, was in their midst and treated as it should be. The spirits were pleased and more triumphs should follow. No mere dance for pleasure could give such overwhelming satisfaction.

Traditions say that most of the Caddoans and southern Siouans had tribal hunts of this general kind for the first hunt of the year, and the custom was known as far north as the Prairie Potawatomi. Even when ceremony was less rigidly followed, reverence for the buffalo was of a religious nature. A Sioux priest prayed to Wakan-Tanka (Sacred Great-one):

> Behold this buffalo, O Grandfather,
>   which You have given to us.
> He is the chief of all the four leggeds
>   upon our sacred Mother.
> From him the people live, and with him they
>   walk the sacred path.[7]

REFERENCES

Rituals for success in the hunt: Hill, 1938 (Navaho); Speck, 1935 (Naskapi).

Honor to game after the hunt: Gunther, 1926, 1928 (Coast Salish, salmon); Hallowell, 1926 (Northern Hemisphere, bear); Lantis, 1938 (Alaska, whale).

See also Anthropological Records, University of California; monographs from museums and universities.

[7] Brown, 1953, p. 79.

WAR CEREMONIES

Before the days of massive resistance against the whites, the fighting which took place among Indians could hardly be called war. It has been described as being essentially a ceremony or a game in which the rules of behavior were more important than the results. This was true in many cases. The brief encounters in which warriors fought for revenge and glory have more in common psychologically with the knightly bouts of the Middle Ages than with the struggles between organized nations in which men fight in armies, sometimes reluctantly, because of patriotism.

Indians had no nations. Even the Iroquois groups, about whom that term is sometimes used, never made war as a body. They had not the organization of a modern state that can mobilize its fighting men at will. The warriors had some kind of official war chief who recruited his followers only through advertisement and persuasion. There was no possibility of a long campaign with a reliable fighting force. After a victory, there was no mechanism for holding conquered land, ruling conquered people, or even for enforcing a treaty. The purpose of the encounter (there was rarely more than one by the same war party) was revenge and desire for prestige. It is no wonder, then, that the rules for gaining such prestige were carefully made and observed. In the Plains area, these observances sometimes were carried to fantastic extremes, such as giving the greatest honor to a man who went into battle unarmed and simply touched an armed enemy with a stick.

Most non-Indians associate Indian warfare with scalping, and they would be surprised to learn how unimportant this was in some parts of the country. Scalps were a record of achievement, equivalent to the written reports of modern days. Yet other means of recording were possible, and Indians took heads or captives according to convenience. Captives were worthwhile to those who had work for them to do and means of holding and feeding them. A few might be tortured and killed, but the number was never large as it was in Mexico. North of the border, torture was usually considered uninteresting unless the victim was brave. To carry the heads home was difficult for a party making a long journey on foot but these were a favorite trophy with canoe people. Scalps were the simplest device for reckoning the enemy slain, and a good deal of ritual grew up around them.

Ritual surrounded every act of an attacking war party (in defense there was little time for ceremony), and to understand the ceremony clearly, we can divide the expedition into three phases. The first phase was that of preparation, when the spirit power was obtained for the volunteers. The second came during the expedition itself, when there had to be supernatural means to ensure safety and success. These two necessities were provided for in almost every tribe. It was in the third phase, the return and victory celebration, that we find the most obvious split between the individualistic hunters and the organized planters.

This was the time when the warriors recounted their exploits and received honors, which generally included a new name. It was the time when the women came into their own, taking charge of the booty and venting their fury on everything that came from the enemy. Was it regarded as simply a time of relief from stress, dedicated to boasting and gloating? This was the usual hunter attitude. Or was it a solemn point in the proceedings when enemy spirits had been brought into camp and must be expelled with all means available? This, in various degrees, was the attitude of the planters.

The two attitudes appear in North America in every kind and degree.

My survey begins in the West and North. Those who think of THE Indian as super-warlike may be amazed to find that, in almost half the hunting-gathering area, there were almost no arrangements for war. The solitary hunters and little groups of gatherers were too busy with the food quest to manage anything but occasional quarrels or murders. Even some California tribelets, after a squabble with their neighbors, treated the killings in war like murders to be paid for rather than justifiable revenge.

The only groups with the resources and leisure for real fighting were the wealthy fishing tribes of the Northwest Coast. Prestige was a ruling passion with these wealthy men, and each must constantly show his superiority over his neighbors. This could be done by attacking some non-relative, perhaps taking a head or two, and kidnapping one of his family to be used as a slave. The offended group would, of course, effect a rescue or take revenge, and so a constant feuding went on.

The first two phases of the war project, the gaining of spirit power before the trip and on the way, were attended to carefully. It was likely that prominent men in this coastal area had been visited by a War Spirit. The leader probably had one visitation, and he tried to get as many War Spirit protégés into his canoe as possible. Before leaving, he and perhaps his followers fasted for four days, bathed in cold water, and rubbed themselves with rough branches after the local custom. Also they kept away from women, for female influence was as deadly to the warrior as to the hunter. Fasting went on, according to some accounts, for the first four days of the canoe trip. This going without food before strenuous endeavor has always puzzled the non-Indian. It would hardly be useful in a long campaign, but before a short battle or a ball game it seemed to raise the spirits of the contestants. A doctor has told me that a short fast does the same for his modern patients, providing they are healthy to begin with.

For success on the trip, the party took a shaman who must fast not only beforehand but until the enemy was near. The Tlingit carried little effigies of cedar bark which they maltreated as they hoped to maltreat the enemy. Their wives at home did the same, for women could work useful magic as long as they were not in contact with the warriors. Attention to the Supernatural ended with the attack following which the party paddled home, usually with heads and captives. A triumphant feast was in order at which time the heads were exhibited. A Makah of Cape Flattery made a most effective victory song as he swung an enemy head by its long hair and jeered:

> The only reason why I do not cut off your head
> Is that your face would have a crying expression
> When I carried the head.[1]

There was nothing religious about this taunt. Nor was there any ceremony when the heads were placed on poles outside the village and left to rot.

The next western group wealthy enough to play the war game were the buffalo hunters of the Plains. They attended carefully to the first phase of the adventure, for few men would think of joining unless they had had a vision. There were war societies whose founder had received a spirit's visit and whose members sometimes made special vows of bravery. Still, they did not fight as a unit but as separate individuals.

The volunteer instigator of the party might have gained supernatural help long ago, but if not, he went out to "cry" for it. He had some token from his spirit helper and so, probably, had every man of the party. It might be merely a feather or perhaps a shield with emblematic design. That shield, which had been made by a holy man with prayer and singing, gave far more protection than the mere leather disk. The warrior in the heat of battle might call out a vow: "Oh Sun, let me kill an enemy! Let me gain honor! I will build a sweat lodge for you! I will donate a robe! I will torture myself at the Sun Dance!"

The third phase of the war party, again, was secular. These nomadic people had little use for slaves in the early days and no place to keep heads. Even scalps might be thrown away as soon as they had been used to claim honors. Sometimes striking the post,

[1] Densmore, 1939, p. 186.

recounting exploits, and changing names were done with no trophies at all. The only element of religion was that the boaster might call upon the sun to witness his truthfulness. Ever afterward, he would recount these exploits on festive occasions, this serving as a substitute for a written record at a war office.

The farming Indians of the East were the scalpers par excellence, and I suspect they were the original ones. Their warriors pulled all the hair from their heads except the scalp lock that waved above their blackened faces with its decorative feathers. They needed scalps as records, for their war parties were sometimes so large and scattered that no man could know about another's exploits. Moreover, these were an organized people. Their war party was a solemn affair, ritualized in all its phases. But ritual was for the group, not the individual. The average warrior did not really need a vision or a token, though he might have them. Vision was the function of the group leader who sometimes did not fight at all but devoted himself to ceremony. He carried the group fetish that was surrounded with taboos and was more powerful than that of any single man. Last of all, the war trophies were not simply material for boasting but were surrounded with religious observance.

There were many variations in this pattern, from the western part of the Woodlands, which was nearly as informal as the Plains, to the area of Iroquois, who came to fight on such a gigantic scale that many observances were forgotten, to the Southeast, where ceremonies were developed in amazing complexity. It is a cause for deep regret that more ceremonies of the ancient, organized peoples of this area were not collected in the native language before they faded away. The only full text we have is from the Osage of the southern prairies. The chants, songs, and rituals recorded by a part-Omaha Indian occupy four volumes, and even so they are not complete. Surely the Osage were not unique in these imposing rites even though they boasted of being:

> A people among whom there were none that were craven,
> A people that permitted none of their enemies to live.[2]

[2] See La Flesche, 1939, p. 646.

If we could retrieve more ritual from the Osage neighbors, Siouans, Caddoans, and Muskogeans we might find that ancient Indian war poetry, with its striking metaphors and its sonorous repetitions, could rival that of the Norsemen.

The ritual condensed or, rather, suggested here, is that decided upon by a group of elders although the warriors would be volunteers. The elders were something like a College of Initiates chosen after an arduous probation of fasting, achievement, and vision. To the Osage, they were the "Little Old Men," little being a term of endearment. The Old Men were the keepers of tradition, who chose the War Priest and supervised all the complexities of the war ceremonies. In their house of assembly they sat in two groups, people of the Sky moiety (the ceremonial half) at the north end of the house and people of the Earth moiety at the south. No tribesman could forget the tradition of the descent from above when he saw this seating arrangement and watched how, in a ceremonial march, the Sky people always started off on the left foot, Earth people on the right.

The Little Old Men chose the War Priest for the occasion, or he might volunteer. Then he chose a sponsor from his moiety who would guide him through the coming ceremonials. We shall hear about sponsors again among the planting people for they were necessary for anyone entering a society, and the war priesthood was practically that.

The first act of the new war priest was to obtain a vision (unless he was a volunteer who had just had one). He was sent out to fast and wail and to smear his face with earth after the Osage custom. It was the black bear who had taught the tribe this custom, so the visionary scooped up earth with his hand as the bear was said to have done with his paw. A song describes how he addressed the earth:

> My grandfather, I draw thee into my hand.
> My grandfather, I crumble thee in my hand.
> My grandfather, I color my face blue with thy body.
> My grandfather, I touch my head with thy body.[3]

[3] La Flesche, 1925, p. 277.

FIG. 1.—*Salish girl wearing the fir-boughs and goat's wool blanket that signify her adolescence. Reproduced by courtesy of the National Museum of Canada, Ottawa.*

Fig. 2.—*Menstrual lodge, by Capt. S. Eastman.* Schoolcraft, *Part 5, opposite p. 70. Reproduced by courtesy of the Denver Public Library Western Collection.*

FIG. 3.—*Plains Indian women mourning the dead. The woman at left is cutting her hair with a stone knife. The first at the right is scratching her arm with a bristle brush, and the one behind her thrusts a skewer through her arm. Painting by Capt. S. Eastman in* Schoolcraft, Part 5, *opposite p. 168. Reproduced by courtesy of the Denver Public Library Western Collection.*

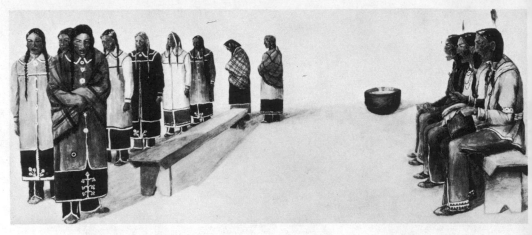

FIG. 4.—*Iroquois Dance of the Dead, in the longhouse. The dancers, or marchers, are women, while men beat the drum and sing. Water color by Ernest Smith. Reproduced by courtesy of the Rochester Museum of Arts and Sciences, Rochester, N.Y.*

FIGS. 5 and 6.—*Typical conjuring lodges in which a shaman receives his spirits and questions them. The first one is constructed of birchbark strips, made by the Ojibwa Indians, and the second of skins, made by Eskimo of Hudson Bay. The lodges are placed over the shaman; there is no opening except at the top, where the spirits enter, often shaking the tent. Figure 5 is from an imaginative drawing by J. C. Tidball, in Schoolcraft, Part 1, p. 428; Figure 6 is a drawing by Lucian M. Turner, from "Ethnology of the Ungava District, Hudson Bay Territory" in* Eleventh Annual Report of the Bureau of Ethnology *(1889, 1890), Fig. 85, p. 274.*

FIG. 7.—*Medicine dance of the Winnebagoes. Members of the medicine society hold otter skin bags, containing the magic shell with which they kill and bring to life. Painting by Capt. S. Eastman, in* Schoolcraft, *Part 3, opposite p. 286. Reproduced by courtesy of the Denver Public Library Western Collection.*

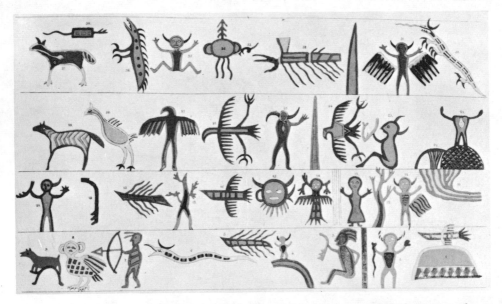

FIG. 8.—*Figures on a birchbark strip used as mnemonic systems for a* wabeno *shaman who was also a member of the Grand Medicine Society. Sketch by Capt. S. Eastman, in* Schoolcraft, *Part 1, opposite p. 373. Reproduced by courtesy of the Denver Public Library Western Collection.*

FIG. 9.—*Spirit Canoe Ceremony of the Snuqualmi, Fort Washington,
1920. The upright boards are paraphernalia prepared for each shaman in
accordance with his vision. Placed in two lines, they represent a canoe.
Reproduced by courtesy of the Museum of the American Indian, Heye
Foundation, New York City.*

FIG. 10.—*Tlinkit shaman at his incantations. (Reproduced from an old illustration, source unknown.) Reproduced by courtesy of the National Museum of Canada, Ottawa.*

Fig. 11.—*The* Hamatsa *or Cannibal Dance of the Kwakiutl. The neo-phyte, with wreath and decorations of cedar bark, enters the house in the character of a cannibal. Reproduced by courtesy of the Chicago Natural History Museum.*

FIG. 12.—*Members of Iroquois False Face Society. They wear masks representing the Disease Spirit, whose face was contorted when the culture hero caused a mountain to fall on him. The masks now bring power to cure disease. Masked healers enter a house crawling and spread ashes from the hearth as purification. Reproduced by courtesy of the American Museum of Natural History, New York City.*

FIG. 13.—*Opening the Sacred Bundle. Ernest Spybuck, Shawnee, Okla.
Reproduced by courtesy of the Museum of the American Indian, Heye
Foundation, New York City.*

FIG. 14.—*Medicine Pipestem Dance. This was the famous calumet dance. The removable stems of calumets or pipes were decorated with eagle wings. It was performed by chosen youths representing eagles when one tribe visited another for peacemaking or trade. Painting by Paul Kane, in* Wanderings of an Artist in North America (*London*), *1859, opposite p. 425. Reproduced by courtesy of the Denver Public Library Western Collection.*

Fig. 15.—*Decorated stem of the calumet. The brown-feathered stem represented the female eagle; it was used in the Pawnee Hako Ceremony.* Annual Report, Bureau of American Ethnology, *Vol. 22, Part 2.*

FIG. 16.—*Buffalo Dance of the Mandan Indians in front of their medicine lodge, by Karl Bodmer. From illustrations to* Maxmillan, Prince of Wied's Travels in the Interior of North America (*London*), *1847, Plate 18. Reproduced by courtesy of the Denver Public Library Western Collection.*

FIG. 17.—*Scalp Dance of the Minatarees. Painting by Karl Bodmer. Reproduced by courtesy of the Denver Public Library Western Collection.*

FIG. 18.—*Scalp Dance of the Dacotahs, by Capt S. Eastman. The scalps held up are stretched on willow circlets.* Schoolcraft, *Part 2, page unnumbered. Reproduced by courtesy of the Denver Public Library Western Collection.*

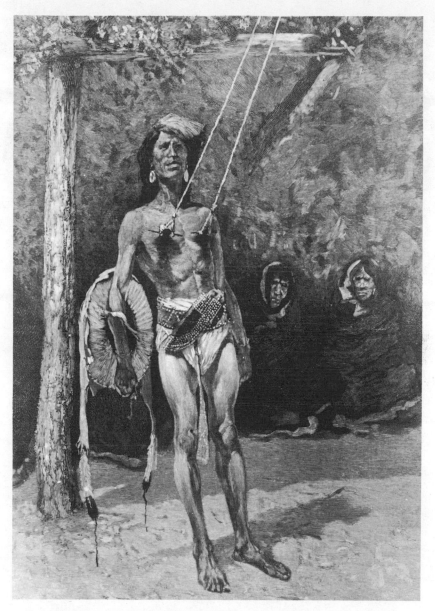

FIG. 19.—*The ordeal in the Sun Dance among the Blackfeet Indians, by Frederic Remington. From* Harper's Weekly (*December 13, 1890*), *p. 473. Reproduced by courtesy of the Denver Public Library Western Collection.*

FIG. 20.—*Great Feather Dance of the Iroquois. This was one of the many performed during every Iroquois ceremony. It may originally have been a victory dance. Water color by Ernest Smith. Reproduced by courtesy of the Rochester Museum of Arts and Sciences, Rochester, N.Y.*

Fig. 21.—*Temple pyramid, Mississippi Valley. Model at Chicago Natural History Museum.*

FIG. 22.—*Iroquois women drag their robes around the cornfields. Iroquois women, who are the planters, drag their robes over the cornfields at night to protect the cornfields from vermin. Painting by Capt. S. Eastman, in* Schoolcraft, *Part 5, page unnumbered. Reproduced by courtesy of the Denver Public Library Western Collection.*

FIG. 23.—*Model of Mound Builder Culture. Reproduced by courtesy of the Museum of University of Oklahoma, Norman.*

FIG. 24.—*Pawnee sacrifice to the Morning Star. The maiden represents Evening Star, patroness of agriculture. The piercing of her heart by an arrow (note archer at right) symbolizes planting. Model at Chicago Museum of Natural History.*

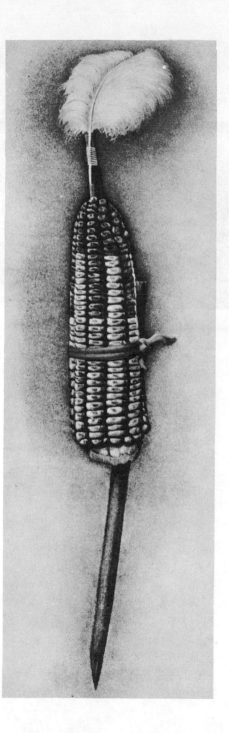

FIG. 25.—*Mother Corn. The decorated ear, carried on the Pawnee ceremony of adoption, has the tip painted blue to symbolize the heaven, dwelling of the Powers. Four blue lines coming from it are the paths by which the Powers visit man. From the* Annual Report, Bureau of American Ethnology, *No. 22, Part 2.*

Fig. 26.—*Hopi Indian Snake Dance. Model at the National Museum. Reproduced by courtesy of the Smithsonian Institution, Washington, D.C.*

FIG. 27.—*Pueblo altar. The design on the floor is made with colored cornmeal. Baskets contain prayer sticks and cornmeal; other ceremonial materials are lying at left. Model at Chicago Natural History Museum.*

FIG. 28.—*Pueblo Deer Dancers. Reproduced by courtesy of the American Museum of Natural History, New York City.*

FIG. 29.—*Boys' initiation among Shoshoneans of southern California. The head of the clan draws a symbol of the world for the boys' instruction. Drawing by Velino Herera. Reproduced by courtesy of the United States Bureau of Indian Affairs.*

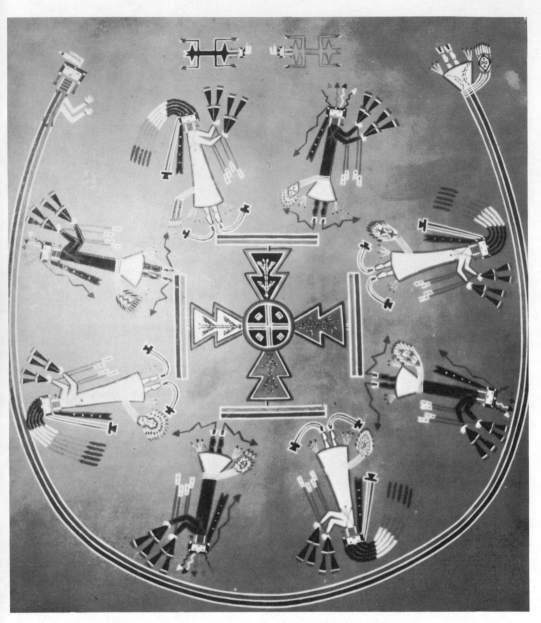

FIG. 30.—*First sand painting of the Navaho Water Chant. Rain boys in kilts and rain girls in long garments, with pouches depending from their waists, hold feathers in each hand. In the center is a pool of water from which corn plants in the four colors spring in the four directions. The whole is surrounded by a rainbow, and two representations of Big Fly guard the opening. Reproduced by courtesy of the Museum of Navaho Ceremonial Art, Santa Fe, N.M.*

Fig. 31.—*Iroquois False Face Ceremony at New Year. Reproduced by courtesy of the Rochester Museum of Arts and Sciences, Rochester, N.Y.*

FIG. 32.—*Indian dead at Wounded Knee, South Dakota. Indians were fired upon by the military in fear of an uprising connected with the Ghost Dance. Reproduced from the collection of Fred and Jo Mazzulla, Denver, Colo.*

FIG. 33.—*The Ghost Dance of the Oglala Sioux at Pine Ridge Agency, South Dakota. Drawn by Frederic Remington from sketches made on the spot. Appeared in* Harper's Weekly *(December 6, 1890), pp. 960–61. Reproduced by courtesy of the Denver Public Library Western Collection.*

Fig. 34.—*Kickapoo Peyote Ceremony, as drawn by a Shawnee Indian. The "road man" holding feathers sits at the rear or western side of the tipi. Before him is the crescent-shaped earth altar, holding the "chief peyote." The man at his left taps the water drum while the next man holds the staff and sings. In the center, the fire man fans the fire as a group member bathes in the cedar smoke for purification. Reproduced by courtesy of the Museum of the American Indian, Heye Foundation, New York City.*

The song is longer and more imposing, with repetitions that I have omitted. The refrains are welcome to those who have no printed word for reference, but most moderns get more flavor from the words without them. Moreover, we do not have the time that Indians had.

The priest candidate was allowed four days for wailing, seven if necessary. Of course he returned successful, since the Little Old Men knew how to choose. He was given a drink of water by a representative of the Water Clan who must first recite the ritual telling how water became their totem. In the same way, he received corn gruel from the Buffalo Bull Clan, for corn was first given to the Osage by the buffalo. He was now the Sacred One of the War Party, and on the morrow the four days of preparation might begin.

The Sacred One of the War Party could not participate. He was endowed with a ceremonial pipe and with the sacred hawk fetish in its basket that represented the whole domain of sky and earth. With these he camped in a hut outside the village where food was brought to him twice a day. Here he besought Wakonda for aid and awaited omens. The actual leadership of the party was handed to eight captains, four from each moiety, who were appointed by the Little Old Men. The honor was great and they gave goods (later horses) in recognition of it. Carrying insignia of office, they danced before the village, their bodies painted black, the color of war, and their scalp locks passed through a foxtail roach. Eight wives had worked and borrowed to see that their men were magnificently decked in kilt, leggings, and moccasins embroidered with porcupine quills. Appointed heralds had called for volunteers:

> Men are gathering to sing the songs
> If thou art a man, go thither!

Then, with the usual hypnotic repetition they chanted: "Eagle men are gathering; feather men, deerskin men, men of the fires."[4]

Excitement must have mounted to fever pitch as, twice a day, the eight war captains circled the village—the Sky moiety going in

[4] See La Flesche, 1925, pp. 217–18.

one direction, Earth in the other. They wore their paint and finery and carried the staves with eagle feathers waving. Now and then they stopped to drum and sing:

> Our brave young men have found in me
>> their leader [repeated three times].
> Oh war priest, they are eager to meet the foe
> To defeat and triumph over him![5]

More and more volunteers in war panoply joined the procession, and the people came out to cry for them as they passed.

Every act of preparation during those four days was performed by the appropriate clan, with a recitation of ritual. Each man, woman, and child in the village was involved in some task, dignified by chant or prayer—preparing food for the warriors, making moccasins, bringing wood for the ceremonial fires, and making charcoal for paint! All were religious rituals, giving importance to the performer and charging him with enthusiasm.

When the warriors finally left, the whole village accompanied them a little way toward the west—the enemy country. There the final chants were sung by the Little Old Men and a dance was performed by the women, who threw their loom sticks out toward the enemy. The Sacred One of the War Party threw down bunches of grass, chanting:

> Oh ye valiant men
> Behold this bunch of grass, the number of its blades!
> My supplications are for the lives of enemies
> Equal in number to these blades of grass!
> Equal to the number of blades in all these bunches!
> This is the theme of my constant supplication,
>> Oh ye valiant men.[6]

The warriors then stepped out over the bunches of grass—Sky people on the left foot, Earth on the right.

During the expedition, the Sacred One of the War Party walked and camped away from the others, carrying the sacred hawk fetish. It was he who bore the burden of ensuring success, eating

[5] See La Flesche, 1939, p. 21.   [6] See *ibid.*, p. 75.

and sleeping as little as possible and awaiting visions. If he had one of ill omen, they all turned back. If all was well and he felt the enemy to be in his power, he fastened the fetish on the back of the chief captain. Some accounts tell of eight fetishes, one for each captain.

The above items are only a sample of the extended ritual that unrolled as the war party departed and returned. The Osage took scalps, heads—sometimes limbs—and prisoners, since they had plenty of work in their fields for extra hands. On their return, all were handed to the Sacred One of the War Party who again went away to fast (according to one account he mourned for the slain enemies seven days), while his sponsor and the Little Old Men handled the victory ceremonies.

This third phase of the war project was as fraught with ceremony as were the other two. Captives were handed to the Peace Clan that, at least in extant accounts, painted them ceremonially and installed them as tribal servants. Scalps were ceremonially cut into strips by the Little Old Men as they sang:

> Lo, it is a spirit, mysterious, I ask you to distribute . . .
> I come desiring you to distribute this mystic spirit.[7]

A strip of the "spirit" was given to each clan that owned a hawk fetish and tied around the fetish bundle. Then bits of flesh from the slain enemy were offered to the four winds, thus speeding his spirit onward. After this came the well-known ceremony when the warriors recounted their exploits and received new names. They were let off lightly by having the war priest achieve purification for the whole party. In many southeastern tribes warriors, before their triumph, had to undergo a period of seclusion with fasting and emetics. In Virginia, the man who had scalped for the first time had to fast and use a scratching stick as did the adolescent girl. It has been noticed before that such a retreat was a familiar pattern at times when supernatural danger was imminent.

The mild treatment of captives by the Osage seems to set this tribe apart from its southeastern neighbors. All these people could use workers in their fields as well as wives to increase the tribal

---

[7] La Flesche, 1925, p. 307.

population. The majority of healthy young captives, it seems, were so employed, usually after a ceremony that removed the enemy magic. Old people might be killed and brave men dramatically tortured. In fact, the brave man expected this and prepared his death song in preparation for it.

Here we cannot but notice the ceremonial similarities between Indians in the Southeast and Mexico. Whether there was communication of some sort around the Gulf of Mexico is a subject for informed discussion that has no place here. We shall, however, notice various likenesses to practices in Mexico and on the northern coast of South America. One intriguing item is the arrow sacrifice of the Skidi and the Natchez. This involved tying a captive spread-eagle to a rectangular frame and shooting him to death with arrows (see Chap. 11). Other Mexican customs were the personal ownership of a prisoner by his captor and graded titles and decorations for the victors.

These torture victims, especially chosen and coddled before they were dispatched, are reminiscent of those the Aztec sacrificed to the sun. This type of sacrifice was not the rule, however. The torture of brave warriors reported throughout the Southeast and among the Iroquois, migrants from that area, usually had nothing religious about it.[8] It developed into a dramatic entertainment for the women who were the chief actors. Here there is a real difference from the Aztecs, who felt that even the tortures they sometimes used were acts to influence the gods. Their wholesale slaughtering was necessary to "feed the sun" and was carried out quickly by a few expert priests. The Creek and Iroquois women, reputed to be the fiercest torturers, acted simply out of vindictive fury against the slayers of their menfolk. This psychological difference between Mexico and the Southeast provides intriguing material for study.

As we move westward, along the Mexican border, emphasis in the war project changes drastically. The Pueblo and Piman Indians were farmers, it is true, but their environment was not the

[8] William M. Beauchamp, in *A History of the New York Iroquois* (New York State Museum Bull. No. 78), 1905, p. 180, comments that early missionaries said that the Iroquois devoted slain prisoners to the God of War.

lush and fertile country of the East. Their corn fields were often small patches salvaged from the desert and existed only by grace of the late summer rains. This was the only farming country north of Mexico where the work was done by men rather than by women. No wonder, when a Hopi farmer might have to run ten miles to an available bit of moist land near hidden water.

Such people, like those of the true Desert, were too busy to fight for conquest. The Pueblos had had occasional squabbles among themselves and later with gypsy Athapascans who stole their corn and women. Pimans (Pimas and Papagos) had Apaches to contend with and, further west, the warlike Yumans. Both Pueblos and Pimans stated openly that they hated war. Their feeling about the enemy, who seemed to thrive on battle, was that they must be inhuman—a nation of sorcerers. It is natural then that, instead of an elaboration of the first two war phases, there was great emphasis on the third. And this did not mean boasting and name changing. Such luxury was dwarfed by the overwhelming necessity of removing enemy magic from men and trophies.

The Pueblos, which we come to first, were perhaps the most tightly organized groups in North America. In some score of villages, each with a few hundred inhabitants, three different languages and several dialects were spoken. Each village was a complex of interlinked clans, societies, or both, with officers who were almost permanent and whose duties were more religious than civil. They had traditional war gods such as the twin Children of the Sun—all but the Hopi, whose war patron was the god of death. They had a calendric round of ceremonies, in which those for the war cult took their place among others, with regular fetishes, altars, and a sacred meeting place. The brief war expedition and the single warrior were swallowed up in this mass of ceremonial. They were small items compared with the warriors' duty of fighting witches, keeping the ceremonies true to tradition, even influencing the hail and sleet as well as human fertility.

Memories of war practice are now vague, but they seem to have included ceremony and offerings before the party left and songs in the field to give the men courage and distract the enemy. The events in which every movement was carefully ceremonialized began with the warriors' return. The scalps and bits of clothing they had brought were handed to the women, thus relieving the warriors of their influence. Then followed ten days for the Zuni (twenty-five for the Hopi), during which the scalps were first abused, then their magic removed so that they could be adopted and used as charms for what these planters needed most—rain and crops. Said the Zuni scalp chief, as he deposited the valuable objects in their appointed place:

> Indeed, the enemy,
> Though in his life
> He was a person given to falsehood,
> He has become one to foretell
> How the World will be,
> How the days will be.[9]

In fact, the taking of such a dangerous trophy brought blessing of waters, riches, seeds, powers, strong spirit, long life, and old age. The scalper himself was in danger from the scalp and must go through an initiation into the Bow Priesthood. This rite involved fasting and continence like that observed by the adolescent girl and the mourner. Meantime, there was dancing in the plaza before an altar where all the arcana of the tribe were set out along with images of the twin war gods. At night, men and women gave way to wild joy and to sexual license for, as the scalp chief told them:

> To some little corner
> Where the dust lies thick,
> You will steal away.
> In order
> To procreate sturdy men
> And sturdy women.
>
> .   .   .   .
>
> Indeed, if we are lucky . . .
> Fine rain caressing the earth,
> Heavy rain caressing the earth,
> We shall win.[10]

---

[9] Bunzel, 1932d, p. 680.
[10] Ibid., pp. 679–80.

For this was a time of power and the Zuni had to seize the opportunity to satisfy their prime need: fertility of the earth and of the people.

The agricultural Pimans, further west, had the same fear and awe of the enemy's power. Without permanent war chiefs or organization, they relied on devoted volunteers to organize punitive expeditions against the raiding Apaches. The Papago who undertook such a duty would have had a vision. He collected a few followers, and while they prepared moccasins and ground cornmeal, he stimulated them by accounts of legendary exploits. A favorite one says nothing about a battle but tells of spirit help and concludes:

> There did I pull up and seize and tie together
> All kinds of his [the enemy's] fine seeds, fine clouds, fine winds;
> Then did emerge, thick stalks, thick tassels
> And the undying seed did ripen.[11]

What the Papagos actually took was not even a scalp but four enemy hairs. The Enemy Slayer who had dared this was quarantined, like the adolescent girl, for sixteen days. His wife underwent the same ordeal in a different place and both had sponsors, a pattern very like that in the Southeast. The old warrior who brought the Enemy Slayer his tiny portion of cornmeal every night told him grimly:

> Verily, who desires this experience?
> Do not you desire it?
> Then you must endure its many hardships.[12]

The reason for the Enemy Slayer's desire for this experience was the rather terrifying power conferred by the enemy scalp. With its power and with the songs he had made in seclusion, he could cause and cure insanity—and love-sickness. The four enemy hairs were wrapped in buckskin and made into a little Apache figure by an old Enemy Slayer. I had a great desire to own such a doll, and proposed that it should be made of horsehair, which would be harmless. I bought some beautiful white buckskin, presented it to

[11] Underhill, 1946, p. 179.   [12] *Ibid.*, p. 197.

an old warrior and waited. After six months and repeated appeals, he acknowledged:

> I began many times to do it. Each time, I felt ill and it got worse. Now I know that such a thing is not for me to do. Take back your buckskin and horsehair. Even those I dare not have in my house.

The Navaho and Apache, who learned from the Pueblos, also purify the killer. So did the Mohave and their language mates along the Colorado River, but these were no peaceful villagers. They did allow their women to raise some corn, but the men spent most of their time in war. "As though they loved it," said one missionary. They went out in army formation, with preliminary challenge, and sometimes duels were fought between the leaders in front of the opposing ranks. Among the Mohave, only one man was allowed to take the scalps, and he had to have dreamed the privilege. It is dramatized in one of their clan sagas. The leader asks:

> Among you people sitting here,
> Who has a good dream for taking scalps?

The scalper speaks:

> I here! I arrive . . .
> I will take it, I take his hair, I take it.
> I do it.
> > Here we stand all together.
> > Up we throw it, down;
> > Up we throw it, down again . . .
> > People to come will tell of it.[13]

Once a month the scalp custodian and his sister, having duly purified themselves by fasting and seclusion, invited the people to dance around the powerful trophy and, of course, to breed strong men and fruitful women.

The means of peacemaking were also standardized and ceremonialized. Some hunter-gatherer tribes in California, it has been mentioned, exchanged shell money in a ceremonial dance, each

[13] Underhill, 1936, p. 14.

side paying for the individual enemies it had killed. The Plains Tribes did not trouble about peace after their frequent raids, conducted by small parties. When two large groups met for trading, they might decide on a partnership that lasted only until one happened to offend the other.

Formal peace treaties were characteristic of the planters in the Southeast, the Mississippi Valley and the Prairie. This was the region of the peace pipe, the famous calumet. A full-scale delegation sometimes made a journey from one tribe to another, carrying the pipe and accompanied by dancers and singers. The receiving group feasted the visitors and gave gifts. Then leaders of each group smoked the pipe in the six directions, calling upon the four winds, the sky and earth to witness the pact. In some instances, a member of the host village was adopted by the visiting leader as a son, thus making peace between them a certainty.

Tobacco smoke, puffed toward the world Powers was, in this instance, a kind of incense. I have wondered if it took the place of the human sacrifice that was thought so necessary south of the border.

REFERENCES

Special studies of warfare: Hill, 1936 (Navaho); Hunt, 1940 (Iroquois); Mishkin, 1940 (Plains).

Volumes on Plains tribes giving much attention to warfare: Berthrong, 1963 (Southern Cheyenne); Ewers, 1958 (Blackfeet); Grinnell, 1923 (Cheyenne); Hassrick, 1964 (Sioux); Lowie, 1954 (Plains, general); Lowie, 1935 (Crow); Oliver, 1962; Wallace and Hoebel, 1952 (Comanche).

See also Anthropological Records, University of California, and monographs on tribes from museums and universities.

FOR THE GENERAL WELFARE: THE SUN DANCE

The hunting and gathering people, it has been noted, found it hard to hold large, general ceremonies. Usually they had not enough food stored to supply a gathering nor could they be sure of being in a certain place on a certain day. These difficulties lay so heavily on the tribes of the Desert and most of those in the Arctic that they held no large meetings at all. Plains people had the same difficulty for much of the year. Still, there was one time when food was plentiful, when hundreds of people could relax from the hunt and enjoy both ceremony and recreation. This was the midsummer pause after the great buffalo hunt, the eight days of the Sun Dance.

The Sun Dance has come to be thought of by many whites as one of the most famous and spectacular of Indian ceremonies. That means also that it must be ancient and deeply rooted. Yet as a full-fledged tribal ceremony, it does not go back much earlier than 1800. The last tribe to adopt it, the Utes, began about 1890. This was necessary. The great summer buffalo hunt with its subsequent supply of plentiful meat could not take place until after Indians had become horsemen.

Wild horses had once existed in America but they had disappeared long before the first immigrants arrived. The horses brought by early Spanish explorers died or returned to Spain when their owners did. But in 1598 Don Juan de Oñate came to set up a Spanish government in what is now New Mexico, bringing an army of settlers with sheep, goats, cattle, and horses. Riding was forbidden to the Pueblo Indians who were under the Spanish thumb, but the more distant people were soon grasping at the wonderful new wealth by means of trade, raid, treaty, or the hunting of strays (the *meschinos* or "mustangs" of later days).

In that development was the origin of the Plains Indian of modern history and fiction. Groups that had been planters like the Cheyenne, or Desert food-gatherers like the Comanche moved into the Plains to camp and to hunt buffalo. It was two hundred years before northern groups such as the Sioux and Blackfoot were properly mounted. Even then, the horse population was not sufficient for each warrior to have all the mounts he wanted. One of the main causes for tribal enmity was the stealing of horses.

By 1800 the Plains, hitherto empty for much of the year, were occupied by mounted Indians. Buffalo could be killed wholesale so that hundreds of Indians could camp and celebrate for a week or so. The coming of the horse, the migration of tribes from all directions to the sparsely inhabited Plains, the development of soldier societies and medicine societies with all their paraphernalia, the inception and spread of the Sun Dance all happened within a hundred years or less. As a complete change in the lifeway of thousands of people, this was a record.

The Sun Dance, in its complete form, was a new ceremony for Indians, although it was composed of ancient elements. To understand how it was begun and spread, we must take a lightning look at the High Plains history. The waving grass, high as man's stirrups, began at the edge of the low, wooded country west of the Mississippi and spread to the Rockies. Pioneers who crossed that stretch later used to report how scarce the water was. Farmers who tried to cultivate it complained of the cycle of rainless summers and of the frequent clouds of grasshoppers.

In all, it was not a country for early planters, and except along the rivers, there were none. But it was a paradise for hunters. The huge buffalo herds, the only large animals left over from the days of mammoth, wild horse, and camel, roamed to and fro in thousands. There was meat in dreamlike supply—if men could handle the monstrous prey and could themselves get along without water. They solved the problem by having seasonal hunts not too far from a water supply. And they handled the buffalo by driving them over a cliff or into an enclosure where they could be killed and butchered with stone tools.

This was the typical buffalo hunt until the horse returned to America. There were tribes west of the Rockies that hunted buffalo perhaps only once or twice a year. There were others along the rivers west of the Mississippi who planted corn, sallying forth perhaps twice a year to trap the buffalo by stampeding them over a cliff, or into a corral, or by burning prairie grass. None of these were Plains Indians as we think of them today. Then the whites came, settling not in the Plains but beyond them to the south and east. The result was a striking change in the Plains way of life.

For one thing, the horse was brought back to America. For another, Indians began pushing each other out of favorable places for trade with the newcomers. Along the Great Lakes there was a movement similar to a fall of ninepins as the Ojibwa, supplied with guns by the French, pushed out the Sioux, the Sioux pushed the Cheyenne, and the Cheyenne the Kiowa. Ultimately all—or part of the populations of all—debouched on the Plains. Many people think of the Sioux, for instance, as bred-in-the-bone Plains Indians, born on horseback. Yet in the mid-1700's they were tramping about Minnesota, hunting ducks and a few deer. About the time of the American Revolution, the Oglala crossed the Missouri and traded with the Mandan there for a few horses. They were not roaming the Plains on horseback until at least 1775. The Cheyenne, the great Plains fighters, had some villages still planting corn along the Missouri in 1800.

As these food-gatherers and planters moved out into the Plains and turned into buffalo hunters, they met new tribes from the North, South, and West. They had to give up some of their ancient rites for lack of material and opportunity. Yet they maintained them in some form if possible, and added others as they learned them. Thus the reverence for a sacred pole might well have come from the Omaha with whom it was ancient. Ancient also were the little images of buffalo placed around the pole by children. The custom of "counting coups" or telling war exploits on all occasions had been known for a long time in the Mississippi Valley as well as in the Southeast.

To trace these and other items of the ceremony would be an interesting study, both in history and psychology. They were combined with the ancient Algonkian custom of the vision quest by ordeal. The result was an impressive pageant, with the open plains as the temple and with vegetation and buffalo parts as the equipment. It was distinctly a Plains production, for those sections of the Plains tribes that had remained east of the Missouri did not have it. The Sun Dance was its Dakota name, since the fasting dancers looked at the sun. The Cheyenne called it the New Life Lodge, the Ponca the Sacred or Mystery Dance. With all of them, the purpose of the rites was to renew communion with the earth, sun, and the spirits, and especially with the winds, so that the tribe might have health and fertility and the buffalo might never fail. The self-torture that has made the occasion famous—or notorious —was incidental, used by some tribes and not at all by others. The essential feature of the ceremony was a prolonged dance or exercise by men who fasted and gazed steadfastly at some holy object —the sun, or the lodge center-pole.

Most tribes performed the dance every summer. The following description refers to the Cheyenne. With them, the occasion constituted a vow made in time of trouble or sickness in the family. The result was an opportunity for the whole tribe to join the Pledger of the ceremony in a communal act of devotion. For the Pledger himself, the result was supposedly the end of his trouble. Also, after his days of conducting the ceremony under guidance, he himself became a priest. He would be eligible to guide another Pledger in the future and to receive continuing gifts and honor. Perhaps it is no wonder that someone was available every summer to vow the dance, for if no one did, it could not be held. And if one who had vowed it in time of stress failed to carry through, he would suffer supernatural vengeance.

The ceremony required no permanent temple or paraphernalia, no organized priesthood. Tribesmen brought with them their portable wealth of decorated tipis and one suit of handsome buckskin clothing. A few old men might bring powdered ochre and chalk for paint and a store of eagle feathers. The only official equipment was one "bundle" containing an ancient pipe, some sinew, and dried herbs. Everything else would be procured on the spot, from the very earth whose favor they were ensuring.

With this humble extemporaneous equipment, there developed an elaborate pageant, replete with symbols that honored all the forces of nature. Every move of hand or foot, every line drawn on the ground had its profound and sacred significance. Few words were spoken, but the movements in themselves were a prayer, understood by all.

The organization was equally informal. The Pledger had been in the status of a holy man since he made his vow and had ceased to cohabit with his wife. He had asked some other man who had once been a Pledger to be his instructor. This man acted as chief priest during the ceremony, and one is amazed at all the gestures, movements, and songs he had learned. He would receive lavish gifts for his services. All other former Pledgers would act as his assistants and all would be feasted.

Thus the men handed down the ceremony from one Pledger to another. But one vital link was beyond their power. The ceremony was alive, and must be passed through a living body. So the chief priest, on the night of the altar dedication, must have connection with the Pledger's wife. So it had happened in mythical times when, according to Cheyenne belief, the ceremony had been taught them by a Supernatural. Such behavior was against all custom for Plains Indians, who as a rule regarded chastity with great seriousness. They punished an adulteress by clipping off the end of her nose, so that she was marked forever. The Sioux honored a chaste matron when they felled the center pole by having her make the first cut. This particular connection, however, they regarded as holy, and it was announced to all the camp. The woman sat with the priests, fasted and received gifts like them, and was instructress for the next Pledger's wife.

For the lay members of the tribe, the occasion was a glorious holiday. During the winter, they had hunted in groups or even families. Food had sometimes been scarce. They had had no news. Relatives and lovers might be dead. New hostile groups or new friends might have been met. Gossip, reunion, and feasting went on during the buffalo hunt but they came to full flower in the glorious days when the hunt was over and the meat dried. As prayer and rites went on among the officiants, the rest of the camp feasted, told tales of war, had their children named, consulted their chiefs, made love, and arranged marriages. Anything done at this propitious time had the favor of the spirits, for many times a day the sun, moon, earth, and winds were being brought close by song and picture.

Shouting and singing, the different bands arrived on horseback to be greeted with shouts by those already encamped. The Cheyenne camp was not arranged by clan and moiety, like that of the agricultural Omaha. They did make a circle with an opening to the East, perhaps this was one of the customs learned from the village dwellers. Their bands came riding in with horses and baggage and they took their places in the circle more or less hit-or-miss, although a tradition grew up that the oldest bands sat at the East. The warriors of different bands set up tipis where they could meet and feast. Everyone went about greeting, weeping, and making appointments, for the business of a year would now be transacted.

The officiants went apart solemnly. The tribe's success for the year would depend on their correct handling of the ceremony. Its public phase would not begin for several days, but meantime the equipment was to be made, mostly out of earth and vegetation. It has been mentioned that, in an Indian ceremony, the preparation of material was as sacred an act as the use of it. In this case, the three days of preparation were secret and almost more holy than the public occasion. The participants were the Pledger and his wife, his instructor who now acted as chief priest with his wife, and all former Pledgers who were assistant priests. In ancient days, it would seem that each of these had an assistant who performed the actual work while his principal gave orders.

For these holy people, a special tipi was erected, and while the camp went on with its feasting and singing, they proceeded with the ceremonial making of costumes and altar furnishings. This meant deerskin shirts and rawhide belts for the Pledger and his wife, with a painted buffalo robe for the Pledger. A buffalo skull, such as was plentiful on the Plains in the early days, had its nose and eye cavities stuffed with grass as a spell to give the animals plenty of grass for next year. A rawhide "paper doll" was cut out to represent a sacrificed enemy. Some rawhide rattles were made, and various sticks were cut and painted.

With half a dozen men working, all this might have been done in half a day. But performing the manual labor was only part of the purpose of this "lone tipi." Before any task was started a pipe must be ceremonially filled and smoked, with motions made toward the sun, the earth, and the four winds. Even the tamping was ceremonially done with a specially prepared stick wrapped in buffalo hide, symbols of vegetation and meat. Each time a piece of material was touched, the worker's hands must be sanctified. This was done by the chief priest, who touched his finger to Mother Earth, then to his tongue, took a bite of sacred root from the medicine bag, then spat lightly on the worker's hands. Every placing of an object was made with four pauses, signifying completion. The whole procedure in the lone tipi was a repetition of the creation and arranging of the world by the Creator.

While this mythical performance was taking place, the lay members of the tribe had their duties also. A huge lodge was to be erected, its skeleton of poles like that of the earth lodges the Cheyenne had used in their planting days. This work was done by the warriors in all their paraphernalia and provided many occasions for reciting their war deeds. First a tall cottonwood tree must be located for the center pole, and this was done by a man who had been a successful spy in an enemy camp. The whole camp then went in procession to cut the pole and bring it home, the warriors who felled it telling of their felling the enemy. At the camp a hole was ceremonially dug for the pole, and with four movements it was erected. Then the warrior societies, shouting and singing, brought and set up the other poles and rafters. Tipi covers were commandeered to spread over them. Some tribes, however, left the shelter roofless and leaned green boughs against its sides.

Toward evening of this third day, the Cheyenne priests left their lone tipi to set up an altar on the ground at the west of the public gathering place, the New Life Lodge. The altar consisted of the decorated buffalo skull as a call for good hunting, plum trees, and berry bushes as a call for vegetation. There was a crude sand painting with lines of red, white, black, and yellow to represent earth and sky; four painted hoops to stand for a rainbow, the call for rain; and upright painted sticks to represent the Cheyenne on one side of the altar, their enemies (painted white for death) on the other.

The sacred ones took their seats behind this altar and had their last drink of water for several days. The Pledger and his wife had been fasting during the preparations, but their instructors had been feasted. Now all would fast until the ceremony was over. Processions of women would bring food to the lodge daily, but it would serve only to provide morsels for sacrifice. It would be carried out again to feed the onlookers, who would thus have their share of blessing.

There was furious drumming and singing around the altar as the people realized that the days of creation had been successfully passed and preparation for the future could begin. Now came the features that have made the ceremony famous. A number of men had vowed to dance, fasting for as long as the chief priest had fasted when he was a Pledger—two or four days. With the Cheyenne, the men came from the military society of the Pledger, along with some volunteers. Other tribes selected them in various ways. Each votary had selected an instructor who painted him differently every day, decorated him with sage and feathers, and gave him an eagle-bone whistle. For this he was well paid by the votary's relatives.

The dancers rehearsed on this first evening and conferred with their instructors. The dance consisted of occasional marches around the lodge, but for most of the time the men simply rose up and down on their toes, gazing steadfastly at the sun or at the center pole. All day and part of the night, they danced and rested alternately without taking food or water. The eagle-bone whistles that they blew constantly represented the Thunderbird and were used to call for rain and vegetation. Also, the eagle was a patron of war, and thus was being brought close to the warriors. When their ordeal was over, they induced vomiting and took a sweat bath. Powerful supernatural help should now be theirs.

A more strenuous ordeal was that of the men who had vowed self-torture. This was not a necessary part of the Sun Dance and many tribes did not use it at all. The United States Government forbade all Sun Dances, on the assumption that the practice was destructive. Although muscles were cut and men often fainted from the ordeal, the injury was not permanent. It was probably no worse than the torture inflicted on themselves by medieval monks. To the Indians, it was a sacrifice of what was most precious to them, their own flesh. It was meant to convince the Powers of their earnestness in seeking supernatural help. A man vowed to suffer in this way when he needed help in trouble or for future success.

The dancing and the self-torture went on for two or four days while outside the lodge there were fasting, singing, and minor ceremonies. Families, at this time, had their children named or their ears pierced. The forty-four chiefs (ten for each division were named) joined the four general chiefs for consultation. Marriages were arranged. Young men and maidens made acquaintance during the dancing and parades. Warrior societies feasted, told of their exploits, and made vows for the future. For the women, there was endless cooking and carrying, yet they seem to have been proud of their function. During the recent fighting in Korea, I heard a sergeant say: "You know, we sergeants are running this war." The matrons, without whose services the ceremony would have stopped, may have felt the same way.

Table 1 shows some of the Sun Dance elements as used in different tribes. We can recognize practices belonging to the vision, to the wonder-working shaman, and to war, all surrounding the central theme of a prayer for plenty. In fact, this dance was a great ceremonial edifice, built on the foundation of a firstfruits rite. This is an interesting example of the way new Indian ceremonies could arise when the situation called for them.

One summer in the early 1960's, I saw the Sun Dance of the Northern Arapaho in Wyoming. It was held in the old-time roof-

TABLE 1

PLAINS INDIAN SUN DANCE

	Kiowa	Ute	Wind River	Crow	Blackfoot	Sarsi	Gros Ventre	Arapaho	Northern Cheyenne	Southern Cheyenne	Oglala	Ponca	Arikara	Hidatsa	Assiniboin	Plains-Cree	Plains-Ojibwa	Sisseton	Canadian Dakota
Procession																			
Blessing					x			x	x	x	x								
Dance																			
Preliminary dance	x		x					x	x	x	x				x				
Chiefs designated	x								x	x									
Dance in altar				?	x	x		x	x										
Sun gazing											x	x						x	
Sunrise dance		?	x					x	x	x	x	x						x	
Sustained by pole		x	x				x	x							x	x	x	x	
Dancing out								x		x									
Circling										x			x	x					
Fanning	x									x				x					
Torture					x	x	x	x		x	x	x	x	x	x	x	x	x	x
Pledger tortured											x	x							x
Tethering to posts				x		x					x								
Objects suspended					x	x		x		x	x	x	x	x		x	x		x
Animals led							x			x	x	x	x	x	x	x			
Flesh sacrifices					x	x	x			x	x	x	x	x	x	x	x		
Drumming on hide	x				x		x	x		x	x			x					
Sham battle					x	x													
Warrior's fire			x	x	x		x	x		x						x			
Ears pierced								x	x	x									
Wife surrender								x	x	x						?			
License								x				x							
Food offerings								x	x	x		x							
Children's clothing	x	?			?		x	x											
Blessing spectators					x											?	x		
Prayer for principals		x	x															?	
Prepared drink	x		?					x		x			?						
Vomiting induced			?					x		x									

Reproduced from Leslie Spier's *The Sun Dance of the Plains Indians: Its Development and Diffusion*. Anthropological Papers of the American Museum of Natural History, XVI, Part VII, 1921, p. 473. Reprinted with the permission of the American Museum of Natural History.

less lodge, walled with cottonwood saplings and having a center pole ceremonially erected. In the crotch of the pole were the sacred objects: the bunch of willows, the digging stick, the buffalo robe on which the eyes of the dancers would be fixed during their ordeal. There were nineteen dancers, their splendid, hairless torsos painted yellow or orange, with markings to represent the sun and the Four Old Men, the winds. There was no cutting of the flesh but, for almost four days, they went without food and water. At intervals, they stood in line, the white-painted sponsors in the center. Up and down they moved in unison, tufts of eagle down bobbing on their heads. The birdlike cries of eagle-bone whistles sounded tirelessly in unison as the singers roared out the songs and each brought his single drumstick down on the big drum with sledgehammer blows.

Sponsors, dancers, and spectators were modern farmers who had come in cars and trailers. They used canvas tents and modern camp equipment. Their announcements were made by a public address system instead of by the old-time camp herald. The dancers had covered themselves with long white cotton skirts in deference, perhaps, to the modesty of old-time white officials. But the panels which hung over these were brilliant with all the shades of scarlet, emerald, and purple that Indians could not obtain in ancient days. And why not? The effect was striking, and it is as natural for Indians to change their costumes with the advent of new materials as it is for whites. The goal of the ceremony, too, was changed. Although the rituals were the same, the yearning of those who performed them was not for more buffalo but for a general blessing. They were communing with the Supernatural in a way that had for them all the sacred associations that churchly prayer and song have for whites. I wish that such a moving way of treating holy things need never be discarded.

There were other backgrounds favorable enough for the resident Indians to build simple rites for firstfruits into an imposing ceremony. One such was northern California, a land of tall trees and salmon streams. There the Yurok, Karok, and others held a pageant that has been called World Renewal. It may have grown out of a ritual for first salmon or first acorns, as practiced by their less forunate neighbors. The Yurok-Karok group can be called hunter-gatherers, but the salmon were so plentiful that they could have permanent villages along the streams with wooden houses and large meeting rooms, or men's clubs. Their ceremony, therefore, was concentrated in a house or near it, not at a temporary camp as the Sun Dance was. Nor did they make their equipment out of the earth and the vegetation at hand. Their paraphernalia were handsome obsidian blades and white deerskins, collected by the groups' leading families over the years.

The display of this man-made wealth at different villages quite obscured the ancient rites for firstfruits and most of the local dances had no connection with them. However, in addition to the dances, a lone formulist went from place to place, recalling the journeys of the first people, the man-animals, who had settled the locality. His journey and recitation were meant to re-create the ideal conditions of those early days. This formula or spell was the basis on which a unique ceremony was built up. It was made in America, as the Sun Dance was and as we shall find that the corn dances were.

Farther south, the Kuksu and Hesi ceremonies of the Pomo and their neighbors were also local developments. The actors were masked unlike any others, either in the Northwest or in the Pueblos. Also there was here and farther south, a group initiation for boys unusual in the rest of the country.

It has been stated that Indian ceremonies were never entirely original inventions. They were, however, original assemblages; each ritual combined various ancient usages with new ones suited to the situation. Ceremonies for the general welfare are an excellent example of combinations using very different elements, old and new, but all for the same purpose.

REFERENCES

Sun Dance in different tribes: Bowers, 1950; Anthropological Papers of American Museum of Natural History, New York.

For further information on world renewal ceremonies, see Barrett, 1917; Heizer and Whipple, 1962; Kroeber and Gifford, 1949; Loeb, 1932; Merriam, 1955.

15

PLANTING BEGINS

With the planting Indians, we come into a blaze of sunlight. Hunter-gatherers had, indeed, revered the sun but without any definite ceremonies. In their mythology, the orb of day might be trapped for man's use or kept in a box and stolen by some clever animal. Their migrations were timed not so much by summer and winter as by the changes of the moon which marked the migrations of birds and the rutting of animals. To planters, however, the sun was the actual source of life. In their thinking, he might be the Father, who begot mankind on Mother Earth as the plants were begotten. Or he might be the delegate of an even more potent Creator. In any case, the sun must be constantly watched and propitiated. Especially at the solstices, life or death for man's world might depend on his turning properly and ceremonies might be necessary to assist him.

Almost as important as the sun was his earthly representative, fire. Hunter-gatherers admitted the relationship of fire to the sun by keeping their menstruating girls away from it. They cherished their fires and carried embers carefully from one camp to another. But they could not keep a perpetual flame burning. Nor could they gather at regular times to renew it. For many planters, however, sun worship and the ever-burning fire were essential elements in religion.

These elements were often shared with fellow Indians in Mexico. It has been pointed out that the planting areas in the United
States were the northern rim of a huge corn-raising area which
stretched far into South America. In those warmer countries, the
ancestors of corn, beans, squash, and a number of other vegetables
grew wild. Hunter-gatherers in Mexico had begun to domesticate
the wild ancestor of maize sometime near the beginning of the fifth
millennium B.C.[1] Thousands of years were needed before that wild
grass with its few small kernels could become the "life sustainer"
which later Indians called it. Gradually, in the hands of one group
after another, it was improved, hybridized, fitted to different cli-
mates. Other plants were added and, by 1500 B.C., Mexico was
dotted with agricultural villages. With the new source of food
there developed gradually the arts of pottery and of weaving with
native cotton.

The villages grew into cities, with powerful rulers and a class
organization. The plan of these cities should be of interest to us,
for it traveled north with the corn. So did many customs and items
of ceremony, for perhaps they all seemed equally powerful to
hunter-gatherers adopting a new lifeway. The so-called city was
rather a civic center, a plaza surrounded by public buildings and
dominated by one or more temples. These were not large but they
were impressive, for each was mounted on a pyramid whose mass
was, perhaps, four or five times that of the building. Most people
on hearing the word pyramid think of Egypt, but here were not
the squat structures of the Pharaohs, built of huge stone steps.
Mexican pyramids were built of rubble, sheathed with stone, with
the temple like a small excrescence at the top. It was reached by a
flight of stone steps on one side, or perhaps on all sides, but few
people climbed those stairs. Only the priests and the sacrificial victims were present at the temple; the congregation waited below.

Other public buildings were dwellings for priests and rulers.
The plaza was for public gatherings and nearby was the ceremonial ball court. This game migrated north along with the corn
and the temple and blossomed into different forms with the various
groups. In essence, it involved two teams violently struggling to

[1] Coe and Flannery, 1964, p. 651.

Map IV
Extended Culture Areas
Planting in North America

Lowland
Extensive Planting

Lowland
Less Planting

Highland

throw a ball toward opposite goals, without touching it with hands or feet. In Mexico, the ball was of rubber and the players bounced it to and fro with hips and knees. Before the game, they fasted and called on the gods for power. So did the Cherokees, before a somewhat similar game, a thousand years later.

Outside the center were the fields and dwellings of the farmers. These had a somewhat different pattern in highland country or in lowland, a pattern which was continued as the plants moved north. In the treeless high country, workers' dwelling could cluster around the center. Beyond were the fields usually watered by irrigation from river or lake. The Aztecs had some gardens actually *in* a lake. In the forested lowlands, planters used the ancient worldwide system of slash-and-burn. This meant girdling the trees with stone axes, allowing them to die, then burning the brush and planting in the ashes. After some years, rain washed away the mineral-rich ashes, underbrush grew up, and the fields had to be abandoned. Thus they and the peoples' dwellings moved farther from the city's center.

The Mexican cities grew rich. They developed social classes, as we can tell from the rich funeral goods given to certain individuals. Our accounts of daily life and ceremony in such cities are all proto-historic; still, the Aztecs, from whom the fullest accounts came, insisted that they were following ancient customs. These accounts tell of a trained priesthood containing several degrees. They tell of a warrior class wearing special insignia and giving public performances.

There was a calendric round of ceremonies, many of them seeming glorified examples of firstfruit rites. Several honored the corn at different stages of growth. Others appealed to the rain gods, of whom there were many, living on the mountain tops. These Tlalocs had a chief and perhaps four principal gods living in the four directions. They ruled a green paradise which was one of the Aztec afterworlds. Also there were gods of fire, of war, of death, of the wind, and of the arts. There was an earth goddess and an all-knowing deity who was almost a Supreme Being.

The Aztecs paid honor to these divinities with magnificent processions and dances. In their temples they kept undying fires which were renewed at stated intervals. They burned a kind of incense made of copal gum. Sometimes all the people fasted; they drew blood from their tongues and ears. But the outstanding tribute to the spirits was human sacrifice. In the Old World, too, most planting people ritually killed human beings, perhaps as a re-enactment of the yearly death and rebirth of vegetation. The Aztecs killed a man and stripped off his skin as symbolic of the husking of corn, and they sent weeping children as messengers to the rain gods. Their mass killings, however, were a gift to the sun. In their belief the orb was not a supreme being but one of the early gods, given power from the bodies and the blood of many other gods. Therefore, a constant stream of blood was needed to keep him on his rounds. They fought their battles largely to get prisoners who would supply it.

Aztecs, the late comers to Mexico, were the most violent in their cult of human sacrifice but we gather that this way of pleasing the Supernatural was common all over Middle America. Sacrifice, in the sense of tribute from inferior to superior, is not the proper term. The person killed was often treated as a god before he was dispatched. He was told that he was to go to the gods, just as we have seen all the dead told in the Great Lakes region. Like them, he was to carry messages from the people about the crops, rain, or victory for which they longed. Many a victim was willing to die with the hope of such apotheosis.

Even this feeding of the sun did not guarantee that Aztec life would continue without disaster. Every fifty-two years came a crucial date called the "binding of the years." It marked the cycle of Venus which must have been calculated by the priests, but for the people it was the end of a world period. When this fatal date arrived, the sun might cease his rounds and life would end. The remedy was a new fire which, perhaps, meant the regeneration of the sun. In preparation for it, says a native account:

First they put out fires everywhere in the country round. And the statues, hewn in either wood or stone, kept in each man's home and regarded as gods, were all cast into the water. Also . . . the pestles and the . . . hearth stones [upon which the cooking pots rested]; and everywhere there was much sweeping—there was sweeping very clean. Rubbish was thrown out; none lay in any of the houses.[2]

The priests in ceremonial costume marched to a hill near the city and there they sacrificed a captive in the usual way, by cutting open the breast to tear out the heart. In the bloody cavity, the new fire was made while crowds of people watched. They expected their doom if the flame did not catch. When it did catch, a great bonfire was lit to flash the news. Runners with torches carried the flame by relays to the most distant villages. In the city, a fire was ignited in the temple of the war god and torches lit from it brought new fire to every house and temple.

Other groups in Middle America also had new fire ceremonies, rain gods, and maize rituals. News of these developments was carried north through the years to alter the customs of Indians on both sides of the border. The news came from different areas, highland and lowland, each with a slightly different culture or, at least, different emphasis on the culture. The travelers, traders, or conquerors who brought the news generation after generation moved north by various routes and reached different parts of what is now the United States. Hunter-gatherers there already had their old established customs, their mythology, and their ways of dealing with the Supernatural. New usages that seemed linked to the new food-wealth were adopted where they were congenial. But they were not adopted intact. Thus planting ceremonies north of the border may be so different that they seem to have no relation to their southern predecessors until we catch a glimpse of rain gods, of an undying fire, or of a sacred ball game. Then we can recognize descendants of Middle American ceremony but descendants very like those in a human lineage where the ancestral genes have combined with others to produce individuals each of whom is unique.

[2] Sahagún, 1953, Book 7, p. 25. Quoted with permission of the School of American Research, publisher, and Charles E. Dibble, translator.

REFERENCES

Domestication of corn: Mangelsdorf, MacNeish, and Galinat, 1964; Coe and Flannery, 1964.

Domestication of cotton: Smith and MacNeish, 1964.

Developments in Mexico which influenced United States Indians: Armillas, 1964; Braidwood and Willey, 1962.

Similarities between Mexico and southern United States: Mason, 1943; Moreno, 1943.

Mexican ceremonies: Sahagún, 1953; Thompson, 1933; Vaillant, 1947.

16

PLANTING CEREMONIES: THE SOUTHERN WOODLAND

In pre-white days, the section of North America stretching from the Atlantic to the Mississippi and from the Great Lakes to the Gulf of Mexico was almost wholly forest. It was threaded with streams which made communication easy. It abounded in fish, game, and wild plant food. The southeastern section especially (see map, p. 18), with its mild climate, was a land of plenty for hunter-gatherers. True, there was no wild corn, wild beans, squash, or even tobacco. Still, the Indians of Muskogean and related languages who roamed the area could live handsomely without the labor of cultivation. They probably knew about corn, and travelers may even have brought in a few ears. But the wizened little cobs—which were all the "life sustainer" could produce in its early centuries—could hardly tempt them to the routine life of farming. In fact, there were no signs of corn cultivation in the whole Eastern Woodland until almost the beginning of the Christian era.

We do not know how corn first was introduced in the Southeast or when. This narrative therefore must pass directly to the consideration of the place where the earliest signs of cultivation have been found, which is nowhere near Mexico. It is in the very heart of the Eastern Woodland, the valleys of the Illinois and Ohio rivers. This is the area of the famous Mound Builders once thought to be a mysterious race that flourished in America before the Indians. Excavation has now shown that they belonged to well-known eastern groups, the Siouan, Iroquoian, and Algonkian, and their earthworks were often the burial mounds or barrows described in Chapter 8. Since barrow is the accredited word for such a structure and since mounds of many sorts are to be met with in the course of Indian history, I propose to differentiate these burial mounds as barrows and their makers as Barrow Builders.

There must have been a concentration of people in the lush river valleys and some students have suggested a stimulus from the south. But the burial barrows are those familiar among northern peoples, only raised to huge proportions. They are enriched with handsome grave goods which show fine craftsmanship and a wide trade, but there are no temples or plazas. The barrow—or sometimes several barrows—stands alone and students have trouble finding where their makers lived. Finally some thatched villages have been located in Illinois, and separate farmsteads in Ohio (some of the dates most recently proposed for these are: Early Woodland, Adena Phase, 400–100 B.C.; Middle Woodland, Hopewell Phase, 100 B.C.–A.D. 750).[1] It would not be hard to imagine processions coming from these dwellings at stated intervals and bearing the "souls" of their dead to be interred as the Huron did. The mass secondary burials were treated in various ways but sometimes one individual was buried alone with specially rich gifts as might befit a chief or a high priest. This sign of class structure, as well as the immense amount of work done on the barrows, indicates a large and disciplined population.

We should expect such a population to be agricultural, yet the signs of corn are still scanty. Perhaps the people moved away to

[1] Prufer, 1964, p. 94.

hunt for part of the year, as later Indians did in that locality. At home, their women did plant some seeds of sunflower, pigweed (*amaranth*), and goosefoot (*chenopodium*). Sometime after A.D. 1, they had pumpkin and, finally, a little corn. The identity of another crop must be guessed at, although not a shred of it can be found. This crop too came from the South and, because of its great quantity, I wonder if it arrived even before the corn. It was raised not by women, but by men, and was used not for food, but for ceremony. It was tobacco.

The presence of tobacco is inferred from the immense number of pipes found in the graves. These are not the simple tubes of bone or clay long used by medicine men for ceremonial smoke blowing. At the Hopewell sites in Ohio the pipes are both of clay and stone, molded and carved in elbow shape, "platform" shape, and effigy shape with figures of birds, men, and animals. Of course, any mixture of dried leaves could have been used in them, as were the sumac and red willow, the kinnikinnick of later days. But I cannot believe such magnificent smoking apparatus would have been manufactured for a tasteless substitute. The substitute must have come into use only later when people who had learned to use tobacco could not get it. And this efflorescence of pipes, unlike previous finds, may well indicate the first importation of tobacco.

The plant did not grow wild east of the Mississippi, although some coarse species did sprout here and there in the west. The home of tobacco was in South America and even the Mexicans had to import it. Neither they nor our southeastern Indians got the modern commercial variety, *Nicotiana attenuata*. That came somehow by water to the West Indies and only reached North America when the Spaniards brought it. The kind used in Mexico and the Southeast was *Nicotiana rustica*[2] whose fumes were strong and almost intoxicating. Some southern Indians raise it still, always in remote plots and away from women. One of my colleagues tried it and his comment was: "Why, four puffs of that would knock you over! I wonder how they ever managed six."

Four solemn puffs to the four directions was the custom, as the

[2] Driver and Massey, pp. 260–66.

pipe was passed ceremonially from hand to hand. Sometimes two puffs were added for the zenith and the nadir. Old accounts sometimes speak of the dizziness or drunkenness induced by the smoke but there is no tradition that narcotics were ever mixed with tobacco. The smoke was incense. Also it was a means to vision and to communion with the spirits. Our Indians did not have the copal or other gums which furnished incense in Mexico. Nor did they have the hallucinogens—peyote and the mushroom *teyhuinti*. Tobacco took the place of all of them. In time, it came to be used also as a confirmation of oaths and a pledge of amity. When men partook of it in company, it had the function of a loving cup.

The Hopewell pipes are little more than a bowl mounted on a short tube. We cannot tell whether they had the two-foot stem which went to make the famous calumet (from the French *chalumeau*, a reed), but a long stem would have been useful with such an acrid smoke. It is tempting to imagine that the calumet had its rise when the Barrow Builders of Ohio received a sacred incense-plant from the south. It need not have arrived with the corn, since its origin is so different. Perhaps it came earlier or, at least, was seized upon earlier by people who had plenty of wild food but were eager for ceremony.

The custom of barrow-building spread along river valleys in all directions. There are instances of several mounds grouped together, surrounded by a fortification. And there are mounds which are not barrows but are in the shape of huge animals, perhaps clan symbols. The effect of the stimulus first felt in the Illinois River Valley spread far and wide, carrying new arts and customs. Certainly it carried the calumet. Throughout the East and into the West wherever tribes had influence from the East, its use is reported. As we observe the planting ceremonies in that area one of the first items to look for is the calumet.

The custom of barrow-building spread down the Mississippi and through our southern states. Some barrows are scattered through this region but there are also some very different structures—temple pyramids in the Mexican style. The earliest-known is in the Mississippi Valley at the mouth of the Red River. It is dated at

A.D. 500,[3] by which time corn had fully developed into a nourishing grain and new settlements had sprung up in many planting areas. The people who built the Middle Mississippi temples were not an army of immigrants. Scholars assert that they were old residents speaking Muskogean, the general language of the Southeast and unlike any in Mexico. Perhaps a few ideas or a few travelers came to fertilize their old, workable customs for it is that kind of crossing which does produce new behavior.

At any rate, the temples multiplied along the Mississippi and along the Gulf Coast. This is a lowland country, almost a continuation of that in eastern Mexico (see map, p. 156). The natural arrangement was slash-and-burn agriculture for the corn, beans, pumpkins (*cucurbeta moschata*), and tobacco which were the only southern plants imported. At the center was the plaza, with the elevated temple, public buildings, and ball court. The whole plan was very like that of the Huastec, the nearest planters along the Mexican coast. We need not go into the controversy over whether the bearers of corn and ceremony arrived by sea or by land. We merely note that in these settlements the pottery was of Mexican type and that favorite artistic themes were the Mexican jaguar, eagle, and serpent.

Those settlements have long been in ruins. We should have few clues to the life they fostered if it were not for a few survivals. One of these was the Natchez tribe on the Mississippi which was thus described by a French visitor in 1700:

". . . the cabin of the Great Chief . . . is raised to a height of 10 feet on earth brought thither . . . Before that of the chief is the temple mound, which has a circular shape, a little oval, and bounds an open space about 250 paces wide and 300 long."[4]

Strung along the streams nearby, Iberville reported scattered hamlets where the people raised corn, beans, and pumpkins by the slash-and-burn method. Out in the fields, they improvised a ball court.

Their wooden buildings and unwalled ball court are a rustic

[3] Sears, 1964, pp. 265–66, 270.

[4] Swanton, 1946, p. 638.

simile of stone edifices further south. The Natchez also shared in
the complex of customs which the Mexicans had developed around
their planting ceremonies. They had sun worship, undying fire,
human sacrifice, and a ripe corn ceremony. They also had the calumet and some social and religious ideas which seem peculiarly
their own.

The Natchez had a class society, consisting of a ruling family,
two grades of nobles, and a mass of commoners. The ruler was
called the Sun and claimed to be descended from the orb itself.
The Sun usually married his sister, after the fashion devised by the
Pharaohs and the Incas, to keep the line pure. Rules of descent
were so arranged that his female children kept the Sun rank, but
male descendents, through the generations, were absorbed by the
commoners. Such an autocracy would provide a background for
belief in a supreme Being and the Natchez, apparently, worshipped
the sun. They had a temple—only a wooden affair on a low platform—but it housed an undying fire, with two guards who were
killed if they neglected it.

The temple was also an ossuary which enshrined the bones of
former Suns. These, alone, went to the sky after death; common
people had no afterlife. To overcome this disability, some of them
elected to be killed when the Sun died and be buried near him.
Here is an example of the retainer sacrifice, which we suspected
from the mound burials. The Natchez sometimes sacrificed a war
prisoner by tying him to an upright frame and shooting him with
arrows, an echo of Mexican practice but nothing like the mass
executions performed by the Aztecs. They made peace in a way
unknown in Mexico, by smoking the calumet. The ceremony was
like the one the Prairie tribes carried out later (see p. 194). The
reed stems, decorated with feathers, were removed from two pipes
and delegated warriors danced, waving them like eagle wings.
Then the pipe was smoked to the directions with a vow of peace.

Every summer, the Natchez held a firstfruits ceremony before
eating the first ripe corn. According to one account, the warriors
cultivated a special cornfield which no one else was allowed to
touch, and built a special granary nearby. Others tilled their own
fields but eating their new corn was taboo until the feast had been

held. The scene of the feast was a cleared field near the granary and there the warriors built temporary cabins for their families, with large ones at each end for the Sun and the war chief. On the appointed day, the families went to camp in these cabins, carrying cooking utensils. The Sun was borne there on a litter by relays of warriors.

The first act of the day was making a new fire by the ancient method of the twirling stick. We gather that the cooking fires of the families were lighted from this. On a word from the Sun, the women ran to the granary with their baskets and received corn from the warriors. Each one, then, husked her family's portion, pounded it, and made the customary porridge. Another word from the Sun was necessary before all could begin, at the same time, to eat. The pounding, cooking, and eating would continue until the corn supply was exhausted, perhaps several days. Different accounts say that people also brought other food which they shared.

Interim activities were those of which we have already heard. One was the ball game. The ball was "the size of a fist" stuffed with moss and covered with deerskin. The Sun and the war chiefs headed the two sides, each of which might contain several hundred men. The game was to hit the ball with the hands, never letting it fall or be held, and to send it against the cabin of one's own side. This is something like the Mexican game already mentioned and versions of it will be found all through eastern North America.

An even more popular activity was "striking the post" familiar on the Plains under its French name of "counting *coups*." It is probable, however, that it was practiced by the Natchez and their compeers before the Plains group had their war behavior organized. Perhaps it was a faint reflection of bloodier war triumphs in Mexico.

The "post" to be struck was as high as a man, and across its top was laid a calumet with the red stripe on the stem which indicated war. The warriors rushed up to it in order of rank, striking it with a war club and, with each stroke, proclaiming some valiant achievement. Boys who had never been to war told what they intended to do and thus were pushed to action. The evening was given up to circle-dancing and to love-making. The magic which would make new tribal members was usually a concomitant of victory.

The Natchez were conquered by the French in the late 1800's and their members dispersed among other tribes. In the meantime most of the temple-pyramid people were gone and new groups were moving in. One of these was the Creek, a federation of tribes from further west who made their farms along the creeks of Georgia and Alabama. The Creeks were well organized, but their federation was not an autocracy like that of the Natchez. They had no temple and their religious officiants were shamans of various kinds. Still, their mother-clans and their agricultural ceremonies were characteristic of planting people. The beings they revered were the sun, fire, and even a greater one known as the Master of Breath. This last was a vague figure, living in the upper world of which the sky forms the floor. The earth, according to Creek myths, had once been submerged and animals had dived for it as in the tales known further west. However, when we come to the genesis of other animals and men, the familiar plot takes a new turn. Most animals and all human beings existed in spirit form in the sky world. Thence they came down to take fleshly form, but the animals did not come first. They were sent down after Man, to be his helpers and messengers. Tales do not agree on this, for the Creeks are a people of mixed ancestry and traditions. Yet the descent from the sky is a usual belief in much of the Woodland country. The Natchez allowed it only to their ruling family, but the more democratic newcomers included everybody. We know little more about Creek theology except that they thought of the winds and stars as spirits and the sun as the Master's symbol. The animals they hunted as they must have done in food-gatherer days. Now, however, they had leisure to flatter the deer and game birds with fine costumes and dramatic dances. Throughout the season they had firstfruits ceremonies for different plants and animals, but the crop that merited important rituals was corn and the ceremony in its honor was the "boskita," known to the whites as busk.

They followed the usual custom with firstfruits, of not touching the crop until after the ceremony. A family whose corn was ripe early would live on roots and even starve for a day or so rather than break the taboo. They even refused food cooked on the same fire as the forbidden crop. Before the ceremony, women cleaned all the dwellings and put out the fires. They were not to share in the ceremony proper, even though it was they who had done most of the corn-raising. They seem to have shared the feeling of the Papago women that their sex needed no ceremony. When I talked to them, I found they had a quiet pride in the fact that without their practical function of cleaning and cooking the rites could not operate.

The men had more strenuous duties, since the corn ceremony was the beginning of a new year. They were to purify the town of debts and quarrels. They were to fast and purge their bodies to be worthy of the new fire. There was exaltation in thus achieving well-being for the group, but also there would be drama, learning, merrymaking, and a chance for distinction. In this yearly gathering of people from far and near, almost every need of the personality was satisfied. First, there was the happiness of reunion. Friends and relatives came from distant farms and from other towns, perhaps bringing the first news people had had for a year. Men and women separated, each group turning to its work with gossip and laughter—and tears, too, since there were deaths to report.

Every male over the age of puberty went to the busk ground, the penalty for absence being a fine paid in skins. Preparing for the ceremony gave responsible work to every approved male. Younger men cleared the ground and surrounded it with a fence with openings at the four corners. Here children would appear with messages and women with food. Men would not leave until the ceremony was over. Youths were sent to bring the four logs for the ritual fire and the various herbs for emetics, each taken from the east side of a bush or tree. Older men prepared booths as the Natchez did, but these were for men only. The Creeks had a class organization but it was built on merit, not birth. There were four "beds" or tiers of seats, the occupants being officials, including a chief, speaker, feast manager; "beloved old men" past the war age;

warriors and youths. Each class was divided according to clan and moiety. By noting where a man sat and also his paint and feathers, one could tell his rank and history. Here the men would sit or sleep for the appointed number of days, fasting all the time.

The first day was the peace day, when all debts must be settled and quarrels ended. Any not attended to must be forgotten, so that the new year could start clean. I have said earlier that the spirits did not concern themselves with men's ethical behavior. This was how the hunter-gatherers conceived the situation, although they found themselves forced to ethical behavior nonetheless. Those who revered the sun or the sky had a wider view presented them. Sun and sky were everywhere used as witnesses of oaths or of truth-telling since they could see everything. The Creeks seem to have taken a further step in deciding that the Sky Power also wanted honesty and dependability. These qualities were also needed for a successful town government. Town officials were present to judge any disputed case; to prepare themselves for duty, they fasted and took an emetic. This was the "ten-herb brew," not the famous black drink which would be used on the morrow. Betweentimes, they gave moral discourses, a custom which we shall find prevalent among eastern planters.

Next morning at dawn began the day of purification. A medicine man, dressed in white buckskin, made the new fire with a wooden drill. It had to be of four logs from the four directions, their butts pointing to the quarters whence they had been brought. When a blaze was going, youths lighted torches and ran to the corners of the square where the women waited with torches of their own, ready to run home and light the household fires. They and the children might eat, though not yet of the new corn, while the men fasted and purified themselves.

The means of purification was the famous black drink made of cassine, *ilex vomitoria*. It was mixed ceremonially by the medicine man, chosen from a group whose visions enabled them to blow power into an herbal brew. He pounded the cassine roots on sanctified stones, mixed them with water from a running stream and cooked the brew over a small fire. Before lifting it off he breathed into it through a tube a formula whose ancient language the

Creeks scarcely understood. It was addressed, they told me, not to the cassine or the corn but to the One Above who gave the corn.

Youths took the pots as they came from the fire and passed them around the square, first to the chiefs, then to the warriors in order of rank. As each man received the conch shell of liquid, an officiant gave the boskita cry, *yahola,* and the man did not drink until it ended. One white trader felt sure that he was saying *Jehovah* and that the Creeks and their neighbors were the lost ten tribes of Israel. The men drank and vomited at least four times during the day. The cleansing must have been complete, for when I saw it, I was reminded of a hydrant. Containers were passed out to the non-participants but they did not drink. They washed their hands and faces and the women washed their children.

It seemed odd to me that the Creeks chose a bitter purge when they might have made a fermented drink from the corn itself. In fact, planting Indians in Mexico and South America did make corn beer but those north of the border seemed never to have learned the secret. I gathered finally that emetics from various bitter herbs were an old custom in the Southeast and several tribes used them. Even the Great Sun is said to have taken them while fasting and praying for rain. The Chickasaw said that the moon, a male, was pale because he had neglected "to take his bitters." And one Florida group took bitters at ceremonies even though they were not planters.[5]

Purification might last one day or, in some towns, several. Then "the busk was destroyed," fasting ended, and the new corn was cooked. After that, other functions of the ceremony came to the fore. There might be a hunt, with a feast in honor of the game killed. There might be a mock battle. Boys were scratched with a garfish spine to make them brave, and the town chief or clan head gave them a moral lecture. A whole day might be given to "striking the post" when every warrior recounted his exploits. New titles and the right to wear special decorations were handed out to those who had achieved in the past year. To strike the post at this time and to receive his man's name was the ambition of every boy.

There were dances at night, by men alone, by women alone or,

[5] Swanton, 1946, p. 764.

later, the uproarious stomp dance, when all formed a line together with their hands on each other's shoulders. The leader called out a phrase as he stamped around, winding the line into a tight spiral, and the chorus shouted a response. I defy anyone to take part in this dance without feeling almost madly intoxicated. There were ball games of men alone or men against women. Finally the whole party "went to water." This was a regular Southeastern custom which ended every ceremony. It meant that a group, with a "doctor" at the head, went to one of the streams in which the country abounded. There the doctor recited a formula and the people splashed themselves or even jumped into the water.

Here and there in the Southeast and north as far as Virginia, were groups with one or more features like those of the Creek. Information about them is vague for as one white pioneer admitted: "[The whites] care nothing for the Indians excepting to get their lands, . . . they really consider all study concerning them as egregious folly."[6] For our next clear picture of corn ceremonies, we move to the North.

REFERENCES

Early history of the Southeast: Fairbanks, 1952; Griffin, 1952; Jennings, 1952.

Hopewell culture: Griffin, 1964; Prufer, 1964.

Temple mounds: Sears, 1960, 1964.

Description of individual cultures: Swanton, 1911 (Lower Mississippi), 1928b (Chickasaw), 1928a, c (Creek), 1931 (Choctaw), 1946 (southeastern United States); Witthoft, 1949 (corn ceremonies in Eastern Woodland).

[6] Witthoft, 1949, p. 66.

17

PLANTING
CEREMONIES:
THE IROQUOIS

The news of corn and tobacco spread north, east, and west through hunter-gatherer country. Tribes which had had no fixed residence began to settle down for at least part of the year and to build some dwellings that could not be carried about by canoe or by dog traction. Their old myths and ceremonies gradually made room for the new food and its traditions. These fitted into the ancient tales so that, generally, corn was thought to have been provided by the culture hero and its ceremonies were "from the beginning."

The most impressive planters in the Woodland and, in fact, in North America, were the five nations of the Iroquois: the Seneca, Cayuga, Onondaga, Oneida, and Mohawk. In historic times their domain was the lush country of central New York State. They also claimed the Ohio Valley—"the Beautiful" in their language—and it is thought that some of them, at least, may have been among the ancient Barrow Builders. They spoke a language related to that of the Creek. They had some customs like the blowgun, the ball

game, and fish poisoning that spoke of a southern past, and shamanistic societies that look northern. A mixed people! But the Iroquois
have been in the Northeast since A.D. 1200,[1] and their conquests absorbed many different people. Their federation of five tribes (later
six) has the most complex organization of any Indian group.

We are not left in uncertainty about Iroquois beliefs, as we
sometimes were about the Southeast. There are volumes on the
subject, some of them written by educated Iroquois. Yet the
material does not come straight from the fountainhead of ancient
myth. There have been two tributaries to its flow, and the amount
of change they induced we cannot tell. One resulted from the
arrival of Jesuit missionaries in Canada, in the early 1600's. By that
time, the Iroquois were already settled in what is now New York
State while their relatives, the Huron and others were in southern
Canada. The Jesuits were indefatigable workers, eager to save
souls, but also eager to understand the Indians' own religion. They
have recorded many of their theological discussions with intelligent Iroquois. The Indians often professed to find their own theology sufficient, but one wonders how many changes of attitude
crept into it undetected. The ceremonies to be described will
hint at some of these changes.

The other influence was a prophet from the Iroquois' own
ranks. Ganiodayo, or Handsome Lake, lived nearly one hundred
and fifty years after the Jesuit work had ended. By 1799, the
Revolutionary War was over. The Iroquois, some of whom had
sided with the British, had lost much of their land. They had no
chance to hunt or fight and their primitive methods of farming did
not support them. Handsome Lake had been a hopeless alcoholic,
as had many others, but he had a vision.[2] He told his people, as
many Indian prophets have done since then: "Go back to the old
ways. Keep up the ceremonies decreed by the Creator." That
meant giving up alcoholism and modern dancing, though the wise
prophet did not discourage white man's plows and white man's
schools. So earnest was the prophet's message that many tribesmen
did go back to the old ceremonies and have continued them to the
present. However, they were the old ceremonies as interpreted by

[1] Griffin, 1964, p. 254.   [2] See Deardorff, 1951.

Handsome Lake. What flavor they may have absorbed from modern thought we cannot tell, nor can we tell how much has been discarded. As celebrated today, in a house with wooden floor and with the sacred fire in an iron stove, they are still full of dignity. Farm people in calico and overalls go through some fifty dances, solemn, warlike, or picturesque in their imitation of animals. Corn is cooked and distributed. Tobacco incense is burned. This is a living religion.

The Iroquois origin myth begins like that of the Southeast, with the Sky People whose world is on a disk above the earth. In the southeastern myths all earth's inhabitants, including most animals, came down from the sky; but in the Iroquois tale only one woman made the descent. (Longfellow has introduced her to us as Nokomis.) She fell toward an earth that was covered with water; the water birds saw her coming and spread their wings to float her down. Then they dived underwater and brought up earth according to the usual earth diver story. The Great Turtle, one of earth's original inhabitants, offered his back to support the new land; and he has always been a spirit highly revered by the Iroquois. The sky woman was already pregnant and she bore a daughter. Later, the daughter bore a son, whether by Turtle or the North Wind the myths cannot agree. Here we have a culture hero who was half of the sky people and half, perhaps, of earth. He had a twin brother who was one of those companions that so often appeared in the northern tales as a mischief-maker. This one, however, was not merely incompetent or naughty. He was malicious and as near to a devil as any character to be found in Indian tales.

Sapling, the name of the good brother in one version, went about creating people, plants, and animals out of the *orenda*, the supernatural power which was within him. The bad twin was not merely mischievous, like Coyote, but a near-devil, hostile to the Creator and to mankind. Such dualism is unusual in Indian thought. So is the picture, to be met later in Iroquois ceremonies, of the good twin, the Creator, now located in the sky, receiving offerings and "always watching carefully what they do, the people on the earth."[3]

[3] See Chafe, 1961, pp. 43, 45.

The Iroquois believed in other spirits that are familiar to us: the four winds and the thunders, which in this case are a number of birds with flashing eyes. There was a water monster who lived under Niagara Falls and seized all who came near. There was the hideous demon who brought disease, but who was conquered by the culture hero. The demon was forced to let the False Face Society wear masks to imitate him and thus conquer the disease he brought. There were shaman societies to deal with other diseases, and these exist to this day. Handsome Lake, the renovator of Iroquois religion, wanted to emphasize only the good, however. The succession of ceremonies that he prescribed constituted paeans of praise to all the good things that had been created.

For these ceremonies, there was a corps of managers who approached the position of priests. They were called Keepers of the Faith, and their duties were to see that the ceremonies were carried out in good order, and, often, to lead them. They were chosen from mature and upright members of the tribe, both men and women.

The Iroquois had apparently rid themselves of woman-fear in ceremonies. It is well known that their matrons had a good deal of political power as nominators and censors of chiefs. Women also owned the houses, where their husbands and their daughters' husbands came to live with them. As household head, a grandmother performed what might be called family prayers, for the Creator had directed that "she . . . the most ancient one . . . as often as she shall again see the new dawn of daylight . . . she shall say customarily, 'We greet one another repeatedly. . . . Now then, we will unite our minds to give thanks repeatedly.'" She gave thanks for all the fruits of the earth, for "those who habitually come from the West" (that is, the Thunderers, for thunder, with the Iroquois, was not one great bird but many), and finally, for the light of day, the sun. It will be seen that the Iroquois used special sacred terms in their prayers and speeches. Finally the grandmother asked that all "should pass through the day in peace, and that thus it should continue to be."[4] This was the standard

4 See Hewitt, 1928, pp. 564–65.

thanksgiving speech given by men on other occasions, and there were, of course, adult men in the household. Still, the woman householder had ceremonial precedence.

Women were present at all public rituals and joined in the dances. It is true that their function was the usual cooking and serving while the men did the speaking and singing, but the women sang in the rites of their own curing societies and in those of the society of women planters. Iroquois women did most of the work on the crops as Creek women did, but not because the men were busy elsewhere. Their power of fertility was needed for plant growth. A woman could work magic by walking around the cornfield at night, dragging her garments over the ground. The women planters had dances for the corn, beans, and squash, which were spirits, "our supporters," and also for the wild fruits. I have seen their matronly, full-skirted figures in the blackberry dances, circling like galleons in full sail while the men sang.

Honors to the food spirits were paid regularly throughout the season, interspersed with curing rites and social dances, and with what might be called political rites, such as changing names or naming children. Thirty-three dances with their different steps and songs have been described.

At Tonowanda, in New York State, the ceremonies began in early spring with that for the maple sap. Then followed those for corn planting, the wild strawberry, ripe green beans, ripe sweet corn and corn harvest (or bread dance). At midwinter came the new year ceremony, longest and most important of all.

As with the Creek, the new year was a time for wholesale cleansing, but there was no emetic involved. The cleansing was a moral one, by confession. Weeks before the ceremony began, every man, woman, and child confessed in public. The rite took place in the longhouse, a large replica of the Iroquois' own wooden dwellings that was used as temple, council house, and general meeting place. A Keeper of the Faith presided. First, he held up a string of white wampum and told all the wrongs he had done since the last confession. Wampum was used by the Iroquois instead of a signature to confirm treaties, for its white color meant peace. Without it, words would be useless, like a contract not notarized. When one man had finished, the string was handed to the next Keeper of the Faith and so confession might continue for several days until everyone present was purged of wrongdoing.

Then came another form of purging, the Dream Feast or Feast of Fools, as the whites often called it. This was a cleansing of thoughts, not of deeds, when the fears and worries of the year were brought into the open and cured. Before it began, the ashes were raked out of every hearth in preparation for a new fire. This was done by two male Faith Keepers who were called "Our Uncles the Big Heads." Big Head meant one who was disturbed in mind, perhaps from contact with the Supernatural.

Many were so disturbed. This was a time when all the troubles and problems of the year could be remembered and expressed. The expression took the form of dreams and no one has yet decided to what extent these were unexpected or to what extent the constructions of an anxious mind. At least, there were days when people went about asking others to guess what they had dreamed, for the dream or the hallucination must be quieted by someone other than the dreamer. Once, it is said, a man dreamed he was taken prisoner and burned alive by the enemy, an anxiety that might well haunt any male. To cancel the threat, the villagers enacted a mock execution and erected a scaffold, put him on it, and even started a fire. He could then walk off with peace of mind.

In recent years, a woman dreamed that she sponsored the game of snow snake (sliding a snakelike stick across the snow), which meant that she gave a feast for the players. Someone made her a miniature snow snake and after that she feasted the players every year. It was a positive act that must have given comfort, like penance enjoined by a priest. All new dreams had to be quieted in this way before the end of the ceremony, and the remedies for old ones repeated. Otherwise, the dreamer would fall ill; but, worse than that, the coming of spring might be delayed and the whole community would suffer.

This was a different treatment of dream, vision, or hallucination from that of the hunters. They had thought of the vision as each man's personal means of getting help from the supernatural. The Iroquois planters made everyone's mental worries a group matter. The whole group must help with the cure or the whole group would suffer. Here again, the women were responsible for seeing that all was properly done. A Faith Keeper called at each longhouse to ask its matron about the dreamers in her family, past or present. Five days of the festival might be occupied in this general catharsis. In the meantime, the medicine societies held meetings to renew their power, and the False Faces, the curers par excellence, visited every house to drive out diseases.

The town was clean, physically and morally, and now began the traditional four ceremonies, the "greatly prized matters" ordained by the Creator as a duplication of those held above by the Sky People. They took place in the morning, for the Iroquois felt that ceremonial power lessened as the sun declined. In the afternoon there were games and dances, for all "the people now upon the earth" must be rejuvenated at this time of renewal. At night, each family carried home its portion of corn and meat that had been cooked by the women Faith Keepers.

In the longhouse, the moieties sat on benches at the opposite ends of the house, while the singers straddled a bench placed down the middle. Singers, if possible, were to be of two moieties, one calling out the first phrase of a song and the other answering before they shouted together. Songs consisted mostly of syllables but now and then they conveyed a sharp, bright picture:

> Blossoms on both sides . . .
> Wolf runs along the rim of the gully.[5]

Instruments were sometimes tortoise shell rattles in honor of the Great Turtle. He it was in some myths who had fathered the Creator, and in others had offered his back to support the floating earth. Sometimes there was a cowhorn rattle (once bison?) or a water drum. This last, an earthen pot partly full of water with a deerskin tied over the top, was a device of the planting people, for most hunter-gatherers did not make pots.

First of the "greatly prized matters" was the Great Feather

[5] Kurath, 1964, p. 102.

Dance in which men, wearing the ancient deerskin cap with its single feather, cavorted in the traditional war dance. Then might come the individual blessing chants. This was a democratic procedure during which every man present rose to tell of his experiences during the year. At one time he had recounted war exploits. Later he listed his blessings, and, if he could not think of any, he at least told jokes.

A specially important rite was the Drum Dance of Thanksgiving. A short version of it began every ceremony and there was a long one at green corn time, preceded by confession. At the new year it was particularly important. Then every item in the Iroquois world must be remembered and honored or the world would be like a machine with some parts unoiled. So say modern Iroquois. The Faith Keepers chose a speaker with a good memory and a good voice, and well he knew what responsibility rested upon him. Here were no murmured spells which no one could understand. He spoke loudly about what they all knew.

First he urged the people to be thankful for each other. Fierce conquerors though they were toward outsiders, the Iroquois spoke constantly about love and peace among themselves. And they needed these things if their little communities were to survive. Then came the thanks to the earth, "our mother who supports our feet," and after that, says one Iroquois report, the speaker "thanks upward," mentioning grasses, plants, water, trees, birds, animals, the three sister-spirits, corn, beans, and squash; then the winds, the thunderers, the sun, the moon, and stars; then Handsome Lake the prophet and, finally, the Creator himself. Each section of thanks ended with "and our minds will continue to do so." At intervals during this catalogue of blessings, a "whooper" gave a loud call; then the water drum sounded and the singers began a song, such as the following: "On earth it grows our life supporters.[6] The men rose one by one and the women followed to circle the singers' bench in one of their dignified processional dances. Then came an offering of tobacco, placed on the fire as incense. The Iroquois raised tobacco, and in their belief its smoke went directly to the Culture-Hero-Creator, making a path for

[6] *Ibid.*

prayer. The grandmother of the Creator, who took corn from her body, had herself gone up in that way but such flight was forbidden to human beings. "Only the Word" the Creator had told them, "and also only the Mind will be able to go on high ... and the smoke will arise and then one shall speak."[7]

This speaking in thanksgiving sets the Iroquois apart from most other Indians. Verbal expression of gratitude was not an Indian custom, and in fact few tribes had any words for the purpose. A gift or a kind deed was reciprocated by gift or deed, often with nothing said about obligation. Almost everywhere the same attitude was held toward Supernaturals. Firstfruits were honored not by thanks or prayer but by praising them or dancing to imitate them. The dance was a form of praise but also it was sympathetic magic, bound to produce a new crop of food. Had the Iroquois, in the course of tribal organization, developed an attitude different from that of most hunter-gatherers? Or had they adopted some of the behavior of early Christian missionaries they had known, Jesuits in the seventeenth century, Quakers in the eighteenth? Even though they were not converted, the white man's attitude toward his Creator might have seemed good to them.

In early times, tobacco was not the only sacrifice. Some reports tell of a white dog that was raised for the purpose, and known, in the usual ceremonial metaphor, as "the Trussed Thing."[8] It was ritually painted, had confession wampum hung around its neck; then it was strangled without loss of blood. Finally, it was brought on a litter to the longhouse, and with songs to the Creator, it was burned. The smoke went to the skyworld, carrying the loyalty and hopes of the village.

The last of the four required rituals was the Grand Betting, the throwing of dice from a wooden bowl. This was in memory of the game played by the Creator against his evil brother, with the world at stake. Generally the moieties played against each other, and it was a religious duty for each man to wager his most valuable possessions as the Creator had done. The Creator himself had directed them: "When my father's clansmen who are alive

---

[7] Hewitt, op. cit., pp. 552–53.   [8] Ibid., p. 561.

upon the earth will be amusing my mind [with this game] . . .
you must employ therein what is of your utmost toil, whatever
thing of what you are in the habit of using, you will spare that."[9]

The people were always "father's clansmen" to the Creator.
He, of course, belonged to his mother's clan, the Sky People,
since the Iroquois were matrilineal. They obeyed his dictum, betting all they had, and the game might continue for days.

REFERENCES

Prehistory of the Northeast: Griffin, 1964.

Iroquois customs and ceremonies: Chafe, 1961; Fenton, 1936; Hewitt,
1903, 1928; Morgan, 1901; Speck, 1949; Wilson and Mitchell, 1959; Kurath, 1964.

[9] *Ibid.*, p. 564.

18

PLANTING CEREMONIES: GREAT LAKES AND UPPER MISSISSIPPI

"These people are not very far removed from the recognition of the Creator of the world."[1] Thus wrote Father Claude Allouez, in 1667, about the Fox Indians of Wisconsin. The Fox, with the Sauk, Potawatomi and other Algonkian groups were part hunters and part planters who had never before received a missionary. Yet, the enthusiastic Jesuit exclaimed: ". . . they acknowledge in their country a great spirit, the maker of Heaven and earth, who dwells in the country toward the French."[2] And, three hundred years later, a white scholar averred: "Whatever may ultimately be shown to be the case among the tribes of other areas, there can be no doubt as to the antiquity of the Great Spirit among the Central Algonkians."[3]

This Great Spirit was not the mysterious Power spoken of in the South who either was the sun or dwelt within it. He was a being

[1] Skinner, 1923, p. 34.   [2] *Ibid.*   [3] *Ibid.*

in human form, called by the Algonkians the Great or Gentle Manitou. He not only created the people and "made them to move"[4] but he was concerned for their welfare. The Fox pictured him as calling his subordinate spirits together for instructions about helping mankind. This is a more definite concept of deity than we have met with among either planters, hunters, or hunter-gatherers. It results, perhaps, from the mingling of many religious patterns; for this area near the headwaters of the Mississippi was a sort of woodland pocket, bounded on the north by the Great Lakes and on the west by the plains. Many migrant tribes made their last stop here, so that there was an accumulation of customs and beliefs from the most primitive to the most advanced.

We must think first of the primitive hunters, with their vague concept of supernatural power but their intimate contact with the animals whom they met in vision. This general attitude may have taken millennia to develop and become established. Toward the beginning of the Christian era the barrow culture began its spread. Ultimately much of this northern Woodland was filled with mounds for burial and perhaps for clan symbols. Whether the hunting people took part in this new development or only watched it is matter for speculation. In any case, when that culture faded away after some eight hundred years, it must have left them with some knowledge of agriculture—and of tobacco and pipes. Mark the pipes for, in later years, the Great Spirit, Gitche Manitou, was described as smoking one at his place in the heavens.

In the barrow culture period, there was movement throughout much of America north of Mexico. Someday, archaeology may unearth the causes for moving in war, immigration, or change of climate and thus give to Indian prehistory a more definite shape than it has at present. What we can record here is movement from the great centers of the Mississippi Valley. We can even point to the Siouan-speaking Winnebago as a possible spearhead and wonder how much their orderly clan system and their lofty picture of a Great Being has to do with that background. Finally, in the 1600's came a horde of Algonkians fleeing before the Iroquois. The Ojibwa, many of whom had been hunters in Canada, had a

4 See Michelson, 1930, p. 61.

legend that they had come all the way from the Atlantic coast. Also, in the 1600's and the 1700's, French missionaries and travelers moved down the Mississippi.

Here is a combination of traditions from which we might expect many individual religious patterns. The wooded country, with its long established hunting customs, however, seems to have prevailed. Most of the tribes did some planting and increased their agricultural activities as they moved south, but they never arrived at full-scale planting ceremonies. To the average tribesman, the vital parts of the religious pattern were his vision, his animal guardian spirit, and the token which gave him confidence and self respect (see Chap. 10). Individuals had such tokens and clans had them, handed down from some successful ancestor. Perhaps the focus of religious belief was still on this means of power.

But in some of the societies and some of the clan legends, a quite different picture appeared. It is here that we find the Great Spirit, the Gentle Manitou. He lives in the Sky world but he is not mysterious and invisible. The Fox pictured him and his assistants as taking human form when they appeared in visions, just as the animals did. Moreover, they gave to him the character of a hunter-gatherer chief, who looked after his people and whose authority was dependent not on hereditary right but on public opinion.

> He who made us to move . . . he the Great Manitou . . . Verily when he observed that he had determined the life of the future people to be too short, he must have said, "why, there will be a great disturbance when they begin to meet their death. Verily at the time when they begin to lose sight of each other they will make a hue and cry. And it will be my own fault."[5]

So this very human deity, who was dependent on mankind as mankind was on him, took measures for his peoples' welfare. He gave them tobacco.

Nicotiana rustica, the tobacco of the Barrow Builders, was so strong as to have a narcotic effect and early travelers often spoke of Indians being intoxicated by it. The Woodland Indians, when they first made its acquaintance, must have felt the resulting

[5] *Ibid.*, p. 61.

euphoria to be magical and they attributed to the spirits the same yearning for a smoke which they felt themselves. Therefore, when Gitche Manitou presented mankind with this powerful herb, he was allowing them a tool with which to coerce the Supernaturals, from the lowest to the highest. For he "kept not one pipeful for himself."[6] This coercion, without prayer or sacrifice, has a flavor of primitive magic. It is different from the attitude of some southwestern Indians who regarded the ascending smoke as a message to the spirits and did not ask them to smoke for themselves.

Tobacco was cultivated by men, in small fields from which women were debarred, and it was used only for sacred purposes. The dried leaves were sprinkled on sacred objects and on people engaged in ceremonials and they were smoked in the calumet. For smoking purposes, the adulterants red willow and osier were sometimes used if the tobacco supply was small. In time, the smoking practice spread and adulterants and even substitutes became common. But for ceremonial sprinkling, only the sacred herb could be used.

The beings who received these gifts were the Great Spirit and the natural phenomena—the four winds, sun, moon, thunders, and the water-spirit, who was to be feared as well as honored. Also, there might be powers (respectfully called grandfathers) in any rock, grove, or waterfall and early explorers noted how often the Indians left gifts for these in passing. One spirit was not a natural phenomenon. This was Our Grandfather Fire who, said a Potawatomi song: ". . . stays here with us all our lives . . . He was here before us, and he will be the last to leave this earth."[7] Could this cult of fire indicate a concept brought from the country of the temple pyramids? If so, the hunter-planters had given it a homely form suitable to their own way of life. They had no public building where an undying fire could be kept but fire had its place in the center of every dwelling, where the family gathered around it. So Our Grandfather knew all the doings of men, all their wishes and even their secret thoughts and these he repeated not to the sun but to the Great Spirit himself. Therefore, the Great Spirit had com-

[6] See Skinner, 1924, p. 25.   [7] *Ibid.*, p. 202.

manded, he should have the first whiff of tobacco.[8] After all his years on earth, Fire was an old man and people treated him gently. They did not spit in the flames nor throw in rubbish. They saw the smoke going out through the smokehole and knew that the old man was sending word to the sky.[9]

The Wisconsin Indians grew corn, beans, and squash. Many of them held some rites at planting time and harvest, and forbade planting or eating the ripe food until these had been held. Nevertheless, the crops did not take first place in these rites. The chief interest of these hunter-planters was war. It was in the interest of war, rather than agriculture, that the clan bundles were opened and offerings were made. The ceremony resembled an eat-it-all feast such as hunters had normally given when times were plentiful. That described below was given at harvest time by the Bear Gens (a patrilineal clan) of the Fox tribe. It honored the sacred pack which a vision-seeking ancestor of theirs had received from a buffalo.[10]

The scene was the house of the clan leader, a rectangular bark structure such as Fox families used in summer. At one end was a platform where the leader and bundle-keeper sat with their clansmen. All day, they drummed, sang, and called on the manitous, while men of their hereditary clan waited on the guests and danced. The hosts did not eat but a number of men and women were invited as guests and it was understood that the spirits ate with them.

The feast was white dog boiled with corn, for both these foods had been given by the Great Spirit when he gave tobacco. Perhaps the dog was a substitute for the human sacrifice of other days, for one Indian called the animals "a price for their [the peoples'] lives."[11] Indeed, they were treated very much like the human sacrifices made by the Natchez and the Aztecs. That is, they were exceptionally well treated until the time of death. Then they were decorated and dispatched, being told that they were messengers carrying the peoples' wishes to the spirits. The Fox sent messages

[8] Michelson, 1930, p. 27.
[9] *Ibid.*
[10] See Michelson, 1930, p. 93.
[11] Michelson, 1929, p. 51.

by their own dead in the same way. What they asked for was not rain or crops but long life, village security, and that "when the Manitou hangs war upon the sky" each devotee might have one slice (that is, a scalp).[12]

All day the guests feasted in relays, being careful never to spill a drop of food, since this would be disrespectful to the spirits who were feasting with them. The hosts did not eat but sang and addressed the spirits, or the leader made one of the traditional long speeches. At stated intervals he asked the ceremonial attendants and some male and female guests to "seek life by stamping."[13] The Fox felt that the dance and the dance songs should be quiet and dignified. Some Potawatomi songs, however, have a wild flavor like these which honor their Man Bundle:

Now we all move, we're moving with this earth.
The earth is moving along, the water is moving along.
The grass is moving, the trees are moving, the whole earth is moving.
So we all move along with the earth, keeping time with the earth.[14]

And,

I am dancing, dancing earnestly to the Great Spirit,
And dance and dance till I can dance no more.[15]

Besides the clan bundles, there were personal bundles which might be opened at any time with proper ceremony. Those who had visions and bundles from the same spirit sometimes formed a society and developed a secret ritual.

The Grand Medicine Society, the Midewiwin (Chap. 9), may first have been formed in this way. It was an association of those who had obtained great spirit power and perhaps had gone through several stages of instruction. In later days membership could be obtained through heredity or election and, of course, payment. Full members had the power through their magic token, a shell or an otterskin, to kill and resuscitate whom they pleased.

Each tribe had its own version of the society's origin, often connected with the creation myth. That myth, in the Lake country,

---

[12] See *ibid.*, p. 21.   [14] Skinner, 1924, p. 177.
[13] See Michelson, 1932, p. 121.   [15] *Ibid.*, p. 178.

began with the primal flood, the culture hero, and the earth divers. With some tribes, there was no mention of a Great Spirit. The Winnebago, however, had worked the Great Spirit, the culture hero and the Medicine Society into a complicated theology based on the idea of reincarnation.[16] Their version of the myth, like that of the Fox, tells how the Creator, having made man, was troubled by man's unhappiness. But the gift he gave his people as a solace was not merely tobacco. He sent down helpers to solve man's problems.

Four deputies descended from heaven for the purpose but all failed. Then, by his thoughts, the Manitou created Hare. We are familiar with the arctic hare of northern tales who was both Culture Hero and Trickster, and many outside the Medicine Society thought of him as such. The Society thinkers, however, bisected the character, leaving Nanabozho to go through the rabbit's adventures while Hare was made in human form as a savior. "Try with all your strength," the Creator urged him. "If [these others] spoil my creation for me the earth will not be good. This light and life will not be good."[17]

Hare went down to earth and, to have a real kinship with human beings, he entered the womb of a virgin. Even there, he heard the people weeping and shrieking, so he burst out prematurely, killing his mother. He destroyed the evil ones and thrust them down under the earth, and his grandmother (earth or fertility) produced corn and tobacco from her body. But the people, his uncles and aunts, still mourned because their life was short. So he gave them the final gift put in his power by the Creator, the gift of reincarnation. "If any of your uncles and aunts does well," the Supreme Being had told him, "he can come back [on earth]. I will always keep the door open."[18]

So He-whom-they-call-nephew gathered the good spirits together to establish the medicine lodge. He used tobacco, "the means for obtaining life," and he "tied life and light into them."[19] The spirits taught the proper dances for ensuring a succession of lives and, as they left, each rubbed off some of his light and life on

[16] Radin, 1950, pp. 9–10.
[17] See *ibid.*, p. 10.
[18] *Ibid.*, p. 14.
[19] See *ibid.*, p. 47.

the doorposts. The lodge was thus invulnerable and the people, if they carried out the rites, would be able to be born and grow old over and over again. Hare went back to the sky, saying: "What I wished for my uncles and aunts, it is accomplished."[20]

REFERENCES

Prehistory: Griffin, 1952.

Descriptions of individual tribes: Blair, 1912 (Potawatomi); Densmore, 1929 (Chippewa); Hallowell, 1934 (Northern Salteaux); Hoffman, 1891, 1896 (Ojibwa, Menomini); Jenness, 1935 (Ojibwa); Kinietz, 1940 (Huron, Miami, Potawatomi, Chippewa); Radin, 1923, 1950 (Winnebago); Skinner, 1923, 1924 (Sauk, Potawatomi). Also monographs from museums and universities.

Fox customs and ceremonies: Michelson, 1925, 1927, 1929, 1930, 1932.

[20] See *ibid.*, p. 18.

19

PLANTING
CEREMONIES:
THE PRAIRIE

The Spiro Mound, built perhaps as late as A.D. 1300–1400 was one of the largest and latest of the structures erected by the planters of the Middle Mississippi. It has been so ravaged by curio hunters that we cannot tell the purpose of the round chamber within it, held up by cedar posts and with conch shells lying in a circle on the floor. We know that out of it have been taken axes of native copper, yards of cloth made of wild grass, and pottery whose decorations show elaborate costumes reminiscent of Mexico. Perhaps, as some students think, there were new influences coming from the south in these later years of the temple builders, for the relics abound in such symbols as the jaguar and serpent, the "weeping eye," and the human hand, all common in Mexico as well as in the Mississippi Valley.

Such objects might have been left by people as sophisticated as the Natchez but along with them are weapons and grinding stones of the sort used by early buffalo hunters on the Plains. The nearest groups who might have been responsible are those of Caddoan speech, the Caddo, the Wichita, and the Pawnee. All of them, when whites knew them, were part-time buffalo hunters and part-time planters. In the summer, they camped on the Plains but in the winter the Pawnee, at least, lived in solid, earth-covered houses. These were grouped in villages and the villages were federated, like so many in the Southeast.

About the religion of the Caddo and Wichita, we know little, but fifty years ago a Pawnee priest gave for publication a moving description of his people's religious pattern. Here are no vague references to a Master-of-Breath whose nature and function must be surmised. The Pawnee reverenced a Supreme Being, Tirawa-atius, who lived in the highest heaven. Below were three other heavens, the first containing the Winds; the second, the Sun; the third, the Stars. From his height Tirawa "threw down" to men everything that was needed, but He, himself, was never seen. "Tirawa-atius is the father of all things," explained the painted priest in his buffalo robe. "It is he who sends help to us by these lesser powers, because they alone can come to us so that we can see and feel them."[1]

This mighty being created the earth. Rather, he had it done by his servants Wind, Cloud, Lightning, and Thunder. They sang to form the land to shape it, then scattered seeds and made rivers. Morning Star, a young warrior, and Evening Star, a maiden, united and had a girl child. Sun and Moon had a boy, and these two children were the first human beings. The four Air Powers made others and gave them the sacred bundles that were at the heart of all Pawnee ceremonies. The stars, thought of as people, were bidden to look after the human race, and each of them was the patron of a village. Animals appear as patrons of the medicine societies, but they are no longer the powerful First People of the earth.

We recognize here some of the main beliefs of the planters but there was another that linked the Pawnee directly to Mexico. They practiced human sacrifice. It was not done in quantity after the Aztec manner, for the victim was only one captive maiden. She was tied spread-eagled to a wooden frame and ceremonially killed

[1] See Fletcher, 1904, p. 109.

with an arrow through the heart and a blow on the head from a sacred war club. Then every man and boy shot an arrow into the dead body. This was a rite for fertility, and the maiden should be called a messenger rather than a victim. According to the Skidi, the one Pawnee band that kept up the practice, the maiden represented Evening Star, the patroness of vegetation. Her soul went to her husband, Morning Star, who clothed her with the colors of dawn and set her in the sky. Their reunion meant the renewal of growing things on earth.

In Mexico, too, the sacrificial victims were often messengers, treated as Supernaturals even before their death; they were glad to be certain of a place in the sky. We may remember that the dogs killed by the Fox were also messengers, and some Great Lakes Indians simply waited to send messages by their own family dead. We wonder whether the trait of victim-messenger might once have been more widely held among the temple-pyramid people of the Mississippi. The Natchez, some old pictures show, burned a male captive on a frame, but this was by way of torturing an enemy. In fact, through most of the East and North torture and revenge seem to have superseded the message to the spirits.

The Skidi used the maiden sacrifice even in historic times, when one of their chiefs put an end to it. By that time the Pawnee had moved to Nebraska because of the inrush of whites after the Louisiana Purchase. They continued to be part-time planters and part-time buffalo hunters (now with horses instead of on foot), but they kept their organization, which was like that of the southeastern federated groups rather than that of the simpler hunters around them. They remembered it and continued many of the stately rituals even after they came back to a reservation in Oklahoma.

The Skidi had a succession of ceremonies lasting all summer but they cannot be called planting ceremonies. True, the corn was honored, but the activities that held Pawnee attention were the buffalo hunts and the trading trips. These took place after the corn had been planted and they needed special spirit help. In the winter it was felt that the spirits had gone far away and could not hear the people's wishes. They returned to Pawnee country in early summer with the first thunderstorm. At that time Thunder, who was the messenger of the gods, roared over the prairies awakening everyone to ceremonial life. The Pawnee priests then met to make offerings and divine the future. They sang a hymn to the Paruxti, the Thunder:

> They sang this song above, they have spoken,
> They have put new life into the earth.
> Paruxti speaks through the clouds,
> And the power has entered Mother Earth.
> The earth has received the powers from above.[2]

This was repeated fifty-six times with variations. Then men were sent outside to look at the stars and see if the summer would be good. They almost always reported they saw plenty of buffalo in the future. Then a buffalo heart and tongue were cut into nine pieces that were offered along with nine small sacks of tobacco to Tirawa and his assistant Powers.

The Pawnee made great use of tobacco in ritual, as the Woodland tribes did. Not only was the dried herb offered in packets to the spirits but it was smoked in pipes with a bowl of stone or clay and a long reed stem. Such a pipe has become known to whites as a calumet. On some ceremonial occasions, the calumet stem was four feet long and the bowl so large that it had to rest on the ground, with the smoker in a squatting position. In that case, the smoke was blown like incense to the Powers above, to the Earth, and to the Four Winds. Sometimes the bearer of the pipe danced with it, offering the mouthpiece to the Powers in succession.

The calumet stem was differently decorated according to its purpose—war, peace, or trade. For war, the stem was red and the chief feathers were those of the male eagle. The warriors danced around the pipe before starting on a raid, then smoked it in succession. For a peace treaty, the stem was blue and the feathers those of a female eagle. This peace pipe was the equivalent of a passport when one tribe visited another and Father Marquette, who saw it in use reported that "the Sceptres of our Kings are not so much

[2] Linton, 1922a, p. 10.

respected."[3] Less impressive pipes were used in trading or in confirming any promise.

On some ceremonial occasions, the decorated pipe stems were used without the pipe and it seems possible that such feathered staves had a long history apart from that of smoking. Two dancers waved them in a special calumet dance, in which they simulated the movements of mating eagles. Two such feathered staves were an important feature of one Pawnee ceremony of which we have an impressive description. This was the peacemaking ceremony in which one group visited another and gifts were exchanged by way of cementing a treaty. We have heard of this with the Natchez and Osage. I suspect that it may have been an occasion not only for peacemaking but for trade, as new tribes moved into the Southeast.

The peace journey of the Chaui sub-tribe, which has been called the Hako, was a religious occasion. A member of the host village was adopted by one of the visitors as a son, thus binding the two villages closely—an excellent device in turbulent times. I wonder if the planters along the Mississippi used it with the wilder tribes around them, and if this was one way in which corn was distributed. In any case, corn was important in the Pawnee Hako journey and Mother Corn, in the shape of a decorated ear, led the way. One of the songs sung to her says, in free translation:

> The Mother leads and we follow on, . . .
> She leads us as were our fathers led
> Down through the ages.[4]

For this journey, one man volunteered as the adopting Father, and he and his family paid the considerable expenses. The Father was usually a chief but if not, a chief had to be present, since no one else was allowed to carry Mother Corn.

The party was an impressive one as it set off on foot across the prairie. At the head walked the chief, carrying Mother Corn wrapped in a wildcat skin. At his side walked the Father and the Hako priest with his assistant, carrying the two "breathing tubes

[3] Hoffman, 1891, p. 153.　　　　　[4] Fletcher, 1904, p. 300.

of wood," the calumet stems. The pipes were decorated from one end to the other with symbolic feathers. That nearest to Mother Corn had, among others, a brown eagle's wing signifying the mother bird which hovers near the nest. The other pipe was the protector of the party and represented the father bird with a white eagle wing. Behind the priests walked two medicine men with other eagle wings for sweeping away evil; then some thirty singers with their drum. Finally came the men, women, and children of the Father's family with the loaded ponies carrying gifts and food supplies.

The procession plodded over the prairie for days, the leaders silent and looking straight ahead. They stopped to contemplate every new feature of the landscape, for, as the priests explained, Tirawa is in all things. "Everything we meet as we travel can give us help and send help by us to the Children [the group to be visited]."[5] The singers then chanted a hymn in the Plains style, with almost no words. To the accompaniment of the drum, the human voice used like a wind instrument, a flute, or tuba, uttered exclamations and onomatopoetic sounds, each replete with significance for the hearers. Only one or two articulate words were used to drive home the meaning. Thus a hymn to the trees begins: "*Wira uhaki, wira uhaki.*"[6] *Wira* is a qualifying word, meaning that an object is long. The -*ra* in *wira* means at a distance, yonder; *uhaki*, something that is in a line. The one articulate word, which comes later, is *katuharu*, trees or woods. This has been interpreted:

> Dark against the sky yonder distant line
> Lies before us. Trees we see, long the line of trees,
> Bending, swaying in the breeze.[7]

As they proceeded, the priest appealed constantly to Mother Corn to be sure that they were on the right road. Mother Corn could fly straight up to Tirawa, for it was he who had sent her down to earth in the first place.

The Children, as the people of the host village were called, had of course been notified, since they would have to make large gifts. It is said that a group sometimes refused the honor as being too

[5] *Ibid.*, p. 73. [6] *Ibid.*, p. 74. [7] *Ibid.*, p. 303.

expensive. Usually they accepted, however, and had a lodge prepared for the visitors. The peace pipe was smoked, and there were reciprocal feasts. The visitors, who were all called Fathers, sanctified their lodge by imposing processions, with singing and waving of eagle feathers. One night, after feasting the Children ceremonially, they called on visions to visit them from the sky. A hundred voices sang the almost wordless invocation that has been interpreted:

> Holy visions!
> Hither come, we pray you, come unto us, . . .
> Holy visions!
> Near are they approaching, near to us here, . . .
>
> Holy visions!
> Now they cross the threshold, gliding softly, . . .
> Holy visions!
> Now they touch the children, gently touch them.[8]

The crux of the ceremony was the adoption rite. The chief figure here was not the leader of the Children's village but a child of his, preferably a small boy. The little one was anointed, painted, and given symbols of long life and success. Then two young men danced with the feathered calumet stems that represented the eagles who made and guarded the nest. The child was given the sacred objects used in the Hako, including the ear of corn. Perhaps the Pawnee themselves had received their first corn in this way, and perhaps they had given loads of meat and skins in return for it as the Children gave the Fathers.

Even though the purpose of the journey was the practical one of trade and peacemaking, the officiants felt themselves endowed with a sacred responsibility, sponsored by the spirits and by Tirawa himself. Their ritual was as solemn as though practiced in a temple, yet much of it savored of a hunter's lifeway rather than that of planters.

Mother Corn, although she is technically the center of the ceremony, has a prominence more theoretical than real. The hymns about her do not feature the necessity of corn as a life sustainer.

[8] *Ibid.*, p. 319.

Rather, she is appealed to for her magic properties as a guide and an intimate of Tirawa. A more vivid interest goes to the feathered staves, with their rich symbols of the hunter's life and there are touching songs concerning the mother eagle and her nestlings. Even the vision, that mainstay of the hunter, had a place in the ceremony. But the concept has been ceremonialized. The visions of the Hako did not come to individuals through their own efforts. They were brought to everyone through a communal ceremony and at the bidding of Tirawa.

The picture of a Supreme Being, revealing himself through nature, is one of the most moving that we have from any Indian group. It is truly regrettable that we have so few other descriptions from the Southeast and the neighboring areas in the words of the Indians themselves. If these were available, perhaps we should have a better understanding even of the Master-of-Breath and the being "behind the sun."

There is another group of hunter-planters whose contacts must have been different from those of the Pawnee but who share the trend toward complex organizations and impressive ceremony which we attribute to the planters. These are the Siouan-speaking people who, in historic times, were strung along the eastern Plains just west of the Mississippi. This low-lying, fertile country, which early travelers described as blossoming with wild flowers, is threaded with streams flowing into the Mississippi and, in the valleys of these streams, there were villages long before the whites arrived. The people of these villages raised corn, beans, and squash and lived in solid, earth-covered houses. Also, they sallied out onto the plains to hunt the buffalo on foot.

These were not nomads, partially converted to settled living. Their organization, their planting, even the kind of corn they raised speaks of an eastern background. The Omaha and their relatives the Osage were organized as tightly as any group in the Southeast but not in a federation of villages. Offices and duties depended on kinship as they do with nomadic people, but all operated within a network of ritual.

These tribes divided all nature into two parts, the sky and the earth. Every animal, plant, and natural phenomenon belonged to one of these and so did every human being. Each tribe was divided into moieties (ceremonial halves), the Sky People having duties connected with ceremony and Earth with practical matters. Each moiety was composed of clans (with descent through the father, as with most hunting people). Each clan had its duties in almost every activity of the tribe, and also taboos governing its food and work. It had special face painting, a list of clan names to be given the children and even a special hair cut which clan boys wore until adolescence.

Their account of origins brings man down from the sky, as in many southeastern tales. (But myths differ, so do not expect complete coherence.) The Osage Black Bear clan had a ritual describing the descent of these pre-human spirits as they floated down from the topmost of the layered worlds.

> The little ones were to become a people,
> It has been said, in this house. . . .
> They sat in great perplexity,
> For in the first of the great divisions of the heavens
> They thought to make the abiding place of the little ones.
>
> They sat in great perplexity,
> For in the first divisions of the heavens
> It was not possible for the little ones to abide.
> They had made their first downward soaring.[9]

They made "downward soarings" through the second and third divisions of the heavens, and at the fourth they came to earth, which lay engulfed in water. They alighted upon seven rocks of different colors and

> The rock that was black in color,
> Spake to the little ones of its great age,
> Spake to them, saying: Verily, my little ones
> Shall come closely to me for protection
> As they travel the path of life . . .
> They shall enable themselves to see old age
> As they travel the path of life.[10]

[9] La Flesche, 1921, p. 220.
[10] *Ibid.*, p. 221.

The red rock then promised protection. The water beetle, the water spider, the "water strider," and the leech all promised their powers.

> When the little ones make of me their bodies,
> They shall be free from all causes of death.[11]

None of the creatures, however, could help "the little ones" over the water that submerged the earth. (There are no earth divers in this account.) Finally the Great Elk appeared and

> Threw himself suddenly upon the water,
> And the dark soil of the earth
> He made to appear by his strokes.[12]

With four of these tremendous movements, he cleared away the water and gave "the little ones" dry land for their dwelling. He then bade them take the various-colored soils, which his hooves had thrown up, to paint their faces in time of war. Even the seeds of corn, in the myths of the Omaha and Osage, were provided by the elk or the buffalo.

Their harvest ceremony was appended, like an afterthought, to the buffalo hunt. The spring planting ceremony was brief. A special red corn having sacred power was in the care of a certain clan. When planting time arrived, a member of this clan went through the village, distributing grains of this corn and calling out that work should begin. The clan which guarded the corn was also custodian of the sacred pipes—another possible link with the East.

Such customs were not developed during a hunting and gathering life. We shall follow with interest the discoveries of archaeology which suggest an earlier eastern home for these people. The Omaha and Osage have traditions of coming down the Ohio River to the Mississippi, then turning upstream and finally northwest as far as Minnesota. They have long sagas about moving and fighting, with an end for the Osage in Oklahoma and for the Omaha in Nebraska. It would be surprising if many ancient customs had been kept through so many changes and contacts. We know that, along the route they or other Siouans followed, there

[11] *Ibid.*, p. 222.   [12] *Ibid.*, p. 225.

are burial mounds of various shapes and sizes. We know that fifty years ago the Omaha method of burial was a small mound for each person.[13] Can they have shared, even from a distance, in the life-way of the Barrow Builders?

We remember the abundance of pipes in the barrows. So many and so elaborate were they that it seems there must have been some special ceremonies connected with them. Pipes were used by the Natchez, and French travelers have mentioned them all the way along the Mississippi, but we have no accounts of such con-stant use and such sacredness of pipes as with the Omaha.

The tribe had two sacred pipes, acquired in the mythical past. They were kept by special custodians and lodged in a special tent when the people traveled. They were ritually smoked before a council meeting of the seven chiefs, first to the Sky moiety, then to the Earth. The duties of lighting the pipe and cleaning it be-longed to clansmen who had received their function in the mythi-cal past. The whole ritual of the pipe took four days to tell and could be confided only to a chief of blameless life. A man who once used the pipe without such sanction died soon after.

Besides these, there were numbers of other pipes, all carefully wrapped and kept by clans or society heads. When tribal or clan members quarreled, a chief had only to lay a pipe between them and they had to desist or find themselves outside the law. A pipe was smoked at the beginning of every feast and the ratification of every agreement. It was used in the welcoming of visitors and on peace journeys like the Hako. Individuals used it in imploring the spirits, for the Omaha and Osage had the hunters' custom of the vision quest and the spirit guardian, at least for warriors. So uni-versal was the offer of tobacco smoke, with the Omaha, that it seems to have replaced other gifts to the spirits. There was no human sacrifice. Only occasionally do we hear of a dog being sac-rificed in certain societies.

On occasion, the Omaha puffed smoke or offered the mouth-piece to individual spirits such as the sun or the winds, but these creatures, as well as the stars and winds, had all been created by

[13] Fletcher and La Flesche, 1911, p. 592.

Wakonda. That name has been mentioned before, as an extension of Wakan, the impersonal power believed in by so many of the hunter-gatherers. Wakonda, Wakanda, or Wakonta, according to how white scholars heard the word, would seem to mean a concentration of power. Was that power focused in a person? One might almost think so on reading the words of a Kansa, another Siouan tribe: "Wakanda has indeed been looking at me";[14] or those of an Omaha chief to his successor: "If you get in a bad humor Wakanda will do so [the same] to you."[15]

But the term might also refer to any mysterious Power or to all of them together. Some Omaha wise men named seven Wakondas: the Above, the Below, Darkness, Sun, Moon, Morning Star, and Thunder. One shaman insisted that he himself was, at times, Wakanda. Perhaps the word shifted in meaning as the concept of a Supreme Being has shifted in many other religions. When the Osage stood at their doors at dawn and cried to Wakonda perhaps they were using a covering term for all possible Powers. Later, missionaries used the term as a translation for the Christian God. And a few years ago a ceremonialist of the Dakota Sioux said in prayer:

> Grandfather Wakan-Tanka [Great Wakan]! You are first and always have been! Everything belongs to you! It is You who have created all things! You are one and alone![16]

REFERENCES

Spiro mound: Hamilton *et al.*, 1952, with comments by Griffin.
Caddoan area: Sears, 1964.
Culture and ceremonies: Dorsey, 1884, 1894 (Omaha); Fletcher, 1904 (Pawnee); Fletcher and La Flesche, 1911 (Omaha); La Flesche, 1921, 1925, 1930, 1939 (Osage); Linton, 1922*a*, 1922*b*, 1923 (Pawnee).

[14] Dorsey, 1894, p. 374.   [15] Dorsey, 1884, p. 361.   [16] Brown, 1953, p. 46.

20

PLANTING
CEREMONIES:
THE PUEBLOS

For the Pueblos of New Mexico and Arizona, the Supernatural was not an indescribable force, honored with ritual, fasting, and sacrifice but never seen. On the contrary, supernatural Beings danced in the village plazas in summer and in the ceremonial rooms in winter. They carried seeds which were distributed to the people, and the people's officiants, in turn, blessed the supernaturals with the sprinkling of cornmeal. The acts of blessing and kinship were reciprocal.

Pueblo, the Spanish name for village, was applied by the Conquistadores over two hundred and fifty years ago, when they first took possession of the country. It referred to a score or so of settlements whose people spoke four different languages and had varied ways of dealing with family and government. Yet they were alike in being true farming people who subsisted almost entirely by their crops, and whose tillage was done by the men, not the women.

For tillage was no part-time, easy occupation as it often was in the Woodlands. Pueblo country was part of a huge, semi-arid region stretching from southern Colorado to northern Mexico. This Greater Southwest has a few rivers, but away from their banks, the country looks like a near-desert. Nevertheless, it had summer rains, unlike the true desert north of it. So the groups of hunter-gatherers once scattered through it learned about corn and slowly passed the news from south to north. The ancestors of the Pueblos, or some of them, lived at the extreme northern edge of the area, strung through Nevada, Utah, and Colorado. And there, sometime after A.D. 1, they settled down to raise corn.

One of their first dwellings was the pithouse, a sort of cellar with a roof over it, insulated by its earthen walls. Some modern Pueblos still use the plan for their sacred rooms, or kivas. Archaeologists can follow the progress of these pre-Pueblo farmers through flimsy surface houses, to clusters of houses made of stone and sun-dried brick, and finally to large towns. Some dwellings were in cliff openings, perhaps for protection; some in the open with room for a thousand people. Their fields produced corn, beans, and squash, and sometimes cotton and tobacco. House ruins reveal a great deal of pottery and some signs of weaving.

Then came disaster. Toward the end of the thirteenth century a long drought caused an emigration of the planters all around the margins of the Greater Southwest. Groups from Mexico went south, the Aztecs among them, and others probably came north. Pueblo dwellers from the cliffs and the terraced towns streamed south by different routes. We cannot follow all the groups who made up that part of the history of the Greater Southwest. Of those who formed the historic Pueblos, there were two streams. One settled along the Rio Grande and its tributaries; the other was farther west. Perhaps the groups already had differences in language and custom but after this, new resources and new neighbors drew them even further apart. We must think of them as Pueblos of the East and of the West, or of the River and the Desert.

The Pueblos must have brought with them some customs of the northern hunter-gatherers, such as fear of the dead, seclusion of maidens, and the medicine man. Some of these can be traced through the rich ceremonies they developed, for now they had a new impetus to ceremonialism. They were closer to the great cities in Mexico. These were not the lowland cities, with their civic centers and scattered farming hamlets whose influence was so prominent in the Woodland. From Pueblo country, a route leads straight down, over the plateau, to the close-built highland cities: Tula of the Toltecs and, later, Tenochtitlán of the Aztec (see Map 4). Some items of Pueblo ceremony plainly suggest Aztec influence. But that influence was only the starting point. It supplied the spark from which Pueblo imagination took fire and constructed its own ceremonies and the beliefs behind them. Add, after that, some two hundred and fifty years of Spanish rule, then the new desires and slackening of ties which came when the Pueblos found themselves in the United States. Through all this, the sturdy organism of Pueblo religion remained alive, although it changed as living bodies change.

The Pueblo origin myth, still told, is entirely different from that of Woodland planters. For these farmers, human beings did not float down from the sky. They came up from the earth, like seeds, a layered universe being taken for granted. Some groups spoke of a Creator but he—she among the Keres—was of the vanishing type, who retired when the initial work was done. Then the people were made, or born, in the lowest womb of the Earth. In Zuni myth, Sun Father mated with Mother Earth and begat the grotesquely formed ancestors of the people down in her fourth womb. It was he who called them up into the daylight. "Yes, indeed. In this world there was no one at all. Always the sun came up, always he went in. No one in the morning gave him sacred meal. No one gave him prayer sticks. It was very lonely."[1]

Sun Father spoke to his two sons. And here we meet the twin brothers in a very different guise from Hare and Wolf or even Sapling and the Evil One. These were powerful war gods, with no animal traits except the mischief with which they sometimes plagued their grandmother, Spider Woman. They descended into the Earth's womb and led forth the people, along with the priests bringing the sacred tokens which they already possessed. Would

[1] Bunzel, 1932, p. 584.

it be blasphemous to suggest that there might be involved, here, some tradition about the arrival of a group from the South, already equipped with officiants, ceremonies, and sacred objects?

Once above ground, the war gods changed the primitive creatures into proper human form. There were animals with them possessing the same shape they have now, and some were very powerful. On the earth's surface, however, there were no inhabitants except monsters whom the twins subdued. This allusion to monsters, by the way, is common in myths that tell of disposing of primitive inhabitants. The war gods acted as culture heroes, teaching and protecting the people. But the Pueblos pictured them as very youthful heroes who sometimes enjoyed themselves as tricksters. Finally they departed, as most culture heroes did. But, unlike many, they are still impersonated in ceremonies and they have shrines where offerings are laid. In fact, the area around every pueblo is dotted with shrines to various Beings. The Hopi, in particular, pleaded with the United States government to keep Navaho sheepherders out of this land, even though it seemed empty. To them it is a protecting and life-giving envelope, surrounding their villages as air surrounds the earth.

All Pueblos have the tale of emergence from the Underground which they surely did not bring from hunter-gatherer country. What they must have brought was the concept, common to all Indians, of the living personality of everything around them, from bushes to grinding stones. Said the Zuni Sun Priest, announcing the dawn:

> Dawn ancients,
> Youths
> Matrons
> Maidens
> Over their sacred place
> Have raised their curtain.[2]

Note that the Dawn People who raised their curtain were living in a house, just as the Pueblos themselves did. Each Being had his

[2] *Ibid.*

domicile and the Sun had two, in the east and west. No spirit was thought of as floating homeless in the air.

Particularly sacred and powerful was corn. In this semi-arid country, where game and wild plant food were scarce, the grain was a real life-sustainer, whose failure might mean starvation. The Pueblos probably had it in a primitive form long before the Christian era, and over the centuries it developed into handsome cylinders in six colors: yellow, white, blue, red, black, and speckled. They were often used in relation to the six directions: east, north, west, south, up, and down. The same directional order and, often, the same colors, were used in Mexico.

As in other places, the new food was thought to be the gift of the Supernatural. The Hopi had received it from the god of vegetation. With the Zuni, it came from the six Corn Maidens whose leader was Yellow Corn, the earliest-known form. The Maidens left the people once, when corn was being wasted, and it took years to coax them back. Then, like Proserpine, they stayed only part of the year. Keresan pueblos thought of corn as the gift of Iyatiku, their Mother-Creator. Some others seemed to assume that the varicolored Corn Girls and Corn Women came up from the Underground with the people.

The corn ears and even the meal made from them had a power of their own. With the Hopi and Zuni, a perfect ear was the emblem of a ceremonial leader. With its base ritually wrapped in feathers and jewels, it was placed on the altar at ceremonies or laid over a medicine bowl. A corn ear kept a house safe after a death or guarded a newborn child. Cornmeal was sprinkled over sacred objects and sacred officiants like an anointing. It blessed a new house. It made a pathway into a ceremonial chamber. Sprinkled across the road, it barred the way against an enemy. Above all, it was carried by the dancing spirits of rain and fertility and often it was sprinkled before them, to "make their road."

These spirits, called *kachina* in the West, *katsina* in the East, were known in pre-Spanish days in every village but Taos. They danced regularly in the plazas wearing paint, kilt, and feathers reminiscent of an Aztec carving. Of course all but the uninitiated children knew that these were men of the village but they had, nonetheless, supernatural power. The kachinas were explained in various ways. The Zuni story was that these rain-bringers had come from Underground with the people. Periodically, they danced to bring their blessings, but it was found that when they departed, someone always went with them; that is, died. So they decided not to come again but to leave their masks. Usually, all the males of a village were initiated into the cult. While wearing the mask, they had supernatural power but they had to treat it reverently and be purified when the mask was removed.

Pueblo imagination conjured up scores of kachinas, each with its individual character, costume, and function. They lived in mountains, in a lake, or in a canyon. They represented clouds, animal owners, the dead left behind during the Emergence (this part of the belief cannot be charted). They and the weird clowns who sometimes played around them gave every pueblo dweller a visible hold on the world of the Supernatural.

Ceremonies were many and each pueblo needed a huge corps of ceremonial officiants. In fact, everyone performing a public duty was a ceremonialist and there was, until the Spaniards came, no distinction between secular and religious officials. Directing a ritual, settling quarrels, leading a war party or a hunt were all religious functions. The dividing line was not between secular and religious bodies but between clans and moieties, whose membership was usually hereditary, and the medicine societies, which anyone might join.

THE HOPI

Thus far we can go in speaking of all the Pueblos, but in detail there were striking differences. Most noticeable was that between East and West, the villages in the river valleys which came under Spanish rule, and those in the desert where the mailed fist could hardly reach. Most remote of all were the nine Hopi villages, perched now on flat-topped mesas which protrude into the desert like peninsulas into a sea. The Hopi spoke a Shoshonean language like many desert groups, and pottery marks their trail from such desert settlements as Betatakin. That is the trail of *some* clans. Their own legends tell of many of these matrilineal (or mother-descended) clans, coming from many directions, each with its own ceremony.

So a Hopi village was a collection of clans with the first-comer, generally the Badger, at the head and its headman as village leader or "chief of houses." Each clan, theoretically, had built its own kiva, a descendant of the ancient pithouse. For clan members and invited neighbors, this was a workroom, a club room, and a temple, where no woman might come except to clean and bring food or, on special occasions, to be a spectator at a ceremony. The kiva was entered by a ladder through the roof, as Pueblo dwellings had been entered long after the pithouse was given up. On its earthen floor burned the small fire which gave the only light for cere-monies and, near it was the *sipapu*, the opening to the Underworld. Usually this was closed with a stone on which dancers stamped loudly, so that the dead below might hear. On the awesome occasion at year's end when the dead took part in the initiation ceremony for young male tribal members, it was left open.

At least twice a year, each kiva was the scene of the long and solemn preparation that preceded a clan ceremony. Each clan, we have noted, had its own, with a regular place on the calendar. For these rites, the clan headman was the priest, who had a number of initiated helpers. The membership, however, was not quite according to myth, for the initiates were volunteers, some clan members, some outsiders. They could be called a society or even a priesthood. And they were powerful. There was almost no communication with the Supernatural except through them, and through their ceremonies they brought rain and crops. They cured disease, and they also gave it. Most Hopi villages had no individual medicine men. Sick people applied to a society which might send a single member to suck out the disease or perhaps perform a ceremony.

No individual need seek a vision. His welfare was wrapped up with the welfare of the village and that was assured by the calendric round of ceremonies. Even the priest need not seek individual power. Power had been given to his clan or, perhaps, to the ruling family in his clan, long ago. What he had to do was to carry through the rites without error and to lead an upright life, free from quarreling or breach of taboo.

The ceremonial year for the Hopi planters was a series of dramas, picturing seed time, growth, and harvest. It began with Soyal, when the sun was turned back from his southern journey. The Soyal chief watched the shadows on a certain mesa at sunrise and, when they reached a particular mark, he knew the number of days to come before the solstice. Sixteen days before that he had secluded himself in the kiva, and gradually the society members had joined him. They refrained from meat, grease, and salt and from sexual contact, the usual rule for those dealing with the Supernatural. Instead of ancestral robes, they wore a breechcloth. Their feet were bare and their newly washed hair hung free. It was vital, at this time, that they think no evil thoughts. Their minds should be concentrated on holy things, for it was by this secret force that village life was kept safe.

Reverently, with pauses for song and meditation, they prepared their messages to the spirits. Reading and writing had no place in ancient Pueblo life, and messages, even to the Supernaturals, were conveyed by visible symbols. These were placed on what we may call an altar. It was a design in cornmeal, drawn on the floor, surrounded by sacred corn ears and other symbols and with a decorated reredos against the wall. Messages were also sent to the spirits at their shrines. These were the famous prayer sticks. They were lengths of wood with feathers attached, but there was infinite variety in the length and shape of stick, the kind of feathers, and the method of attachment. The prayer sticks were not sent out until they had been treated, perhaps with drops of honey but always with tobacco smoke.

Several kinds of tobacco grew wild in Pueblo country and a little was cultivated for ceremonial use. But there was no calumet. The dried leaves were smoked in a cane tube, cigarette fashion, or in a "cloud blower"—a short, funnel-shaped clay pipe. This was ceremonially filled by a man from the Tobacco clan and lighted by one from the Fire clan. The blowing of smoke on the

offering, from the giver's own lungs, was something like a signature to the message.

There have been changes and omissions in the Hopi ceremonial
year since the time, twenty or thirty years ago, to which most of
my descriptions refer. Yet the confidence which many participants still feel in their rites makes it fitting that they should be
described in the present, not the past.

For sixteen days before the Soyal ceremony, the kiva is closed
to all but the priests, who are busy with altar and prayer sticks.
During the last days, messengers come to every house, carrying
"something to be breathed upon." It is only a cornhusk containing
prayer feathers and pollen, the symbol of fertility, but every
resident of every house breathes upon it, even the children. The
message they send thus to the Supernaturals goes first to the kiva
to be blessed, then to a spring, the residence of spirits.

Next, the seed corn is blessed. Four messengers go through the
town collecting it from the women, for women own the houses
and the stored crops. The bunches of varicolored ears are laid on
the altar. They will be returned after the ceremony, with promise
of a plentiful yield. As each corn collector mounts the ladder to
leave the kiva, he pauses four times and simulates sexual inter-
course. I remember when I worked in the Indian Bureau that a
white official was horrified at this. "Indecent!" was his comment.
"And with children present. We cannot tolerate this."

The Hopi priest who received the complaint looked both
amazed and sad. I do not remember how his answer was phrased
by the interpreter but its import was: "How then do you wish
us to teach our children about the beginnings of life? The man
is a sacred messenger and his act is performed in a sacred place.
How better could children understand that creating life is a sacred act? I have heard that, when white children talk about it,
they laugh. Children in the kiva do not laugh." There are other
dramatic representations of human fertility for, at this time, germi-
nation must be assured for all living things.

During these last days of Soyal, women and children are admitted to the kiva. In the firelight they can see the altar and, perhaps, some symbolic, costumed figure, different ones in different villages. Spectators have described their breathless silence for, on this night, the sun must be turned back or the village will starve.

The crucial act is performed by a man who, perhaps, represents Muyingwa, the god of vegetation. His whole body is painted with white dots representing stars, and there is a huge star made of cornhusks on his head. On a staff he holds a painted buckskin shield edged with feathers, to represent the sun. He leaps and dances about the kiva—note how often the Hopi perform the most sacred acts in a dance—twirling the sun symbol frantically and giving it power for its summer journey.

Stars seen through the roof opening show when the ceremony must end; then comes a tremendous distribution of prayer sticks, to the sun, to the God of the Underworld, and to every house in the village. In the days of preparation men of all the societies had made not only prayer sticks but also the simpler prayer feathers, a handspun cotton string with one feather attached. These were sanctified in the kiva. They are brought one after the other to every house, to be tied on rafters, utensils, on dogs, and even on automobiles. Thus continuous prayers to the Supernaturals are made through the coming months without words.

In February the beneficent power of the kachinas is made evident, for they go through the village with gifts of young bean plants, although the fields are still bare. The beans have been secretly planted in the kivas, kept warm, watered, and sung over. At this Powamu ceremony, each child receives a plant along with a doll in kachina shape for a girl, a bow for a boy.

Another pageant of early spring presents Palülukong, the Great Serpent. Snakes are revered by all Southwestern Indians, but this Being who "comes from the South" is a bringer of fertility, not only to crops but to people. And his gift is illustrated in dramatic terms. It takes clever craftsmen to volunteer for the Palülukong spectacle. It is presented at night in a crowded kiva. There is singing and tramping by costumed kachinas and at intervals a great roar, said to be the voice of the Serpent, is produced by a gourd trumpet.

There is total darkness as the roof opening and the fire are covered. The fire blazes up, and one end of the kiva is seen to be covered with a screen of cotton cloth, painted with flowers and sun symbols. Before it stands a row a young corn plants, forced into growth in a hot room as the beans were. The screen is pierced with one or more holes and through them poke huge heads of serpents. The heads are made of gourds, with globular eyes filled with seeds. The bodies which come wriggling out are puppets constructed by stretching cotton cloth over spaced willow rings, a man's arm within to move them. This is as clever a bit of crafts-manship as any used by the shamans of the Northwest.

The mother of the kachinas (impersonated by a male, of course) blesses the serpents with cornmeal, then offers them her breast, an enactment of the close tie between the Supernatural and fertility. Finally the serpents knock over the row of corn plants, dramatizing the harvesting of crops. Then the room is darkened, the scenery is dismantled and the puppeteers are off with it to another kiva. The miraculous corn plants are handed to the spectators as another gift from the spirits.

At midsummer, the kachinas leave the Hopi villages. They re-turn to their homes, and from there they may visit the dead underground who will now have their winter solstice and will duplicate all the ceremonies held above. Niman, the "Home Kachina" dance occurs at about the time of the summer solstice. At this time, the first of the sweet corn is ripe and the other crops are safely on their way. The kachinas appear *en masse* to dance in the full sunshine and receive the people's thanks.

I watched the Beings appear, climbing one after another over the edge of a cliff below which they had put on their masks. And suddenly those masks did not appear to me either grotesque or childish, as they once had done. I knew now that every mark, every protuberance was full of meaning, from the kind and color of their features to the painted dots which carried the promise of corn or rain. There was no attempt at human beauty. The

Hopi had no Raphael or Michelangelo, nor did they want one. They saw no use in attempting to deify a human face, so the kachina face is something that everyone must recognize as non-human. It produces a thrill that the most beautiful painting cannot possibly evoke. One is in the presence of the unearthly.

There follows the slaying of captive eagles, reverently killed for their feathers and buried in a special cemetery. Then may come the Flute ceremony, when the Flute society visits its spring and fills a gourd with water. More promises! In alternate years, the Snake society also fulfills its promise. Its members swallow medicine and rub themselves with it, then go out in the four directions hunting their clan brothers, the snakes. On an appointed day, they "dance" these relatives, one priest holding a serpent in his mouth while another, behind him, strokes it with a feather whip so it stretches out and cannot coil to bite. The use of an emetic afterwards does not completely explain why the dancers do not suffer from snakebite. Four clansmen finally pick up their guests and carry them in the four directions, where they are left to carry out their obligation of sending rain. The late summer cloudbursts generally follow, and I heard Navahos joke one year: "We had better help the Hopi with their snake dance so the rains can be over before our Navaho Fair."

The time of fruition arrives and there are three dances by women's societies. These belong to clans as do those of the men. The women fast in the kiva like their brothers, but they need a clan brother to make the prayer sticks, since this is not a female function. Their role is to provide food and the basket containers for which the Hopi are famous. So, in their dances, they throw out colorful basket plaques and cooked food. Once this was the famous wafer bread made of cornmeal, but now it may be packages of cereal from the store.

It is plain that the female in corn country has a good deal more scope than she has among the hunters, for Iroquois women also have their own dances. Hopi women officially throw water on the men at certain ceremonies, as rain magic. And the dousing is accompanied by jibes. A female is considered necessary at many

THE PUEBLOS ► 215

a men's ceremony, but any female parts are taken by a man. For the most part, women are the invisible support of ceremonial life.

The year is wound up with a grim and impressive ceremony in which the dead visit the town and youths are initiated into manhood. On this *wüwuchim* night, all entrances to the mesa are closed by a line drawn with cornmeal. Half the town is vacated, although food for the ghosts is spread inside the open doors. In the other half, the women and uninitiated males listen to shouts and running feet, as initiated men patrol the town to see that no spirits have entered but those of Hopi dead. It is on this night, a month before the solstice, that all old fires are put out and a new one ceremonially made. The initiates, wrapped in their blankets, sit watching in the kiva. They are told the story of the Emergence. Perhaps they even see the dead. Their experience, like so many initiations, seems to be an enactment of death and rebirth. Having passed through it they can perform in the great Soyal ceremony; and in former days this initiation was a preliminary to marriage.

THE ZUNI

Zuni, in New Mexico, is the other large desert pueblo. With its mother-clans and its public kachina dances this group, at a casual glance, seems almost the twin of the Hopi. The two are indeed related, but like siblings who share the same bony structure but have different hair color and complexion. A close look at these differences sheds light on the personality and the ancestry of both.

The large Zuni pueblo, combined from six or seven ancient ones, is less than a hundred miles from the Hopi mesas. Yet the Zuni language is entirely different from that of the Hopi and from that of any other pueblo. In fact, the linguists have not yet classified it to their satisfaction. Yet this language has provided us with a glimpse of poetry as impressive as any we have from ancient Europe. Many of the Zuni rituals have been translated, as those of the Hopi have not. Perhaps these articulate calls upon the spirits can help us in translating the Hopi message, couched in symbols.

In the Zuni rituals, recitation often took the place of public drama. The essence of each ceremony was a long retreat by the priests, while pageantry was left to the kachinas. Zuni organization was not a collection of clans but a hierarchy. There was a sun priest and sun watcher, appointed by the war gods themselves. There were two Bow Priests to represent these gods. And there were twelve rain priesthoods, each belonging to a clan, with no outsiders.

There were four principal priesthoods, each in charge of a certain kind of moisture, and they called upon Rain Beings who were not kachinas, but *uwanammi*, dwellers in the clouds. They received prayer sticks and consulted together.

Yonder at the north encircling ocean
You will hold discourse together, touching each other with them [the prayer sticks].
And then also yonder toward the south, toward the east, the north, above and in the fourth womb.[3]

This is in the opposite order from that used in the East, but it is the order for naming gods of the Aztec and Maya. In fact, the Zuni *uwanammi*, are very like the ancient rain gods of Mexico, the *chacs* of the Maya and *tlalocs* of the Aztec. The tlalocs ruled a paradise that received those who died by means of water. And to the Zuni uwanammi went all rain priests who had led a good life.

The uwanammi were never seen except in the form of clouds, but the kachinas were visible beings. And here we are reminded of the lesser tlalocs, local representatives of the Mexican rain gods who lived in every stream and mountain. The kachina masks are not copies of the tlaloc, with his black face and serpents around the eyes. Yet, after seeing many pictures of Mexican divinities, one must recognize a general likeness in the kilt, feather headdress, sash, and decorative bands around arms and legs.

The kachinas may have been of Mexican descent, but their

---

[3] *Ibid.*, pp. 644–45.

development has been their own. For tlalocs did not dance in the Aztec plazas "to make the people happy." Nor did they bring corn to adults and gifts to children as the kachinas did. Rather, weeping children were sacrified to them. The kindly picture of these Supernaturals which the Zuni have evolved is all their own. So are the nursery tales, fantastic and comic, they tell about the happenings in Kachina Village.

Clowns appear in all pueblos as a dramatic contrast to the kachina, but the Zuni *koyemshi*, the "mudheads" are an out-·standing group of sacred funmakers. Their mud-colored masks show innocently foolish faces, but on top of them are knobs containing dust from the footprints of all the townspeople. In their drums are butterfly wings, an irresistible love magic. The koyemshi "play" like children. They mimic the dancers. They eat filth and use indecent expressions. Yet the actors are middle-aged men who fast and plant prayer sticks before every perform-ance. Their function is partly to provide the comic relief that so often lightens solemn ceremonies. It is also a warning. These strange sacred Beings, born of a forbidden union, may commit what seems sacrilege. But let mortals beware!

The clowns play and the kachinas dance all summer long while the priesthoods retreat in succession. They make altars and send out prayer sticks as do the Hopi, gathering the materials and putting them together with a recited ritual. The humble gift of a prayer stick, made of rod and feathers, seems unique with the Pueblos. One wonders whether this gentle form of offering might be a substitute for the bloody ones used in the South. The Zuni sun-watcher, in making his prayer sticks, recited:

> I fashioned plume wands in human form.
> With the striped cloud wing of my grandfather
> Male turkey . . .
> And the wings of all the different birds of summer
> With these four times
> I gave my plume wands human form
> With the flesh of my mother,
> My grandmother yucca fibre, cotton woman,

> Even a soiled cotton thread,
> With these I gave my plume wands human form.
>
> With the flesh of the one who is my mother . . .
> Black paint woman,
> With her flesh making the flesh of my plume wands
> I gave them human form.[4]

It was not only priests who made prayer sticks. Every citizen made one for the sun at the beginning of each moon and planted it in his cornfield. After planting, he had to practice the usual abstinence for four days, or the offering would have no power. He made one for his wife, to the moon, but she did not fashion the offering or fast as he did. She was a provider, who carried the proper food to those fasting in the kiva and who fed the dancers. At every meal she threw bits of food into the fire for the ancestors. If her family was a guardian of masks or sacred objects, it was she who must remember to "feed" them daily with a sprinkling of cornmeal. Without her, the whole system would have collapsed.

The priests, having sent their offerings, called upon the Cloud Beings:

> From wherever you abide permanently
> You will make your roads come forth
> Your little windblown clouds,
> Your thin wisps of clouds,
> Your great masses of clouds,
> Replete with living waters,
> You will send forth to stay with us.[5]

Notice that, here, there is no begging, no pleading from inferior to superior. Nor is there praise and thanks in the Iroquois style. The prayer sticks have been delivered according to contract. The rains *will* come. The Zuni order of life, established in the beginning, allows no place for misfortune as long as taboos are observed.

At Zuni, rain-bringing and curing were separate functions, not combined as with the Hopi. There was a roster of shaman societies, some who sucked and some who worked wonders, like swallow-

4 *Ibid.*, p. 669.   5 *Ibid.*, p. 645.

ing long rods or handling fire. Yet their power did not come from visions any more than that of the priests. It had been obtained by the society's founder long ago and, when necessary, it was renewed by a standardized ceremony. Still, not all the marks of the northern medicine man had been lost. Anyone might join the society, either because he had been cured or because he wanted to share its power. And the societies were paid for their services, as priests were not.

For a full-sized ceremony, the society set up an altar. We have spoken of altars before and mentioned the design which might be traced on the floor in cornmeal or colored earth. The medicine altar is especially interesting because it was often so elaborate— and because it may have given suggestions to the Navaho. Many people think of the art of ground-painting as a Navaho invention, since this tribe has brought it to such a glorious climax. Yet there were ground paintings in northern Mexico, southern California, and in most pueblos, perhaps as early as anything done by these late arrivals in the Southwest. California paintings used moss and pebbles as well as earth colors. Pueblo paintings were small because of the many objects that also had to be placed on the altar. Yet from such a germ the Navaho may well have received inspiration for their magnificent healing ceremony (see Chap. 21).

An important item on the Zuni medicine altar was the bowl of medicine water, ritually concocted by the society chief. Also, there were bear paws and, perhaps, effigies of the beasts that gave shaman power. These were summoned in counterclockwise order, the same order used by the rain priests and Aztecs.

> Yonder in the north
> You who are my father, Mountain Lion,
> You are life giving society chief.
> Bringing your medicine.
> You will make your road come hither.
> Where lies my white shell bowl.[6]

The summons went in turn to the Bear of the West; Badger of the South, Wolf of the East; the Eagle-with-knives-for-wing-

[6] *Ibid.*, pp. 783–84.

feathers-who-lives-above, and the Burrowing Gopher from Below. There were calls also for six powerful stones: yellow, blue,
red, white, varicolored, and dark, who "held the world in their
keeping."[7] (For the rocks which helped the Osage when they
arrived on earth, see p. 199.) The summons quoted here comes
from the Great Fire Society, and fire-handling, we know, is the
specialty of the northern shaman.

On the last night of the winter solstice, each society called
upon its patrons not simply to bring power, but so that "We
shall become one person."[8] This means spirit possession. And
spirit possession occurred. The male society members, stripped
to the breechcloth, first performed sucking cures on any citizen
who presented himself. Then the various societies exhibited their
wonders, such as stick-swallowing or fire-handling. Some groups
put the skin of bears' legs over their hands. Then these quiet and
organized people growled and rushed about, supposedly turning
into bears. At this one time of the year, shamanism expressed itself fully.

THE EASTERN OR RIVER PUEBLOS

The two eastern language groups, the Keresan and Tanoan,
are among the few tribes north of Mexico that have been able
to accept many of the white man's ways, including his church,
while keeping the core of their own ways and their own religion
alive. Here, we can take note only of the most striking differences manifest in the ceremonies of East and West.

To begin with, heredity has no such firm grasp on the River
People as it has in the Desert. There are few clans in the River
region and often none at all. The usual division is the moiety
(half). A moiety head is elected or he comes from a medicine
society, where membership is voluntary.

The moieties manage ceremonies and each moiety is equipped
with societies and clowns. But there are no pageants all summer
long as in the West. If there are kachina dances, they usually
are not public. The Spanish priests saw to that, when they burned

[7] *Ibid.*, pp. 784–85.   [8] *Ibid.*, p. 784.

the masks and flogged the impersonators. Moreover, rain is not the prime need of these valley people who can use irrigation. What they want is sun for growth of the crops, and often this is achieved ceremonially by racing or pole-climbing. When dances are public, they are performed without masks and are often in honor of the local saint.

For each village has a saint, assigned by its early missionary priests, and many appear on the map under the saint's name. Their residents are baptized, married, and buried by the church, although they sometimes retain membership in a kachina group or medicine society. They also have provided themselves with the secular and ecclesiastical officials required by the Spaniards as a supplement to their own, and by now the double arrangement has often taken successful root.[9]

Westernmost of the River pueblos are the Keresans, located mostly in the Rio Grande Valley. Of the four Pueblo languages, Keres is the one which has puzzled students most. And the Keresan pueblos have a kind of government unique in North America. Their rulers are medicine men. True, we have seen shamans prominent in other places, but here a medicine society man is the town head, the cacique. He receives his standing because he is the head of a particular society. Generally there are four of these, two in each moiety, and he becomes head simply by seniority. So, in time, any man might theoretically work up to the place.

This "father and mother of the people" is a priest as well as medicine man. He keeps clay images of all the villagers in a basket as their female creator did. And he prays and fasts for their welfare. Yet, like medicine men in all the other pueblos, he has participated in a ceremony which has come down in his society. It involves altar, medicine bowl, and cornmeal design. Before it, the society sings, dances, sucks out diseases, retrieves hearts that have been stolen, chases witches and kills them. Also the societies procure rain, take charge of solstice ceremonies, and, at one time, gave power to warriors and guarded scalps.

[9] This is an abbreviated statement, taking no account of Spanish-sponsored officials at Zuni or of more recent Christian missions in all pueblos.

Here, then, among the corn planters, we have the apotheosis of the medicine man. We have seen him as an individual visionary with power direct from the spirits. We have seen him as shaman, chosen and possessed by the spirits. As the wonder-workers found themselves among more organized people, they too began to organize. The history of shaman societies is a long and varied one, each society taking color from the lifeway that it served. Among the highly organized Pueblos, the societies were tamed and organized almost into priesthoods. They retained vague semblances of the shaman abilities to suck, to retrieve lost souls, or at least hearts, and to chase witches. The Keres took the final step of turning a medicine man into a priest.

The other river people did not follow their example. The string of Tanoan pueblos, with their three separate dialects, are spread up the Rio Grande Valley north of Santa Fe. These are the people on whom Spanish rule weighed most heavily, for Santa Fe was the capital of the Conquistadores. They accepted the church and the extra secular officials. At Isleta, the installation of these on New Year's day has become an important ceremony. Their own arrangement is that of moieties, called Summer and Winter or North and South, and the moiety chief is chosen by his people. He is their father and mother for half the year, then gives them over to his opposite number. There is a chance for democracy here and also for factionalism. Both seem to be present.

A beautiful compromise with the white man's ways is the saint's day dance. Spanish priests tactfully named a saint whose day would come in summer when the corn was ripening. On that day, the saint's image is carried from the church and placed under an arbor in the plaza, where town officials sit around to guard it. Out from their kiva flows one moiety in single file, men and women alternating.

Men wear the white kilt with its woven pattern made now only by the Hopi and the long, white, fringed sash called the rain sash. On their breasts hang all the turquoise and silver necklaces that can be borrowed. On their heads are parrot feathers and on their arms, tufts of spruce, symbol of undying greenery. Fox skins hang from their belts in the back, and on their feet are handsome moccasins. The women are—or used to be—barefoot, wrapped in the narrow dark manta which leaves the left shoulder bare. Their cheeks are painted with a small scarlet disk. Their heads are crowned with the light wooden structures called *tablitas*, which are made of thin slats and painted to represent clouds and rainbows.

The performance, like that of the kachinas, is as much a parade as a dance. All remain in place, the men bending their knees and stamping, while the women merely bob up and down. A choir of old men waves toward the sky and the fields, all the while singing of corn and plenty. Finally the moiety retires and the other arrives, in similar costume but with songs of its own. With each one may come the clowns who belong to it, the Quirana or Koshare. These are not mudheads. Some are frightening beings striped in gray and black, their hair tied with cornhusks into two horns. Their play is often a rebuke to evildoers and they represent the dead.

At Christmas time, there is a crèche in each Pueblo church. As midnight approaches on Christmas Eve, most of the women of the village and some of the men may be seen kneeling in the dim light on the stone floor. One year, at San Felipe, I was with them. In the gallery a melodian was playing "Come All Ye Faithful" in a jerky rhythm which could not quite accommodate the Indian mode to that of the Christian hymn. A few female voices quavered the words. Then it was midnight. Outside we heard the sound of the rattle, not quavering but firm and strong with emphasis on the first note as is the Indian custom. With that sound the Deer Dancers entered the church. We could see the horns on their heads, their white shirts and the sticks held in their hands to represent forelegs. The melodian stopped. The dancers pranced up the aisle to the conquering sound of the rattle. They knelt before the crèche. Through the kneeling congregation there went murmurs of content.

21

"STRANGER" INTO NAVAHO

The Navaho have become famous over the country for their "sings," chants or chantways. These are curing ceremonials of three, five, or nine days' duration, in which a tale of salvation from trouble is illustrated by songs, rites, offerings, and sand paintings. These latter are magnificent colored designs made with sand on the ground, and are representations of supernatural Beings. The Beings themselves are called on to put their power into the painting, and from the painting it is transferred to the sufferer of disease or misfortune. The ceremony is given for one person or for a very few, but hundreds attend and share in the blessing.

Such is the Navaho chant as seen today and such it was when reported by the first white observer in 1891. Yet some hundreds of years before that time, the people now called Navaho were skin-clad hunters in the wilds of northwestern Canada or western Washington. This is shown by their language, Athabascan, that was spoken by a great number of tribes occupying the inland country of western Canada and Alaska. Some of those hunters must have made a long trek south to filter in, at last, among the Pueblos. The date of their arrival is vaguely surmised from the ruins of their ancient hogans, tent-shaped structures like those in the North. Some of these abodes are built even now, but are covered, not with skins, but with branches and mud. The earliest hogan found so far dates from the 1300's.

The Pueblos called the intruders by the Tewa term *Apachü*, which means Strangers or Enemies. Later and by degrees some of these Strangers settled among the planters and were known by a term combining Tewa and Spanish as *Apaches de Nabahu*, Strangers of the Cultivated Fields. Others moved east, south, and west and are still called Apaches. That change took centuries. The Strangers (they called themselves Dené or Denay, the People), when they first arrived, had the clothing and dwellings of hunter-gatherers. Their religion was probably of the same simple type, or so we surmise from a study of their relatives, the northern Athapascans. This means there were no great gatherings like the chants we know today, no masked Beings, and no paraphernalia such as sand painting. Some of their Supernaturals were the powerful animals seen in visions, as they still may be by the Apache. They had the familiar sucking shaman and sometimes a wonder-worker of the northern kind appeared. The Strangers feared witches, of course, as did all Indian tribes in greater or lesser degree. Their ceremonies were simple, uncostumed rites concerned with birth and death. Only one stood out as different. The *n'da*, which prepared a warrior for battle or celebrated victory, might have been developed on their trek south. Doubtless it was needed then.

These vigorous wanderers and explorers found themselves, after many experiences, among settled farmers who in centuries had not moved more than the few hundred miles from one village site to another. They found in time a new kind of approach to the Supernaturals, with paraphernalia and priests to assure success so that no individual need await a dream. The result shows that the Navaho—or their thinkers—accepted these intellectual riches. But they were not content with mere copying. They used the Pueblo framework of theology and ceremony, but into it they poured their own feeling for movement and some of the lore of every region they had traversed.

Consider the Night Chant, or *Yeibichai*, one of the ceremonies most often seen by visitors. It features a visit of masked Beings primarily to cure disease, whether physical or psychical. The pageant is sponsored by one man and his clan relations. At a Navaho "sing," as at the Plains Sun Dance, anyone may attend and "if his heart is good" he will share in the blessing.

The ceremony follows the Pueblo pattern: eight days of more or less secret rites and a ninth of public spectacle. The scene of the spectacle, however, is not a suitable plaza or a kiva. It is a barren plateau overlooked by a winter moon, for ceremonies of this type may not be given until cold weather has put the snakes to sleep. A row of bonfires lights the open space between the sacred hogan at the west and the brush arbor at the east that shelters the dancers as would a Pueblo kiva. In the surrounding darkness, small fires light up densely grouped trucks, dilapidated or new, and an occasional wagon or passenger car. Around them cluster the Indians in bright blankets or sport coats, "squaw dresses," or modern frocks.

The *Yeibichai* (last syllable rhyming with *day*, according to Navaho pronunciation) is a prolonged incantation given by Supernaturals to a mortal who was despised by his brothers. It enabled him to cure and so to help others and be respected. *Yei* is the Navaho pronunciation of the Zuni word for spirits. Their own traditions had no word for such masked beings with unimaginable faces. *Bi* means his and *tchai* or *tsai* is maternal grandfather. So it is the grandfather of the Supernaturals who will lead them to the aid of a suffering mortal.

A weird cry in the distance! Then the firelight is blotted out by a file of stamping figures. Grandfather, in the lead, wears buckskin hunting clothes; but the others, in mask and kilt, have a dim resemblance to Pueblo kachinas. Yet they are taller and more wiry than kachinas. Moreover, the sedate, well-drilled Pueblo performers never make that wild swooping movement with the rattle in the right hand that signals the beginning of the song. Nor have the Pueblo songs the range from falsetto to growling bass. The verve of it is so tremendous that one can hardly resist yelling with them.

In the Pueblos, the Powerful Ones would be conducted by a society member who would sprinkle the cornmeal road for them. Here it is the giver of the ceremony, the "patient," who comes from the ceremonial structure to sprinkle each dancer in turn as he passes by. In the days before trucks brought such tremendous gatherings, he fed all visitors during the performance. Only in these recent days of automobiles, when the spectators sometimes come by hundreds, have commercial food stands been allowed.

The dancing *yei* whom I have seen recently were all male. But I sometimes saw an equal number of goddesses, boys dressed as Navaho women in full skirts and velvet blouses or in the old style one-piece female dress. Such characters appear less and less as teams of young men choose to vie in singing and dancing for the prize of a sheep. The chanter provides the masks that have to be made, as in the Pueblos, from the skin of a buck that has not been wounded. The men bring loincloths and jewelry borrowed from all their relatives. The chanter paints them ritually, within a sacred shelter made of boughs.

The dancing, singing, and rattling by different teams will go on all night. To visitors, this *is* the Night Chant. To the chanter and patient it is only a repetition, a final setting the seal on a course of supernatural help that has been carried on for eight days within the hogan. Every day there has been singing, bathing, offerings to the Supernaturals, and finally a supreme act of curing. All this is a re-enactment of the adventures of the mythical hero who first received the ceremony. In the Night Chant it was a mortal, but in some chants it was one of the war gods himself. In any case, if the ceremony is carried out perfectly with all taboos observed and all hearts "good," it is bound to succeed.

The person responsible for its perfection is the chanter. He cannot be called a medicine man, for he does not have a vision, suck out disease, or retrieve lost souls. Nor is he a shaman, for he is not possessed by a spirit. He is a priest who has learned a sacred ritual given long ago to his predecessors. Yet he does not inherit his duties. There is no organized society or clan to train him. He elects himself for the onerous function and pays to be taught. This Stranger-turned-Navaho is an interesting combination of hunter-individualist and planter-ritualist.

The chanter studies with his teacher for many years, learning by rote every tiny detail. Meantime, he collects a bundle of sacred objects: special prayer sticks, herbs, and the Navaho "jewels" of turquoise, white shell, abalone, and jet. He finally is graduated in an impressive ceremony and begins practice for himself. He usually knows only one great rite and a few of the lesser ones, and parts of the Blessing Way that must follow every ceremony to atone for possible mistakes.

Chants can be used for the treatment of almost any disease of body or mind, symptoms being of secondary importance. The real reason for any trouble, in Navaho thinking, is lack of harmony with one's world and with nature. For nature is good, say the Navaho, and so is man, who is a part of her. They have no conviction of original sin. All any sufferer has to do is get back into harmony with his world.

So, when one is sick, unhappy, or out of luck, he may ask to have a Blessing Way, which rids himself of evil and fills him with good. Or he may get a diagnosis to indicate which specialist might be needed by applying to a diviner of a very ancient type —the hand trembler. After song and prayer, this diagnostician simply holds out his hand, turning it from side to side in front of him. In silence he meditates on the possible causes of the petitioner's trouble, on the chants that might be used, and on the chanters. In each case, when the right answer comes to his mind, the hand makes an automatic motion that he can interpret. There is also a stargazer who sees the light of the stars in different colors that have different meanings and there is a listener, who interprets the night sounds. These are relics of northern shamanism, which are slowly disappearing.

The Navaho had no special ceremonial building. In the days of the "forked pole hogan," when a dwelling was constructed in a day out of poles and mud, a new one was made for the curing ceremony. The later octagonal houses of logs were too expensive for that, both in time and material. So the old hogan was cleaned out and sanctified with a blessing ceremony. Now that many

Navaho have modern farmhouses, a group of families is likely to keep a log hogan for ceremonies.

Officially the chant cures only one person. Actually, all his clan and his neighbors help with the expense and share in the blessing. Men who know the songs or the technique of making sand paintings sing with the chanter or work on the paintings inside the hogan. Women may be present, especially if the patient is a woman, but others can help best by working outside. One of their tasks is their standard duty of cooking. The other is keeping the peace and the "good heart" of the company that is so vital.

Another task for the men is that of making sacrifices to the Supernaturals. These are often called prayer sticks, but they are not the Pueblo kind. They are two-inch lengths of hollow reed, stuffed with pollen and bird down and tiny fragments of the Navaho "jewels" that the chanter supplies. Some have called them cigarettes, for they are symbolically lighted with a crystal. Feathers are not attached to them but are wrapped with the sticks in a bundle.

The chant is divided into three periods: four days of cleansing and of invitation to the Supernaturals, four days during which Supernaturals arrive, and a final night of climax. For the first four days of the Night Chant a sweat house is used each morning. In other ceremonies a fire is built in the hogan. The patient sweats by leaning over the fire, nearly naked and covered by a blanket, and the male helpers follow him. Then comes the emesis. An herb brew is passed, all present drink and vomit, then the soiled sand is carried out to the north, the direction of evil.

We could spend much thought on the difference in attitude of Navaho and Pueblos as they present their simple offerings. Both offered their ceremonies to gain protection and help in need. The Zuni, it will be remembered, ask for this help as from an equal with whom they had made a bargain: "I have given you prayer sticks. You will give me rain." The Navaho, although many of their ceremonies include impersonation of the gods, perhaps have not lost all the feeling of the northern visionary whose cry was: "Pity me. I am poor." In the Night Chant, the patient

holds the offering in his hand and repeats, after the chanter, words
that seem like a prayer.

The following is an abbreviated version of one of the Night
Chant appeals made to a number of Supernaturals in succession.

> I have made your sacrifice.
> I have prepared a smoke for you.
> My feet restore for me.
> My legs restore for me.
> My body restore for me.
> My mind restore for me.
>
> . . . .
>
> Impervious to pain, may I walk.
> Feeling light within, may I walk.
> With lively feelings, may I walk.
> Happily may I walk.
> Happily abundant dark clouds I desire.
> Happily abundant showers I desire.
> Happily abundant vegetation I desire.
> Happily abundant pollen I desire.
> Happily abundant dew I desire.
>
> . . . .
>
> May it be happy before me.
> May it be happy behind me.
> May it be happy below me.
> May it be happy above me.
> With it happy all around me, may I walk.
> It is finished in beauty . . .
> It is finished in beauty.[1]

This prayer for happiness, which is sometimes translated "beauty,"
is similar in many of the chants. The difference is in the Beings
called upon, who must all be named correctly and in the right
order.

During the entire ceremony in the hogan, the chanter sings
the repetitive songs that are an essential part of the myth, and
performs the many acts designed to dispel the evil of which the
patient has complained. These include making the prescribed sand

[1] Matthews, 1902, p. 73.

paintings and administering potions and sacred pollen. On the eighth and ninth nights of the *Yeibichai* the teams of dancers perform their own ceremonial acts in public accompanied by the falsetto "*Yeibichai* song."

Rarely do we find myth and ceremony thus marching together as intimately as they do with the Navaho. There are occasions with many peoples when no connection between the two can be seen, and scholars have argued earnestly about what is the cause and which came first. The answer may be, I surmise, that myth is at first fitted to action, and the two develop together. However, during a long history they may grow apart, so that their connection is almost unrecognizable. There is no such separation with the Navaho, perhaps because there has not been enough time for this to happen.

As the illustrative drama goes on, the chanter's songs may mark its emotional high points. Also, the chanter registers his own acts in Songs of Sequence, a familiar style in the Southwest. For instance, during the painting of prayer sticks, he sings:

> A little one now is prepared. A little one now is prepared.
> For Hastséhogan [House God], it now is prepared.
> A little message now is prepared,
> Toward the trail of the he-rain, now is prepared,
> As the rain will hang downward, now is prepared.
> A little one now is prepared. A little one now is prepared.
> For Hastséyalti [Hunting God] it now is prepared ...
> Toward the trail of the she-rain, now is prepared,
> As the rain will hang downward, now is prepared.[2]

This song with its slight variations goes on for four verses. One reason for the repetition was doubtless to help in memorizing. The very ease with which it nested in the listener's mind made it seem personal property as soon as it was heard.

In the second four days, the Supernaturals appeared—by means of sand painting. This art form is sometimes spoken of as a Navaho invention and in its large, magnificent version, it is. However here, as at other points, the Navaho have taken an item of

[2] *Ibid.*, pp. 71, 72.

procedure from the planters and enlarged it to heroic proportions. In contrast, the Pueblo painting was small, laid in an inner room or kiva. Its simple design, in cornmeal or earth colors, showed mostly clouds and rain, other ideas being expressed by clay images of corn ears, animals, or Supernaturals. The Navaho did little work in clay and had no place to store effigies. Their paintings, taking up the whole hogan floor, represented the Supernaturals. The forms of the figures were elongated as in a Byzantine mosaic, perhaps to indicate unearthliness and power.

Navaho designs, made with earth colors on the earth, had to be swept up soon after completion. In fact, the word for them means "the going away of a group," or in other words, a temporary visit of the Supernaturals. According to myth, the original picture was sometimes shown to the hero on a cloud and he was promised that, if he could reproduce it in all its details, power would enter the copy.

To illustrate a chant, there may be a hundred or more paintings of which the chanter will use only four, chosen by him or by the patient. Their size may range from four to eighteen feet wide and the shape may be square, oblong, or round. The Holy People may be placed at the four cardinal points or in a row. In any case, they usually are in pairs—male and female, older and younger. Often the pairs face each other from the cardinal points, and then the usual colors are: east, white; south, yellow; west, blue; north, black. Colors may change, though, in the different chants, and all this the chanter must know.

He must see that the earth colors are collected, ground up, and placed in receptacles. (I once earned my entry into a ceremony by providing abalone shells.) The white is from "white rock"; red and yellow from deposits of ochre; black from charcoal mixed with sand to give it body; blue, or rather gray, from a mixture of white and black; pink from red and white. The chanter, after giving directions, leans back to watch his helpers dribbling color on the ground in fine lines using the first and second fingers of the right hand, guided by the thumb.

The Navaho begin at the center of the design, whereas the Pueblos, in their much smaller paintings, start at the periphery. This has been interpreted as showing a psychological difference between the outdoor, centrifugal Navaho and the indoor, centripetal village dwellers. Or it could be merely a practical matter, since the large Navaho paintings could not be handled by reaching in over a part already done. So that the body might be straight, two painters sometimes snap a string stretched between them to make a mark on the sand. Then the naked body is painted on in red and black sand mixed to make brown. Clothing is drawn on piece by piece, beginning with the feet, for in a ceremony to bring luck to all, movement must go upward. The Supernaturals wear the Pueblo costume of kilt and sash, but may hold weapons, branches, or other symbols, and they may be crowned with clouds or birds.

Sometimes the body of the Rainbow Goddess curves, in an attitude of protection, around the whole painting as the rainbow curves in the sky. Her head and arms are at one end and her feet and kilt at the other, with an opening at the east. Here may sit two guardians, perhaps Bear or Fly. By the time these last figures are finished, twelve men may be working.

Up to now the painting is merely a vessel ready to receive power, as is a mask before it has been blessed. The power comes when the chanter sprinkles it with pollen, then places around it his special plumes and the objects from his bundle. Now it is an altar, but a very different one from that of the Pueblos, where the ground painting is often the least important part of the display.

The patient has been absent while the Beings took form but now he is called in to receive their power—in fact, to be made one with them. He is bathed, dried with cornmeal, and painted with the symbols of the Supernaturals. A turquoise is tied in his hair to represent an inner man, indestructible. Then comes the actual incarnation. Sand from different parts of the figures is pressed against him, especially on the ailing parts. He is made one with the great Beings and shares their power. The sand is swept up and carried away to eliminate the chance of its contact with man or beast.

At last comes the final night, the culmination of all the curative acts. Patient and chanter must stay awake until dawn while power increases within them. The *Yeibichai* impersonators, dressed in grotesque masks and colorfully decorated kilts with as many turquoise and silver necklaces, bracelets, and bow guards as they can accumulate for the occasion, spend the night in public dancing and singing. The rite is ceremonially concluded with the Blue-bird Song.

The patient must not go to sleep until sunset when he enters the ceremonial hogan to sleep for four nights afterward. Certain food taboos are carefully observed until sometime after the ceremony.

On the other hand, the final night of the Mountain Chant presents an entirely different set of events. It might be a spectacle of sword-swallowing or fire-handling, or an exhibition of the magical growth of a plant in a few minutes. These tricks are performed by groups of experts paid for their services, and some-times the audience is well aware of the sleight of hand used. That does not matter. The exhibition reproduces the real miracles done in mythical days and thus summons Power. The more such wonders the patient can afford, the more Power is assured for him and for everyone. If possible, he will have the spectacular Fire Dance performed in which a dozen or more men, their bodies smeared with white clay, race around the blaze and wave burn-ing torches over themselves and each other. Here is a continuation of the wonder-working and the fire-handling of the North, but on a far grander scale.

This night of climax finishes the faith cure, for a faith cure it is. Patients have been known to call for a chant after treatment at the government hospital had apparently failed. Nine days of vomiting, insufficient food, and exposure to cold draughts never-theless left them filled with hope and peace. They pronounced themselves cured. At the end of that final night, when power is supposedly poured into him, the patient comes out to "breathe the dawn." The daily wish is changed to a cry of triumph as he recites after the chanter:

> My feet *are* restored to me
> My legs *are* restored to me.

The chant culminates with: "It is finished in beauty" meaning "All is in accord again."

Would that this exalted experience could somehow be carried over to the problems of modern Navaho life! If some genius of "the People" could change the theme of chants and sand paintings so that they might supply power for the new problems, how many negative attitudes would shift to positive!

The patient, after his experience, undergoes four days of seclusion and continence as do the Pueblos after contact with the Supernatural. In fact, anyone familiar with Pueblo ceremonies notices how closely the Navaho chant follows them in form, if not in spirit. This is particularly true of the initiation into a medicine society that goes through all the stages of a chant: bathing, emesis, body painting, prayer stick offering, meal strewing, the sand painting whose contact brought blessing,[3] and last of all the payment, without which the ceremony could not take effect.

Such similarity could hardly be by chance. Indeed, the Hopi and Zuni once complained that the Navaho raided their kivas and took away sacred objects. However, long acquaintance and intermarriage would give plenty of opportunity for learning ceremonial procedures. And there was one period, after the Pueblo rebellion, when villagers and strangers actually lived cheek by jowl for a generation. It could be said that the Navaho married into Pueblo customs.

But not into their meaning! We can imagine a Navaho, married into a Pueblo family, attending a public medicine society. He might even have been cured by a society and finally joined it, as the custom was. Here was magic for a hunter's needs, far more important than rain, the goal of Pueblo rites. He could imitate the symbolic acts of cleansing, and call to the divinities. This transfer of a complete series of ceremonial acts from one group to another is a fascinating example of religious change. Human groups have always welcomed a ceremony hallowed by use and therefore imbued with power. Otherwise there would not be such similarity in the services of churches whose creeds

---

[3] See Stevenson, 1904, pp. 490–503. At the initiation of the Zuni *O'naya'nakia* society, sand from the altar is placed over the heart of each novice, after which he is sucked for purification.

may be at violent odds. So the hunter-Navaho may have been glad to perform a series of seemingly important acts. Probably they did not know or could not understand the songs that went with them. So they made up their own songs, filled with all the Beings and the incidents of their travels.

The one-day ritual of the medicine society they protracted to nine days. Instead of holding celebrations in the closed kiva, they expanded into an open space before the ceremonial hogan where they would have room to perform more lively rites, and where they could come closer to the forces of the natural world around them. The patient was cured, like the initiate, but he did not become a member of an esoteric group. He procured a blessing that was distributed far and wide. In short, these outdoor people enlarged the scope of the ceremony as they did that of the sand painting.

The songs and myths of a Navaho chant are so different from anything reported from the Pueblos that we can well imagine that the Navaho stranger composed his own. By the Navaho stranger, of course, I mean the thinker or a succession of thinkers who meditated, discussed, and meditated again. They took the Pueblo origin myth, they took the northern tales of vision experiences among the man-animals, they took episodes of magic and bravery from all the regions they knew and fused all these components into a tale of almost Wagnerian grandeur.

Its root is the story of man's emergence from the Underground, a myth of planting people unknown in the North. It says nothing about a trek from the North but the tale has the People appear in the Southwest among the Four Mountains which they revere today. There the *Yei* were already at home, but they were not rain spirits domiciled in a lake or mountain. The Navaho picture them as standing upon clouds or lightning and guarded by the rainbow. They protected the birth and adolescence of Changing Woman (Earth Vegetation?) and that of the twin sons she bore who were sired by Sun and Water.

These twins were the war gods known from the Pueblos, but never, even briefly, do they appear as the mischievous urchins pictured by the peaceful Hopi. They ride on the rainbow to visit the once-mortal Sun, the bearer of a gleaming turquoise shield that he daily carries across the sky. From Sun, after many trials, they receive gifts of the straight and the jagged lightning. With these and with the help of various creatures, they slay the monsters—all but those of age, cold, poverty, and hunger that are needed to prick and stimulate the human race.

Disease, at least, could be overcome, and the many chants of the Navaho repertoire give the means. Navaho thinkers must have worked enthusiastically on organizing this new material. Each main chant has a male and a female branch (nothing to do with the sex of the patient but rather of the strenuous or mild nature of the chant). Also it may have a Holy Way and an Evil-Chasing Way. The various plots separate and rejoin like one of those chains of molecules portrayed by the biochemists.

These plots are the most imposing parts of Navaho religion, the parts fitted into the framework of the planters' lifeways. More ancient ceremonies also survive, amplified by new riches of myth. One of these is the *n'da*, Enemy Way, the only long ceremony lacking the ritual of the sand paintings. Visitors who travel to a "Squaw Dance," held in two places on two nights, are not aware that in the intervening days there has been a war drama. The patient, supposedly a victorious warrior, has been prepared for battle and purified after it. On the nights of dancing the unmarried women choose male partners and are paid. Thus they did when a victorious war party returned and handed over its booty to them.

There was a long time, after the Navaho were subjugated and before the World Wars, during which they did not fight at all. Then they found Enemy Way useful to remove danger from any of them who had had contact with whites. Boys returning from boarding school, girls who had worked in white households would stave off illness and misfortune by this ceremony. There was further use for it after the People had done magnificent military service overseas, and rumor said that the scalp which is finally shot with an arrow upon a rubbish heap was not always an old Ute relic.

The maiden's puberty ceremony is reminiscent of that of the hunter-gatherers. It is now said, however, to be a repetition of the rites performed by Changing Woman under the tutelage of the *Yei*.

So new rituals and new Supernaturals have not been substituted for the old Navaho religious pattern. They have been added to it and perhaps have reflected on it some new color. This may be true of the belief in witchcraft. It flourished in the North and flourishes among the Pueblo. The Navaho, in addition to beliefs which seem ancient, talk of sorcery effected by performing a chant wrongly, and of witch societies like those in Pueblo tales.

The Navaho knew other spirits that probably had been familiar to hunter-gatherers for centuries. The Pueblo know these spirits too, and perhaps they are part of the substratum that was brought from the Old World and subsequently spread over the North American continent. These are the spirits that reside in everything, animate and inanimate, and are ready to help or harm men according to the way they are treated.

Times are changing rapidly for the Navaho, and he needs Supernatural help on which he can call without an expensive chant. Some have found a means in the plant peyote, which came to the Indians "as Jesus came to the whites." They are finding help and brotherhood in the Native American Church.

So Navaho religious feeling has been poured, within historic time, into at least two new ceremonial patterns. We are aware that a process of this kind must have occurred in other tribes, but rarely has it been so short or so easily followed. The Navaho change, with all its causes, would make an absorbing study. We should like to compare its result with that of other hunter-gatherers who started from the same general base but ended very differently. One such tribe, surprisingly, would be the Apache.

These kinsmen of the Navaho came south with much the same rites and beliefs as those of the Cultivated Fields. (In fact, in trying to work back to early Navaho customs, we can use the Apache as a guide.) However, the majority of the Strangers did not settle down to grow corn. Only a few did any planting at all until late in their history. Instead, they roamed—to the Plains, to Mexico, to the West as far as the Piman and Yuman settlements. When they visited the Pueblos, they were interested not in the indoor medicine ceremonies but in outdoor relay racing.

There is no space here for a picture of religion in the different Apache groups. It seems well to point out, however, that these Strangers, who never lived with Pueblo people, did not adopt their ceremonial framework in spite of its beauty and impressiveness. They knew about it, as some of their rituals show. But these only distantly reflect it as perhaps Navaho rites did before their period of intermarriage with the Pueblo.

Apache religion was based on the individual vision. It was not the vision sought after by the Plains people, won by ordeal and fasting. Perhaps hunters and raiders in a new country were too busy for so elaborate a ritual. Visions could come to the Apache in sleep, could be inherited, or bought. And surely these visions were reminiscent of those of the Pueblo. The spirit visitant gave not merely a song and a special prayer. Often he recited a miniature ceremony that was to be carried out word for word. The thunder ceremony, in particular, enabled a man to cure certain ills, to dispel bad luck, and to be paid for his services like a Navaho chanter.

The visitant might be an animal, as in olden times, it might be Thunder, or one of the *Yei* or *gahn* as the Apache called them. The Apache usually pictured only four of these, each representing one of the four directions. Led by Black Gahn whom some called the creator they danced in terrifying black masks to quell an epidemic or give blessing to a maiden. Here is an interesting melee of ideas that are reminiscent of those of the North, of the Desert, of the Pueblo, and of the Navaho. One of the most interesting features is the treatment of the twin war gods, or rather, the war god. The firstborn, Monster Slayer, who always takes the chief part in the tales of the Pueblo and Navaho, is here scarcely mentioned. It is the second born, Child of the Water, who is the supernatural helper to many Apache. One could imagine that the Apache, hearing of this new theology from their kinsmen, decided that they would be different. And wishing to have revelations of a different sort, they *had* them.

The changes in religious patterns only sketched here open an enormous field for future study. Granted that all people have a religious urge, though it may differ in individuals, then what situation makes a new framework acceptable? What works against it? And if the change comes, what is its mechanism? Perhaps Indians themselves will soon help in this little-explored field.

LIST OF NAVAHO CHANTS

Republished by permission of American Folklore Society from Spencer, 1957: Hailway, Waterway, Male Shooting Way, Big Star Way, Mountaintop Way, Prostitution Way, Moth Way, Beauty Way, Night Way (The Visionary, the Stricken Twins), Plume Way, Navaho Wind Way, Chiricahua Wind Way, Eagle Way, Bead Way, Flint Way, Ghost Ritual of Male Shooting Way, Enemy Way.

There are several shorter rituals for special purposes.

REFERENCES

Descriptions of chants with translations: Haile, 1938 (Enemy Way), 1943 (Flint Way); Mathews, 1902 (Night Chant); Wyman, 1962 (Wind Ways).

Description of sand paintings, illustrated: Newcomb and Reichard, no date; Reichard, 1939b.

Descriptions of Navaho life: Kluckhohn and Leighton, 1946; Reichard, 1934, 1939a.

Navaho religion and myth: Matthews, 1897; O'Bryan, 1956; Reichard, 1950; Spencer, 1957; Stevenson, 1891.

Description of Apache life: Opler, 1941.

Apache myths: Hoijer, 1938; publications of American Folklore Society.

22

THE WESTERN
SOUTHWEST

"We Desert People have no rivers," the Papago Indians told me, "so all our water comes from the sky." They did not need to add that this sky water comes at undesirable times and in undesirable amounts. There are a few cold drizzles in winter and, after the rain ceremony, a series of torrential cloudbursts in mid-July. The rain ceremony is known as "pulling down the clouds" and, in my early, uninformed days, I asked, "Could you not pull them down in April? It would give you a much longer planting season." (Of course I did not use the English month name, even then. April, with the Desert People, is the time of the Yellow Moon when the greasewood blossoms.)

The Papago farmers, who were also experienced weathermen, informed me kindly: "There are no clouds in the Yellow Moon." And that is a fact. The brilliant blue skies of early spring do not contain a drop of moisture. So spring for these Indians was "the hungry time" when stored food was beginning to give out. Waiting for the planting season might have been a grim business, but the Papagos were wise enough not to hold a ceremony that was against the order of nature.

The Papago, who call themselves the Desert People, stand as my example of planting Indians in the Western Southwest. They were the tribe least favored by Nature in that torrid and largely barren area that stretches from the Gila River in Arizona to the Pacific coast (see map, p. 156), but their very poverty kept white invasion to a minimum. So most of their religious rites were retained down to the mid-twentieth century, whereas those of more prosperous groups were blurred or lost.

Logically the Papago, along with their neighbors and cousins the Gila Pima, should be studied in connection with the tribes of Mexico. They are at the northernmost rim of a spread of Uto-Aztecan planting tribes that occupied Sonora and parts of nearby Mexican states. Corn was known in this area as early as 3000 B.C., long before it appeared among the Pueblos. Migrations and conquests among the Indians in that area form a long history. When Spanish missionaries arrived in the late 1600's, they found the whole country full of rancherias (villages of small, scattered houses) raising corn, beans, squash, cotton, and tobacco. The Indians became a functioning part of New Spain, using wheat and some cattle and horses, speaking a little Spanish, using some Catholic rituals or, at least, having their children baptized with Spanish names in addition to the Indian ones. Even Mexican independence in 1821 made very little change in their customs. However, the River Pima and the Desert Papago occupied land that could be of use to a growing United States. So the Gadsden Purchase of 1853 added to our galaxy of Indian ceremonies a custom up to that time unknown north of the Mexican border—the drinking of fermented liquor as fertility magic.

Such a ceremony was widespread among planting Indians from Mexico to Peru and generally the drink was fermented from the corn itself. Other vegetal products could be used, however, and in the desert country on both sides of the Mexican border, there was a unique source of supply, the *saguaro* or giant cactus. Cactus cider once a year moistened the throats of men and thus induced the clouds to moisten the earth. But the rainy time was short. For two-thirds of the year, the Papagos reverted to the status of Desert hunter-gatherers.

Their desert, called lovingly the Flat Land, or simply the Land, looked grim enough to the visitor. Gravelly stretches lay between low volcanic hills that glowed with color at morning and evening. Mesquite and palo verde trees were spaced at wide intervals as in a park. Any two that grew close together would have killed one another in the fight for underground water. In some areas nothing could grow but the greasewood, which protects its tiny leaves from the sun by a kind of natural varnish. Near low points, where their fields could get the summer runoff of water, stood the villages.

A hundred years ago their houses were dome-shaped, windowless, and thatched with greasewood. In the thirties, when I shared village life, only the council house had retained the old form. The other were windowless cubes of adobe like those common in Mexican villages. Beside each, however, was the shade, the real living room for hot weather. Crooked, short mesquite trunks, the only posts to be had, supported a roof piled two-feet high with insulating earth.

For the Papago this spot, called "the houses," was home, the place of neighborliness and plenty. But it was so for only half the year. When the crops were harvested and the rainwater reservoirs went dry, ceremonies ceased and neighbors separated. Families who boasted a hunter among them sought the hills. Some worked for the Pima. Others sold pottery or found day labor in Mexico. As a result of their dual lives, the Papago religious life presented a two-sided picture. Seen from one side, they appeared as planting people, with agricultural ceremonies conducted by priestly officiants. From the other, they were typical hunter-gatherers who had songs to bring in the animals and plants, held a regard for the medicine man, the vision, and woman-power, and were instilled with the hunter-gatherers' fear of the dead.

The end of the people's wandering came in June when the first egg-shaped buds perched like birds atop the tall thorny pillars of giant cactus. It grew only in special areas, where Coyote, say the legends, had mischievously scattered the seeds on the southern side of hills. A few strays might have escaped to take root near a camp, however, and some girl returning with her water jar would exclaim ecstatically: "See the liquor growing!"

The fruit ripened in late June and each paternal family had an inherited grove. There they slept on canvas sheets in the open, and all night one old man or another might be heard murmuring the songs that were not to be sung at any other time. In the cool gray dawn, we women were out with our long poles knocking the thorny fruit from its perch. It smashed open as it fell, revealing a crimson jelly with seeds that looked like raspberry jam. When the full day had come, we sought refuge in the shade and boiled the gelatinous mass in a clay jar over a tiny fire. The juice that came to the top was saved to make the magic-working liquor. The seeds were dried and ground for oil and flour.

There was little to eat except wild greens and whatever lean rabbits the men could get. Yet the sense of joyous expectation was such as I have not seen since I was a child awaiting Christmas. Expectations were fulfilled as a moment's rattle of drops spattered against the cooking shelter, evaporating before they touched the ground. From all over the hillside we could hear the cry: "Rain! Rain! Rain! Rain!"

Immediately pots, baskets, and babies were packed in the wagons; and down the hillsides from all directions converged the singing, laughing people. They were going toward food, plenty, comradeship, home. The rains did not come immediately, and the Papagos knew exactly how much time they would have to prepare for the year's great festival. Houses had to be cleaned, sticks and rubbish cleared from the fields. Then, at last, the Keeper of the Smoke, who was both village headman and ceremonial director, called from the top of his arbor. Next day, he said, the jars of juice were to be brought to the council house. Mixed with an equal quantity of water, the magic-working juice would stand for two nights and a day. Old men would watch and sing over it lest there should be injury by witchcraft. And for these two nights the whole village would dance and sing.

The big, domed council house stood away from the village, with a wide clear space before it. Over it on the great night fluttered the string of sacred eagle feathers, never shown except on this occasion. Beside the door sat the old men who would initiate the songs. In the cleared space glowed a tiny fire and there the medicine man sat to see that all went well. All around, up to where the blackness of the greasewood bushes began, sat the people. Women chattered softly together; mothers nursed babies; young men, in all the grandeur of cowboy clothes, stood ready for the dance.

Into the cleared space moved the song leader, with his rattle made, in these days, of a tin can filled with pebbles. He gave it four loud glorious swirls and then started the song. It was *the* song, the rain song of this particular village. I have seen tears come to old persons' eyes at the mere mention of it.

> At the edge of the mountain
> A cloud hangs.
> And there my heart, my heart, my heart,
> Hangs with it.

He began to circle the tiny fire and out of the dark came shadowy forms to move with him, slowly, clockwise, holding hands.

> At the edge of the mountain
> The cloud trembles.
> And there my heart, my heart, my heart,
> Trembles with it.

Then the women slipped out from the greasewood bushes and separated the hands of the men. A woman must know very well whose hand she took at this time for, in old days, the partnership meant a promise. This was a dance of fertility. The song would be sung eight or perhaps sixteen times. Then there might be a pause, while the medicine man lighted his cigarette and looked over the circle. Dark figures moved away among the greasewood bushes. Then a new song began.

> Yonder sits the Shaman of the East
> Holding rain by the hand
> Wind holding by the hand,
> He sits.

It should be understood that these words, when sung, do not have the cameo-like clarity of the translation. Each line is lengthened by nonsense syllables in the usual Indian fashion. Moreover, the harsh consonants are softened so that the word *to-ak*, mountain, becomes *toanga* (rhymes with the English long-*a*). To make the translation I needed two helpers, an old singer and a young interpreter.

Through the night the slow circling continued. The old men might occasionally confer about the next song. The medicine man periodically went to inspect the liquor. When that happened, a wave of tension passed over the seated figures. But all was well. With the first streak of dawn, the medicine man announced: "Go home now. Sleep. Tomorrow we shall dance again, that the corn may grow, the beans may grow, the squash may grow."

Few people actually slept, for Indians do not need to be so regular in their habits. The men hunted rabbits for the coming feast; the women cooked. Official speakers went to the three neighboring villages that would take part in the ceremony to invite their Keepers of the Smoke to be present and to assist in the ritual. The ceremonious invitations and replies were somewhat different for each village, but all were spells that had to be repeated with the utmost accuracy.

Night brought more singing and dancing or, rather, solemn circling. Again, at the pauses, couples disappeared into the bushes and the medicine man inspected the liquor. Eyes followed him toward the council house, and, if he remained too long, a shiver of apprehension passed over the seated figures. (I was present once when the liquor did not bubble. We knew it before he spoke and everyone searched his memory for some breach of taboo. It was learned later that a boy at boarding school had married a girl from another tribe and she was present at the ceremony. I do not know what might have happened but, in the end, the liquor bubbled.) On the night I am describing, the stars were still brilliant when the medicine man announced: "The liquor is made. Go home. Come when the sun is high." He held his two palms parallel. "We shall sit and drink, that the corn may grow, the beans may grow, and the squash may grow."

The sit-and-drink, the most important magic-working cere-

mony of the Papago year, has been fully described elsewhere.[1] It
was sometimes carried out by four related villages that represent,
somewhat arbitrarily, the four directions. Each village was host in
turn, and its Keeper of the Smoke ceremonially invited the other
three. This Keeper of the Smoke was a fatherly headman of the
type found among hunter-gatherers. He presided at council meetings where all the men had their say. He decided on dates of ceremonies, but the only one he "owned" was the sit-and-drink, where
he and his three guests sat at the four directions, each with his male
villagers behind him.

"Do you think," I asked one of them, "that you are like the
shamans in the song, of the East, the South, the West, and the
North?"

I was remembering the Zuni Rain Priests of the Directions.
With the white person's usual desire for synthesis, I was trying to
work out some common theology for the Southwest. What I got
was the usual Papago answer: "I only know we have always done
it that way."

After the company was properly seated, the liquor was passed in
tight-woven willow baskets. Actually, it was a kind of cider, dark
red and often clotted with pulp and seeds. The ceremonial ap-
pointees who passed it might have represented rain spirits for they
adjured the recipients:

> Drink, friend! Get beautifully drunk!
> Hither bring the wind and the clouds.

The Keepers of the Smoke, however, drank sparingly and each
man made a ceremonial speech before he sipped. I had trouble in
translating the speeches, whose meaning was often obscure to the
speakers themselves. Usually they mentioned no Supernatural, but
seemed to be poetic descriptions of making liquor and inviting
guests. They were in the language of the Papagos, but I surmise
that in Mexico where drinking ceremonies were common, there
were many such formalities that are now lost. Only a few of their
speeches suggested the heights of poetry that the Papago some-

[1] Underhill, 1946, Chap. 3.

times reach. The following is part of one made when the liquor
basket was refilled.

> Yonder at the edge of the earth a wind
> Swayed to and fro,
> Well knowing whither it should move.
> The standing trees it went shaking.
> The rubbish at the foot of the trees it
> Went piling high.
>
> Over toward the west it went, and back it turned.
> It saw the earth lie beautifully smoothed and
> finished.
>
> Above emerged a huge white cloud,
> With its head against the sky it stood,
> Then it began to move.
> Although the earth seemed very wide,
> Clear to the edge of it, it went.
>
> From within the great Rainy Mountains
> Rushed out a huge black cloud
> And joined with it.
> Pulling out their white breast feathers they went,
> Spreading their white breast feathers far and wide
> They went.
> Then they stood still and saw.
>
> Although the ditches lying side by side
> Thought they could carry the flow
> With little effort,
> [The rain filled them full and]
> Piled the rubbish crosswise at their mouths.
> Although the flood channels lying side by side
> Thought they could carry the flow
> With little effort,
> [The rain filled them full and]
> Piled the rubbish crosswise at their mouths.
>
> Clear to the west went [the clouds] and back they
> Turned them.
> They saw the earth lie beautifully moist and
> Finished.

> Upon it came forth seed,
> And a thick root came forth,
> And a thick stalk came forth.
> Great broad leaves came forth,
> And well they ripened.
> Therewith was delightful the evening;
> Delightful the dawn.
> Let us all desire only this one end.
> If thus we do, we shall see it.

Only when these rites were over did the rest of the men drink. The liquor fermented in the council house (today known as the "rainhouse") was ceremonially passed, always with the adjuration to "bring the wind and the clouds." By noon the ceremony was over and the real drinking began. Each family had fermented some juice for its own pleasure and there was jovial visiting from house to house. Some men, and even women, were completely unconscious by the end of the day. More often, large doses of the liquor caused vomiting. This was looked on with kindly pleasure and one woman, pointing to a man thus affected, said to me: "Look! He's throwing up clouds!"

There are traditions of quarrels and even killings on this occasion but the only results I saw were vomiting and a sort of hypnotized singing. The whole performance was sympathetic magic (meant to moisten the earth as human beings are moistened).[2] It was a man's duty to drink and vomit as long as he could, for the liquor, like all ciders, remained at the peak of fermentation only a short time. Then it turned to vinegar. All this was decreed long ago, say the Papagos. The liquor had to be made and consumed at this one time of year when the saguaro ripened. Or so it was in the old days.

"It must have been given by I'itoi," ventured one old myth teller, "for he taught us everything we make and do." This I'itoi was a Creator's assistant, a concept found in many tribes. He appeared "somehow" after Earthmaker had created the world out of nothing. Then he bested Earthmaker at the task of making

[2] See Chap. 3.

people, won from him the title of Elder Brother and, after that, Earthmaker disappeared from the scene. I'itoi then slew monsters, including the well-known cannibal woman (see Chap. 5). He taught the people their arts and ceremonies, but in the end he did evil and they killed him. He reappeared from the Underground to deliver them from enemies, then retired to his shrine on Mt. Baboquivari.

In this region, which, so lately was a part of Mexico, it is the liquor which makes connection with the Supernaturals rather than tobacco. The Papagos did raise tobacco of the *N. attenuata* variety and smoked it in cigarettes made of a cane tube. Such cane cigarettes were deposited at sacred places and smoked by medicine men as a prelude to extracting a disease object. Perhaps wild tobacco was used in this way even before the days of corn and cultivation but the Papagos did not credit the herb with such supreme power as it had among the Fox. Nor did the tribes to the north of them as far as we know. Most tribes west of the Rockies had tobacco wild, cultivated, or traded and they also had many substitutes. The pipe was a plain tube of cane, clay, or wood. There was no long, decorated stem and no ritual of filling, lighting, and cleaning.

The Papagos used the cane cigarette at council meetings when it was passed from hand to hand with a kinship greeting. Otherwise smoking was rare and probably the tobacco supply was small. Their main interest during the summer was the corn and its growth was promoted by singing, not smoking. Rains arrived soon after the liquor ceremony and, in this country, they were blessedly regular. After the rock-hard soil had been reduced to mud, little ditches were made in the fields. Then the head of the family poked holes in the ground with his digging stick for corn, beans, and squash and his wife pushed the dirt over the seeds with her bare feet. Tobacco was planted by old men in a secret place; once they also grew cotton. Throughout the summer planters must "sing up the corn." In some villages, this was done by groups of men meeting regularly. In others, the individual farmer walked around his field, picturing in song the results he wanted.

> At the west, the red corn,
> See me!

> I come forth and grow tall . . .
> At the east, the white corn,
> See me!
>
> I come forth and grow tall.

Again, magic was being used as a tool, with no supplication, no thanks, not even the mention of a Supernatural. Nor was there any at the great final feast, given every four years, during which the mountains, the rain, and the crops were celebrated. It was a Pueblo-style performance with masked dancers and a clown probably suggested by invaders who came and went sometime between A.D. 1000 and A.D. 1300. But it was a Papago version of Pueblo pageantry. The masks were made of gourds and, in this hot country, the dancers wore only loincloths. There were images of mountains and fruit, but these were carried out of doors, not shown in a kiva. Thereafter, if no attack by the Apache had to be repelled, the hunting-gathering life began again.

That of the Papagos is the only complete picture of religious rites that we have from the Western Southwest. Their neighbors and cousins the Pima, on the Gila River, must once have had similar ones but through contact with the white man much has been blurred or lost. In Pima country there was once an imposing irrigation system, perhaps developed fully by Indian invaders from further south. We might wonder if there were ceremonies connected with the canals, as there were among the Rio Grande Indians, but no sign of them has survived in the United States or in Mexico.

Settled on the Gila River among the Pima were some Yuman-speaking groups who had moved from further west. These were the Maricopa, Kaveltcadom, Halchidoma, Kohuana, and Halyik-wamai. Their planting methods, crops, and rudimentary ceremonies seem to have been adopted from the Pimas. They gathered cactus fruit and held a drinking ceremony in which the songs were for war, not rain.

The Yuman-speaking tribes of the Lower Colorado might be called planters by reason of luck rather than intent. Their clan migration sagas speak of coming from a less fertile area in the north and generally make no mention of corn or planting. Yet in historic times they were settled in some of the most fertile country in the United States. This was the valley of the Colorado that was, like the Nile Valley, a narrow strip between cliffs. Also like the Nile Valley it was flooded once a year before Boulder Dam was built. This caused a rich growth of the seed grasses the Indians were planting at that time. Also they planted corn, beans, squash, and melons. However, they used no irrigation and the women did most of the work. The chief interest of the men was fighting, and their important ceremonies were connected with war and death.

The Mohave held a general ceremony after harvest, but the accounts given to me make it seem less like an honoring of the crops than a time for peacemaking and commercial exchange among their three geographic divisions. Each man in each division had a partner in each of the others. They exchanged farm products, which might be very similar, but, more importantly, they established a relationship in a possibly hostile territory. During the day there were competitive games and at night clan members from all the divisions united to sing their clan songs. This was a time for unrestricted sexual relations, and one speech that I recorded urged men and women to seek out partners eligible for the marriage relation, but not from their own division. New blood would produce a child "stronger and more active."

West of the Colorado the Desert country continues, with plenty of seed grasses and berries and with small game; but there is no summer rain for corn growing. In fact, the present orange groves owe their luxuriance to irrigation. Here lived people who spoke mainly the Shoshonean language, with one Yuman-speaking group, the Diegueno. They camped in villages near a source of water, a village that usually consisted of two or more male lineages. They subsisted by hunting and gathering; their ceremonies revolved around the vital events of puberty and death. Among these southern California Shoshoneans, there were no planters in ancient days and no planting ceremonies.

REFERENCES

Descriptions of Pima and Papago life: Lumholtz, 1912; Russell, 1908; Joseph, Spicer, and Chesky, 1949; Underhill, 1939.

Papago religion: Underhill, 1946.

Yumans: Devereux, 1961 (Mohave); Forde, 1931; Castetter and Bell, 1951 (Yuma); Kroeber, 1925 (Mohave).

MODERN RELIGIONS

23

Before the white man's coming, each Indian group had religious beliefs and usages that had grown to fit the people's way of life and supply their spiritual needs. Then came upheaval. Ceremonies no longer gave peace of mind and kept man's world in order. Some revival of power was needed, and all over the continent prophets arose, as they have everywhere among distressed people. Their remedies went all the way from attempts to revive and purify the old pattern to proposing a new pattern fitted to the new needs. The two hundred years or less covered by this era of the prophets probably included more religious change than had occurred in the whole millennium before it.

One change came early, while the Indian way of life still had both secular and religious vitality. Then the Indians were as willing to listen to white missionaries as they were to other Indians. They even borrowed elements of the white man's ceremony that appealed to them. Some elements were not appealing, such as kneeling, the lack of dancing, and even the garments thought proper. Yet very often all these were imposed, along with Christian doctrine. And part of that doctrine was profoundly strange, if not repellent. Indians had never considered that mankind was naturally sinful and in need of redemption. To them, as we have seen, all nature was good and man was a part of nature. True, life involved certain ills, such as death, disease, and witchcraft, but these had not come through man's fault. They were due to chance or mischief on the part of some primal being. And other primal beings had given ceremonies for handling them.

If whites had ceremonies for the same purpose, Indians were willing to hear about them. They had always been willing to add on a rite that looked helpful, even if they did not understand its language. On this principle, some of the Pueblos made additions to their ceremonies that can be seen still. This did not happen at first. The early Spanish priests who were sent to save the Indians' souls spoke of the kachinas as devils. They burned the masks and whipped the impersonators. So, in the Rio Grande villages, where Spanish power was strong, the masked ceremonies were held in secret, as they are to this day. But the Indians saw some value in the new deities presented to them, as they saw value in sheep, wheat, and peach trees. They added Jesus, Mary, and the saints to their pantheon alongside their other spirit helpers. Under the priests' direction, they built churches—all but the distant Hopi. They accepted saints' names for their villages and baptism for themselves, with the added power that a Spanish name was thought to give. Chapter 20 has described one of their magnificent corn dances during which the saint looks on and receives reverence.

Other groups, too, accepted the Christian church while still practicing the old ceremonies, as many Pueblos and some Navaho do today. It was when the old lifeway began to disintegrate that the old religion failed to satisfy. That did not mean that they could turn wholeheartedly to the new one. To accept the white man's religion with all the strain of new habits and beliefs, an Indian almost had to feel like a white man and have a white man's history. Instead, he longed for new life, colored by Indian history, to come into the Indian religion.

New life did come. A series of leaders or prophets rose up, one after another, all across the continent. We can follow their appearances, from east to west, as the wave of white settlement rolled on.

Each prophet had a revelation as had Indian dreamers of the past. He fell into a trance, but this dream went further, for the prophet often seemed to die and in that state he met a supernatural Being, as saints have done in trances all over the world. To Indians, however, the trance was especially familiar. It was experienced by the vision seeker who met a guardian spirit, received a song and directions for ceremonial behavior, and a promise of success (see Chap. 10). Such a visionary in former days was a person exhausted or in trouble, and so were the prophets. Often they were drunkards and sinners, for perhaps such men were more willing to be helped than were the leaders of the people.

Thus far, the vision pattern held. However, the Supernatural who appeared was not an animal. It was God or God's messenger —not, perhaps the Christian God, but the prophet's own idea of what God might be. The ceremonial directions he gave were for good behavior by all the people. Sometimes they must abjure all white man's goods and especially the arch enemy, alcohol. Instead of a song, there might be a dance or perhaps a whole ceremony of a kind the prophet knew. The reward of success was not for the prophet alone but for all the people. And this success took on two very different forms, according to whether the Indians felt strong enough to expel the whites or realized that they must endure them.

HOSTILE PROPHETS

The "Delaware Prophet," near Lake Erie, 1762. Helped to inspire the conspiracy of the Pontiac, lost influence with its failure.

Tenskwatawa, Shawnee, Ohio Valley, 1795. Preached immunity from white man's weapons, lost influence after the battle of Tippecanoe.

Smohalla, Columbia River plateau, 1850. Best known of a series of prophets in the area who urged the performance of a traditional dance in honor of the dead. They promised that earth would be destroyed and renewed, whites would disappear and Indian dead would return. Helped inspire Nez Perce war.

Wodzuwob (or Tavibo), Nevada, 1869. Prophesied the disappearance of the whites and return of the Indian dead as a result of a continued dance ceremony.

Earth Lodge Cult, California, 1870 ff. Various prophets preached the

earth would be destroyed by flood and the whites would disappear. The elect could take refuge in semi-underground dwellings.
Wowoka, Nevada, 1886. Dance to cause disappearance of whites and return of Indian dead.

Anyone interested in this list of prophets can see that their message changed as time went on. During the early days, in the Eastern Woodland, their dream was that the Indians themselves would conquer the whites, perhaps by becoming immune to bullets. Successive defeats ended that hope for a time. We might next look for prophets on the Plains, but the tribes there were too busy fighting to think of dreams. Their turn came later. In the Far West, from Montana to California and into Canada, the Indians had met trappers and sailors—and smallpox—long before they felt any crowding. There was a tradition in this country that the earth would be destroyed several times and then reborn. They were prepared for that and they had a special dance which would bring back the dead to enter with them into the new life. The Okanagon of Canada knew that this was near at hand when the first explorers came, for these beings with their strange garments and strange language must have been couriers from the Supernatural. The Indians danced their round dance furiously, either jumping up and down in a circle, or moving slowly counter-clockwise.

Such actions could not be called hostile, but in 1870 a spark was struck in Nevada which changed the Indians' whole picture of the world's end. It would be the end of the whites, while Indians, present and past, would survive. The peculiar name of Wodzuwob, in the list of prophets, indicates the leader of this new gospel. Wodzuwob was a Paiute, in a country already invaded by the whites. This was twenty years and more after the California Gold Rush, and after settlers had flooded into the fertile country around Walker Lake, Nevada. Wodzuwob may have been the one who first preached that world destruction and world renewal would mean the end of the whites. Or perhaps other dreamers had already scented the idea. At any rate, this addition to the old belief made the old ceremony into a Ghost dance. It smouldered for a while, and was taken up here and there by new dreamers like Smohalla. But the menace of white settlement was increasing. In 1886 a spark was struck in Nevada which started a religious blaze.

Wowoka, or Jack Wilson as his employers called him, was a Paiute like Wodzuwob. His people had been hunter-gatherers, living on rabbits, pine nuts, and plant food. When miners and ranchers flooded the country the Indians found their livelihood gone and many saw no hope of making a living except by working for the whites. Wowoka was one of these and doubtless discouraged enough to need a vision. He died not once but twice and when he was resurrected he had seen God. He had been told that a great mass of mud and water would soon roll over the earth, destroying the white men and all their gear. The Indians should dance the old round dance and, as they danced, the flood would roll under them. When it was over, the earth would be green again; animals and plants would be as in the old days, and the ancestral dead would come back. The Paiute danced, day after day, to songs Wowoka composed, such as:

> The rocks are ringing,
> The rocks are ringing,
> The rocks are ringing.
> They are ringing in the mountains,
> They are ringing in the mountains,
> They are ringing in the mountains.[1]

In the meantime, believers spread across the land and delegations came from many different tribes. There were none from the Southwest, for Indians there had long ago made their peace with the new order or else they had not yet felt its full pressure. It was the Plains people who were in need, the onetime buffalo hunters now reduced to subjection and poverty. Tribe after tribe took up the shuffling circle dance and composed words for its slow chanting. Sang the Kiowa:

> My father has much pity for us,
> My father has much pity for us.

[1] Mooney, 1896, p. 1055.

> I hold out my hands toward him and cry,
> I hold out my hands toward him and cry.
> In my poverty I hold out my hands toward
> him and cry,
> In my poverty I hold out my hands toward
> him and cry.[2]

And the Cheyenne chanted:

> Well, my children . . .
> Well, my children . . .
> When you meet your friends again . . .
> When you meet your friends again . . .
> The earth will tremble . . .
> The earth will tremble. . . .[3]

Those who needed the new gospel most tragically were the Sioux. Up to now, they had felt themselves conquerors, the only Indians who had never lost a battle to the whites. They had kept the Bozeman Trail open for ten years. They had demolished Custer's command. But some of their chiefs had seen the change coming. On the promise of tools, food, and clothing, they had accepted a huge reservation where they could still hunt deer, even if the buffalo were gone. There, they had expected to camp as they pleased, meeting the whites on equal terms, while they considered the "new road" at their leisure.

Then, somehow, nine million acres of their best land were gone. The bands found themselves confined on small, separate reservations and treated just like a conquered people. They went through the hardships of drought, locusts, and failure of supplies as did the other Plains tribes. They soon began to divide into two factions: the "friendlies" who were tired and ready to succumb and the "hostiles" who hoped for war. To the Indian agent, they were all rebellious savages. He was a political appointee whose orders were to "keep the Indians quiet," and his usual idea of doing this was to summon the military camped at various forts around the country. The Indians resented these forts located in their old hunting grounds. And they resented the tough little pioneer towns

2 *Ibid.*, p. 1085.   3 *Ibid.*, p. 1028.

crowding close to the reservations. Men in the saloons of those towns spoke of killing a Sioux as "making him into a good Indian."

Delegations went to Wowoka, and in the summer of 1890 the Sioux began dancing. The slow, shuffling circle dance was foreign to them, but they made it more dramatic by placing a dead cottonwood tree in the center to be hung with offerings. The cottonwood, the only tall tree of the Plains, was a symbol of life, ever renewed. Then one of their number began making ghost dance shirts—long garments of white sheeting decorated with symbols in red and with eagle feathers at the elbows. Wowoka had a garment of that sort, which he had said would turn away any bullet, though he averred that no fighting would be necessary. Still, more and more men and women wore the white garment. And more and more fell unconscious during the dance, which might last five days and nights without stopping. The dreamers recovered to tell how they met the approaching dead and all sang:

> The whole world of the dead is returning, returning.
> Our nation is coming, is coming.
> The spotted eagle brought us the message,
> Bearing the Father's word—
> The word and the wish of the Father.
> Over the glad new earth they are coming,
> Our dead come driving the elk and the deer.
> See them hurrying the herds of buffalo!
> This the Father has promised,
> This the Father has given.[4]

There were, of course, groups that did not join in the movement. And there were leaders like old Sitting Bull, medicine man and rainmaker of the Hunkpapa, who remained undecided even when their followers had joined. The white agents could not follow such distinctions. They were nervous and therefore the Indians were nervous. Bands kept moving from place to place and holding councils. More soldiers came. Newspaper men arrived as they had never been able to do with earlier prophets, and the whole country read lurid reports. One careful investigator avers

[4] Miller, 1959, p. 102.

that the tragedy which developed was "a newspaperman's war." It seems likely that, with better-trained officials and with the knowledge of social conditions that we have today, there need have been no tragedy.

But tragedy there was. Probably we shall never know who fired the first shot, for reports differ. There was enough emotional tinder present so that the tiniest spark could have set it afire. There was a skirmish when a frightened agent sent Indian police, the "metal breasts," to arrest Sitting Bull as a suspicious character. The old man was killed, along with several police and camp Indians. The fire had started. Indians were terrified of whites and whites of Indians. There can be no other explanation for the military cordon that surrounded the band at Wounded Knee Creek as they were moving toward the agency under a flag of truce.

Indians were being searched for weapons and a gun went off. Then began the massacre, for it was nothing less. Most Indians had been disarmed long ago and the search produced only a few guns, beside knives and hatchets used as tools. Without defense, all Big Foot's people could do was run—toward the tents or toward a ravine in the distance. Soldiers and cannon were ranged on three sides of them, and some of these soldiers were survivors from the Custer fight. They rushed among the fleeing men, women, and children with the battle cry "Remember Custer!" Some three hundred Indians were killed or died later of injuries. The whites lost twenty-nine men, mostly from their own crossfire since the Indians had no weapons. It is no wonder that some Sioux to this day seem vindictive and despairing.

The Ghost Dance ceased, and with it ceased all hope that the whites would be conquered or disappear. But, contemporaneous with those whom I have called the "hostile prophets," was the series of visionaries who preached a new religion of the Indians' own. It would not destroy the whites but would teach the Red Men to live in the same world with them, accepting such of their products as seemed useful (of course not the enemy alcohol), but receiving supernatural power through their own visions for their own comfort.

PROPHETS OF COEXISTENCE

Handsome Lake, Iroquois, Pennsylvania and New York, 1789.

Washani religion, Middle Columbia River, early 1800's. By-product of Christianity from scattered sources before white settlement. Some threw away property since whites would bring better. Danced on knees, adopted cross, Sunday, hand bell.

John Slocum, Puget Sound, 1881, Shaker religion, still in force.

Feather Cult, Middle Columbia, 1850 ff. Reaction to Shakers with more Indian features.

Peyote religion. Cult from Mexico perhaps via Mescalero Apache. Now a recognized church in the Plains and Southwest.

Ganioda'yo, the Iroquois, lived at the same time as the hostile Delaware prophet but his people had already suffered from the Revolutionary War in which most of them took the English side. He advised them to live at peace with the whites and even to adopt some of their products, such as the plow. He wanted no new religion. God's messenger had simply told him that the people should go back to their ancient ceremonies, purging them of all that was worldly and profane. In this, Handsome Lake had the approval of Quaker missionaries invited by the Seneca tribe. They felt that the Iroquois ideas of God and the "inner light" of conscience was similar to their own and did not require new Christian forms. Handsome Lake's "new road" with the regular feasts at midwinter, strawberry time, and green corn harvest became the official religion and many in the tribes still have no other.

There were few others in the East to preach coexistence, for the early 1800's were years of movement and turmoil. But the Northwest felt the tremors of change and the need for new beliefs sometime before white settlement had begun. In this area there were no large, organized tribes who could trust their own fighting strength. There were little skirmishes among these groups but, in between fighting, each lived a comfortable life in large wooden houses, with plenty of food in the way of fish, game, and berries. Their country was rich with forests, meadows, and rivers. So when white settlement came, it was not in the form of frontier mines and ranches, guarded by forts. It meant towns, sawmills, canneries, hop fields, churches, and jails. By the 1880's, Indian groups were being pushed into a smaller and smaller compass. Attempts were being made to "stamp out" their native customs and settle them on individual farms. Their response was drunkenness and despair.

"We all felt blind those times. . . ."

"I was drunkard—was half starving—spent every cent on whiskey."[5]

There were missionaries in the country, both Catholic and Protestant, doing valiant work. Indians had plenty of chance to see church services and to hear Christianity preached at logging camps. There were some real converts, the missionaries report. But there were also Indians who admired the symbols seen in church and were willing to use them in their own ceremonies, without having to take over the white man's religion. One such symbol was the little brass hand bell used in the Catholic mass and at mission schools. Indians had no instrument which gave such a clear musical sound, and the hand bell entered their rituals to stay. Another symbol was the cross, in the tall, slender form seen on church steeples. Indians had rarely been hospitable to the idea of the crucifixion as atonement. How could they be, when their rituals never included a scapegoat, nor their theology the need of man's redemption? But new rituals grew up here and there in Washington, Oregon, and California, using a hand bell, a cross, and perhaps the long gown worn by some white clergymen.

The visionary who finally brought the coexistence movement to a head was John Slocum, a Squaxin Indian of Puget Sound. His followers started the Indian Shaker Church, which is still active. Like Wowoka, John died and was resurrected twice. The second time he died was in 1882, when he seemed dead for almost a day and friends had come to bury him. His wife Mary approached the corpse and was taken with a violent fit of trembling. John awoke and told how he had seen God and had been bidden to tell the Indians to give up their evil ways. There was nothing about giving up white man's goods in this religion. In fact, it was

5 Barnett, 1957, p. 339.

a gospel of adaptation to the new life. The things to be given up were the old dances and customs and especially anything having to do with shamanism. Indians were to rely on God and Jesus, who would speak to them directly. This was a message especially for Indians and not for whites. It was *theirs*.

The message had what the Indians wanted. Churches were built, with steeples and inside, large wooden crosses and bells. A ceremony developed with an elaborate processional, chanting, and bell-ringing. It was not like any known ceremony, Indian or white. There was preaching by both a leader and volunteers, somewhat like that of a revival meeting; but there the likeness to white customs stopped. The speaker used a low voice as shamans did at a curing ceremony and an interpreter repeated his words. Important meetings were followed by a feast at which people sat in order of rank as at the old potlatch.

The shaking, begun by Mary Slocum, became a regular sign of spiritual power. There are religious sects among the whites who do something akin to it but there seems to be no connection. Converts at a meeting get "the shake" as visionaries used to at the old spirit dance. Like them, the converts break into an original song which the watchers finally join. But the song has a Christian burden. "I am so glad since Jesus came into my heart!" might be sung to an old curing tune although this would be disapproved of if it were recognized. People speak of their particular "shake" as they used to speak of the spirit which possessed them, and many do make their movements in some special way.

The great strength of the Indian Shakers was in their curing power and other miracles. A sick person, Shaker or not, might call them to his house and a group would shake over him for several nights, praying at intervals. Like the old wonder-working shamans, they sometimes found that his soul had been lost or stolen by the dead. Or an evil shaman might have sent his spirit helper into the patient's body. They made no magic flight, unless the shaking dance can be called such, but they somehow restored souls, found lost objects, and foretold the future.

The religion spread through the Northwest and into California and expressed the new belief in the familiar ancient forms, just as the early Christians used forms from well-known religions which had preceded theirs. The Shakers were sure that their help came from God and Jesus, not from the ancient spirits, but this did not mean that they accepted a whole churchly creed. Many of them did not read the Bible "any more than the first Christians did" said one. Some Shaker churches in the state of Washington felt themselves colleagues of the local Presbyterians and wished to be received into their organization. The Presbyterians refused, but the Shakers continue to regard themselves as a separate branch of the Christian church.

Meantime, in the Plains country, a very different church was forming. After the collapse of the Ghost Dance, the despairing buffalo hunters were at last resigned to a religion of coexistence. They found one in harmony with their ancient customs, for it meant a vision, not only for a single prophet but for all participants. This was the peyote cult, whose sacrament involved the consumption of a plant with dream-inducing qualities—in technical terms, a hallucinogen.

Peyote (*Lophophora williamsii*) is a small cactus with a carrot-like root and one or more bulbous growths above ground which look like Brussels sprouts equipped with thorns. The meat of these can be eaten fresh or dried for storage and then soaked. The root can be cut in pieces and brewed like tea. Taken in sufficient quantities, such as forty buttons or one twenty-fifth of a gram, peyote produces hallucinations, in which actual objects are usually surrounded with magnificent colors. An overdose could ultimately draw oxygen from the brain and produce the same symptoms that very high altitudes do, but this would be hundreds of times the amount taken by an Indian at a meeting. The analysis of peyote shows it to contain eight alkaloids, some stimulating, others depressing, so that many cancel each other out. The most important is mescaline, which is already used in psychological and psychiatric experiments. Studies of peyote so far have not ranked it as habit forming. A furor has occasionally been roused against it as conducive to orgies, but it has turned out that the authors of such accusations have never seen a peyote meeting. Nevertheless, nine western states have laws against its importation except for religious purposes, and the Navaho council has forbidden its use.

Peyote as a source of vision has a long history. The Aztecs were using it 400 years ago. The Huichol of northern Mexico had important rites once a year, when they made a pilgrimage to gather the buttons and then ceremonially consumed them. It is possible that in the late nineteenth century the Kiowa or the Apache, both wandering Plains tribes who raided into Mexico, introduced the narcotic to the United States. Several tribes claim the honor, but none admit that they learned about the vision-producing plant from a human source. The tale usually is that some escaping captive or wandering warrior was visited by the plant itself in human form, was told of its powers for healing and for giving visions, and was bidden to introduce a peyote ceremony. The one that has now become standard had nothing to do with any Mexican ceremony I know of. It was definitely a ritual of the Buffalo Plains and it used their equipment. This meant that it was held in a tipi which faced east, while the leader and his ceremonial objects were at the west. Many of the special properties were those used by Plains dance or shamanistic societies: eagle-feather fans, a feathered staff for the leader, white sage strewn on the tipi floor, incense from cedar needles. But perhaps the Kiowa were especially influential. They had a "ceremony of sacred stones" in which the company sat in a circle around an "earthen, crescent-shaped altar" which held stones with spirit power.

Such an arrangement was to be seen at the peyote ceremony. On the altar was a specially large button, the "peyote chief." The leader, known as the Road Man, held a feathered staff and a rattle. Beside him sat the Drum Chief, with a water drum, either a wide-mouthed jar, or, in later years, an iron kettle fitted with a deerskin top. There might also be a Cedar Man, carrying a buckskin bag of cedar needles; and at the door sat the Fire Man. It was his duty to make and replenish the fire of four logs placed with the butts at the center, and the tips pointing in the four directions.

A meeting of this sort has been described in Chapter 1. It ended with the statement from the leader that he prayed for all people, even the Germans.

"Was it Peyote to whom you prayed?" I asked.

"Peyote, God, Christ, Great Spirit. All the same Power."

One should not try to analyze such a cosmic conception as this, but I did attempt it once. "Does your prayer have the same kind of words used in some churches—very humble, begging?"

"Begging?" He looked puzzled. "Talk like a friend. Like to you." The new religion still maintains its Indian pattern.

The Drum Chief also prayed, and sometimes I have heard others do it. Then came the opening song. The Road Man sang it, holding the staff upright in one hand and shaking a rattle with the other.

> Now we begin.
> I look to you.
> Look on me and on these people.
> Help us as we meet here.

Of course the song was repeated four times.

Now the essential ritual began. Starting from the leader, in a clockwise circuit, each man shook his rattle and sang. His left-hand neighbor drummed if he wished, or else the Drum Chief took the position and officiated. Meantime, the peyote was passed. Each of us was instructed to take four buttons. In this case, they were fresh and one pulled off the spines to eat them. I have also eaten them dried or have drunk the tea. The taste is nauseating. No one, certainly, would nibble peyote for pleasure and I have frequently heard the statement: "This peyote is a *hard* road."

No vision came to me; I was too much occupied in controlling nausea. But, as the drumming and singing went on, I saw heads nodding like metronomes. The dull red glow of the fire was hypnotic. Indians have told me that at this time they have seen guardian spirits, as of old. Some saw angels, or God, and had a conviction that they could live better.

At midnight, water was brought by a chosen woman, since carrying water is always a woman's task. She set down the pail with its one tin cup, smoked a corn husk cigarette and prayed.

Then four midnight songs were sung and we all went outside, where the leader blew a bird-bone whistle to the four directions "to tell the birds about us."

After midnight, the atmosphere was very different. We had been working to dispel evil, now we were to accept the good. A lame woman was brought in and each person prayed for her. She ate peyote and was incensed with cedar smoke. More peyote was passed, and one by one the participants testified. It sounded to me somewhat like prayer meetings I have attended, and somewhat like the meetings of Plains societies when warriors recounted their exploits. Now the exploits were less glamorous and more difficult.

"This peyote is a hard road. I used to drink, but now I don't."

"I used to beat my wife."

"I used to leave jobs."

Such were the testimonies. They were often spoken in English because those attending were from five tribes of different languages.

When the first fleck of light showed through the smoke hole the dawn songs were sung and then the food was brought, again by a woman. It was old Indian food—or as nearly traditional as possible—beef, corn, berries, and water. We ate from a common dish; then came the closing prayer and we moved out toward the rising sun.

It is plain that this kind of ceremony is no orgy. It comes close to a church service, yet it is not the white man's conception of a service. Indians have told me with real passion: "It belongs to *us*. Peyote came to Indians, not to the whites." That declaration made me understand how important to an Indian was the social side of church membership. The new Christian convert did not often sit in a front pew, with a well-dressed congregation. He felt that he was herded into a corner, or else there was a special chapel and special service for Indians.

It is no wonder that the peyote cult swept through the Plains, filling the vacuum left by the Ghost Dance. In 1941 the cult was incorporated as the Native American Church of Oklahoma; in

1945 as the Native American Church of the United States. Unlike the old Indian religious groups, this church sends out missionaries. They went from Oklahoma ultimately to the Utes and from the Utes to the Navaho. No stern governing body dictates the kind of service to be held, so each tribe adapts the singing, praying, and speaking to its own background. I know one Indian who goes to a ceremony every Saturday night. He told me: "That's what keeps me going, keeps me happy and working."

Some Christians may not realize how much satisfaction they derive from the companionship of church membership as well as from the worship itself. The Indian religions of Shakerism and Peyote are supplying that companionship which many do not get in the Christian church. Perhaps they will in future, for many Christians are now awakening to this need. Among the Indians, there are today thousands of really convinced church members. Perhaps they will have something to contribute to Christianity's future.

REFERENCES

Messianic movements: Linton, 1943; Wallace, 1956.

Descriptions of special movements: Barnett, 1957 (Shakerism); Deardorff, 1951 (Iroquois); Miller, 1959 and Mooney, 1896 (Ghost dance); La Barre, 1960, Radin, 1926, Slotkin, 1956, Stewart, 1948 (Peyotism).

Studies of change among various Indian groups: Joseph, Spicer, and Chesky, 1949 (Papago); Linton, 1940 (seven tribes); Rapoport, 1954 (Navaho); Ray, 1957 (Eskimo, Iroquois, Yuman); Spicer, 1961 (Yaqui, Pueblos, Mandan, Navaho, Wasco-Wishram, Kwakiutl); Thompson, 1950 (Hopi).

BIBLIOGRAPHY

ALEXANDER, HARTLEY B., 1916. *North American Mythology.* (*The Mythology of All Races in Thirteen Volumes*, Vol. X, ed. LOUIS H. GRAY, Boston: Marshall Jones Company.)

Anthropological Records. Berkeley and Los Angeles: University of California Press.

ARMILLAS, PEDRO, 1964. "Northern Mesoamerica," in *Prehistoric Man in the New World*, eds. JESSE D. JENNINGS and EDWARD NORBECK. (Rice University Semicentennial Publications.) Chicago: University of Chicago Press, pp. 291–329.

BARBEAU, MARIUS, no date. *Totem Poles.* (National Museum of Canada Bull. 119, Vol. I.)

BARNETT, H. G., 1957. *Indian Shakers.* Carbondale: Southern Illinois University Press.

BARRETT, S. A., 1917. *Ceremonies of the Pomo Indians.* (University of California Publications in American Archaeology and Ethnology, Vol. XII, No. 10.) Berkeley: University of California Press.

BENEDICT, RUTH, 1922. "The Vision in Plains Culture," *American Anthropologist* (New Series), XXIV, 1–23.

———, 1923. *The Concept of the Guardian Spirit in North America.* (Memoirs of the American Anthropological Association, 29.) Menasha, Wis.

BERTHRONG, DONALD J., 1963. *The Southern Cheyennes.* Norman: University of Oklahoma Press.

BIRKET-SMITH, KAJ, 1965. *The Paths of Culture: A General Ethnology.*

Translated from the Danish by KARIN FENNOW. Madison: University of Wisconsin Press.

BLAIR, EMMA H., 1912. *The Indian Tribes of the Upper Mississippi Valley and Region of the Great Lakes*, Vol. II. Cleveland: The Arthur H. Clark Company.

BLUMENSOHN, JULES, 1933. "The Fast among North American Indians," *American Anthropologist* (New Series), XXXV, 451–69.

BOAS, FRANZ, 1888. "The Central Eskimo." *6th Annual Report of the Bureau of Ethnology*. Washington, D.C.: Government Printing Office, pp. 399–669.

———, 1930. *The Religion of the Kwakiutl Indians, Part II.* (Columbia University Contributions to Anthropology, Vol. X.) New York: Columbia University Press.

BOGORAS, WALDEMAR, 1902. "The Folklore of Northeastern Asia, as Compared with That of Northwestern America," *American Anthropologist*, Vol. IV.

———, 1904–9. "The Chukchee." (*The Jesup North Pacific Expedition*, ed. FRANZ BOAS, Vol. VII.) New York: G. E. Stechert.

BOURKE, JOHN G., 1892. "The Medicine-Men of the Apache," *9th Annual Report of the Bureau of Ethnology*. Washington, D.C.: Government Printing Office, pp. 443–603.

BOWERS, ALFRED W., 1950. *Mandan Social and Ceremonial Organization.* Chicago: University of Chicago Press.

BRAIDWOOD, ROBERT J., and WILLEY, GORDON R. (eds.), 1962. *Courses toward Urban Life.* (Viking Fund Publications in Anthropology No. 32.) New York: Wenner-Gren Foundation for Anthropological Research, Inc.

BROWN, JOSEPH EPES (recorder and editor), 1953. *The Sacred Pipe: Black Elk's Account of the Seven Rites of the Oglala Sioux.* Norman: University of Oklahoma Press.

BUNZEL, RUTH L., 1932a. "Introduction to Zuni Ceremonialism," *47th Annual Report of the Bureau of American Ethnology*. Washington, D.C.: Government Printing Office, pp. 467–544.

———, 1932b. "Zuni Katcinas," *47th Annual Report of the Bureau of American Ethnology*. Washington, D.C.: Government Printing Office, pp. 837–1086.

———, 1932c. "Zuni Origin Myths," *47th Annual Report of the Bureau of American Ethnology*. Washington, D.C.: Government Printing Office, pp. 545–609.

———, 1932d. "Zuni Ritual Poetry," *47th Annual Report of the Bureau of American Ethnology*. Washington, D.C.: Government Printing Office, pp. 611–835.

BUSHNELL, DAVID I., JR., 1909. *The Choctaw of Bayou Lacomb, St. Tam-*

many Parish, Louisiana. (Bureau of American Ethnology Bull. 48.) Washington, D.C.: Government Printing Office.

——, 1920. *Native Cemeteries and Forms of Burial East of the Mississippi.* (Bureau of American Ethnology Bull. 71.) Washington, D.C.: Government Printing Office.

——, 1927. *Burials of the Algonquian, Siouan and Caddoan Tribes West of the Mississippi.* (Bureau of American Ethnology Bull. 83.) Washington, D.C.: Government Printing Office.

CALDWELL, JOSEPH R., 1962. "Eastern North America," in *Courses toward Urban Life,* eds. ROBERT J. BRAIDWOOD and GORDON R. WILLEY. (Viking Fund Publications in Anthropology No. 32.) New York: Wenner-Gren Foundation for Anthropological Research, Inc., pp. 288–308.

CAMPBELL, JOHN M., 1964. "Ancient Man in a Cold Climate: Eskimo Origins" (review of J. L. GIDDINGS' *The Archeology of Cape Denbigh*), *Science,* CXLV, 913–15.

CASTETTER, EDWARD F., and BELL, WILLIS H., 1951. *Yuman Indian Agriculture.* Albuquerque: University of New Mexico Press.

CATLIN, GEORGE, 1959. *Episodes from "Life among the Indians" and "Last Rambles,"* ed. MARVIN C. ROSSE. Norman: University of Oklahoma Press.

CHAFE, WALLACE L., 1961. *Seneca Thanksgiving Rituals.* (Bureau of American Ethnology Bull. 183.) Washington, D.C.: Government Printing Office.

CHARD, CHESTER S., 1960. "Routes to Bering Strait" (abstract). *American Antiquity,* XXVI, 283–85.

CLEMENTS, FORREST E., 1932. *Primitive Concepts of Disease.* (University of California Publications in American Archaeology and Ethnology, Vol. XXXII, No. 2.) Berkeley: University of California Press.

CODRINGTON, R. H., 1891. *The Melanesians.* Oxford: The Clarendon Press. (Paperback, New Haven: HRAF Press, 1957.)

COE, MICHAEL D., and FLANNERY, KENT V., 1964. "Microenvironments and Mesoamerican Prehistory," *Science,* CXLIII, 650–54.

COLLINS, HENRY B., 1964. "The Arctic and Subarctic," in *Prehistoric Man in the New World,* eds. JESSE D. JENNINGS and EDWARD NORBECK. (Rice University Semicentennial Publications.) Chicago: University of Chicago Press, pp. 85–114.

COON, CARLETON S., 1962. *The Origin of Races.* New York: Alfred A. Knopf.

COUNT, EARL W., 1952. "The Earth-Diver and the Rival Twins: A Clue to Time Correlation in North-Eurasiatic and North American Mythology," in *Indian Tribes of Aboriginal America,* ed. SOL TAX. (Selected Papers of the XXIXth International Congress of Americanists.) Chicago: University of Chicago Press, pp. 55–62.

DAIFUKU, HIROSHI, 1952. "A New Conceptual Scheme for Prehistoric Cultures in the Southwestern United States," *American Anthropologist,* LIV, 191–200.

DEARDORFF, MERLE H., 1951. "The Religion of Handsome Lake: Its Origin and Development," in *Symposium on Local Diversity in Iroquois Culture,* ed. W. N. FENTON. (Bureau of American Ethnology Bull. 149.) Washington, D.C.: Government Printing Office, pp. 77–107.

DENSMORE, FRANCES, 1929. *Chippewa Customs.* (Bureau of American Ethnology Bull. 86.) Washington, D.C.: Government Printing Office.

——, 1932. *Menominee Music.* (Bureau of American Ethnology Bull. 102.) Washington, D.C.: Government Printing Office.

——, 1939. *Nootka and Quileute Music.* (Bureau of American Ethnology Bull. 124.) Washington, D.C.: Government Printing Office.

DEVEREUX, G., 1937. "Mohave Soul Concepts," *American Anthropologist* (New Series), XXXIX, 417–22.

DEVEREUX, GEORGE, 1961. *Mohave Ethnopsychiatry and Suicide: The Psychiatric Knowledge and the Psychic Disturbances of an Indian Tribe.* (Bureau of American Ethnology Bull. 175.) Washington, D.C.: Government Printing Office.

DIXON, ROLAND B., 1902. *Maidu Myths.* (American Museum of Natural History Bull. 17.) New York.

DORSEY, GEORGE A., 1904. *Traditions of the Skidi Pawnee.* (Memoirs of the American Folk-Lore Society, Vol. VIII.) Richmond, Va.

DORSEY, JAMES O., 1894. "A Study of Siouan Cults," *11th Annual Report of the Bureau of Ethnology.* Washington, D.C.: Government Printing Office, pp. 351–544.

DRIVER, HAROLD E., 1939. *Culture Element Distributions: X, Northwest California.* (Anthropological Records, Vol. I, No. 6.) Berkeley: University of California Press.

——, 1941. *Culture Element Distributions: XVI, Girls' Puberty Rites in Western North America.* (Anthropological Records, Vol. VI, No. 2.) Berkeley: University of California Press.

——, 1961. *Indians of North America.* Chicago: University of Chicago Press.

DRIVER, HAROLD E., and MASSEY, WILLIAM C., 1957. *Comparative Studies of North American Indians.* (Transactions of the American Philosophical Society [New Series], XLVII, Part II.) Philadelphia.

DRUCKER, PHILIP, 1955. *Indians of the Northwest Coast.* (Anthropological Handbook No. 10. Published for the American Museum of Natural History.) New York: McGraw-Hill Book Company, Inc.

DuBOIS, CONSTANCE G., 1908. *The Religion of the Luiseño Indians of Southern California.* (University of California Publications in American

Archaeology and Ethnology, Vol. VIII, No. 3.) Berkeley: University of California Press.

DURKHEIM, EMILE, 1954. *The Elementary Forms of the Religious Life.* Translated from the French by JOSEPH WARD SWAIN. 3d edition. London: George Allen & Unwin, Ltd.

EASTMAN, CHARLES A., 1911. *The Soul of the Indian.* Boston: Houghton Mifflin Company.

ELIADE, MIRCEA, 1949. *Traité d'Histoire des Religions.* Paris: Payot.

——, 1951. *Le Chamanisme et les Techniques Archaïques de L'extase.* Paris: Payot.

ELMENDORF, WILLIAM W., 1952. "Soul Loss Illness in Western North America," in *Indian Tribes of Aboriginal America,* ed. SOL TAX. (Selected Papers of the XXIXth International Congress of Americanists.) Chicago: University of Chicago Press, 1952, pp. 104–14.

EWERS, JOHN C., 1958. *The Blackfeet, Raiders on the Northwestern Plains.* Norman: University of Oklahoma Press.

FAIRBANKS, CHARLES H., 1952. "Creek and Pre-Creek," in *Archeology of Eastern United States,* ed. JAMES B. GRIFFIN. Chicago: University of Chicago Press, pp. 285–300.

FENTON, W. N., 1936. *An Outline of Seneca Ceremonies at Coldspring Longhouse.* (Yale University Publications in Anthropology No. 9.) New Haven: Yale University Press.

——, 1940. *Museum and Field Studies of Iroquois Masks and Ritualism.* (Explorations and Field Work of the Smithsonian Institution.) Washington, D.C.

FEWKES, J. W., 1893. "The Pa-lü-lü-kon-ti," *Journal of American Folk-Lore,* VI, 269–82.

——, 1894. "The Walpi Flute Observance," *Journal of American Folk-Lore,* VII, 265–87.

——, 1897a. "Tusayan Katcinas," *15th Annual Report of the Bureau of Ethnology.* Washington, D.C.: Government Printing Office, pp. 245–313.

——, 1897b. "Tusayan Snake Ceremonies," *16th Annual Report of the Bureau of American Ethnology.* Washington, D.C.: Government Printing Office, pp. 267–312.

——, 1900a. "The New-Fire Ceremony at Walpi," *American Anthropologist* (New Series), II, 80–138.

——, 1900b. "Tusayan Flute and Snake Ceremonies," *19th Annual Report of the Bureau of American Ethnology, Part II.* Washington, D.C.: Government Printing Office, pp. 957–1011.

——, 1900c. "Tusayan Migration Traditions," *19th Annual Report of the Bureau of American Ethnology, Part II.* Washington, D.C.: Government Printing Office, pp. 573–633.

FLANNERY, REGINA, 1939. "The Shaking-Tent Rite among the Montagnais of James Bay," *Primitive Man*, XII, 11–16.

FLETCHER, ALICE C., 1904. "The Hako: A Pawnee Ceremony," *22nd Annual Report of the Bureau of American Ethnology, Part II*. Washington, D.C.: Government Printing Office.

FLETCHER, ALICE C., and LA FLESCHE, FRANCIS, 1911. "The Omaha Tribe," *27th Annual Report of the Bureau of American Ethnology*. Washington, D.C.: Government Printing Office.

FORDE, C. DARYLL, 1931. *Ethnography of the Yuma Indians*. (University of California Publications in American Archaeology and Ethnology, Vol. XXVIII, No. 4.) Berkeley: University of California Press.

FRAZER, SIR JAMES G., 1910. *Totemism and Exogamy*. 4 vols. London: The Macmillan Company.

——, 1922. *The Golden Bough: A Study in Magic and Religion*. (Abridged ed., 1 vol.) New York: The Macmillan Company.

——, 1936. *The Fear of the Dead in Primitive Religion*, Vol. III. London: Macmillan and Co., Ltd.

FREUD, SIGMUND, 1950. *Totem and Taboo*. London: Routledge & Kegan Paul Ltd. (Paperback, New York: W. W. Norton & Company, Inc., 1962.)

GARFIELD, VIOLA E., and FORREST, LINN A., 1948. *The Wolf and the Raven*. Seattle: University of Washington Press.

GAYTON, A. H., 1930. *Yokuts-Mono Chiefs and Shamans*. (University of California Publications in American Archaeology and Ethnology, Vol. XXIV, No. 8.) Berkeley: University of California Press.

——, 1935. "The Orpheus Myth in North America," *Journal of American Folk-Lore*, XLVIII, 263–93.

GENNEP, ARNOLD VAN, 1960. *The Rites of Passage*. Translated by MONIKA B. VIZEDOM and GABRIELLE L. CAFFEE. Chicago: University of Chicago Press.

GIDDINGS, J. L., 1960. "The Archeology of Bering Strait," *Current Anthropology*, I, 121–38.

——, 1964. *The Archeology of Cape Denbigh*. Providence: Brown University Press.

GIFFORD, EDWARD WINSLOW, 1916. *Miwok Moieties*. (University of California Publications in American Archaeology and Ethnology, Vol. XII, No. 4.) Berkeley: University of California Press.

GJESSING, GUTORM, 1944. "Circumpolar Stone Age." *Acta Arctica*, Fasc. II. Copenhagen.

GOLDFRANK, ESTHER SCHIFF, 1927. *The Social and Ceremonial Organization of Cochiti*. (Memoirs of the American Anthropological Association No. 33.) Menasha, Wis.

GOODE, WILLIAM J., 1951. *Religion among the Primitives*. Glencoe: The Free Press.

GRIFFIN, JAMES B., 1952. "Prehistoric Cultures of the Central Mississippi Valley," in *Archaeology of Eastern United States*, pp. 226–38.

——, 1964. "The Northeast Woodlands Area," in *Prehistoric Man in the New World*, eds. JESSE D. JENNINGS and EDWARD NORBECK. (Rice University Semicentennial Publications.) Chicago: University of Chicago Press, pp. 223–58.

GRINNELL, GEORGE B., 1889. *Pawnee Hero Stories and Folk-Tales*. New York: Forest and Stream Publishing Company. (Paperback, Lincoln: University of Nebraska Press, 1961.)

——, 1923. *The Cheyenne Indians, Their History and Ways of Life*. 2 vols. New Haven: Yale University Press.

GUNTHER, ERNA, 1926. "An Analysis of the First Salmon Ceremony," *American Anthropologist*, XXVIII, 605–17.

——, 1928. *A Further Analysis of the First Salmon Ceremony*. (University of Washington Publications in Anthropology, Vol. II, No. 5.) Seattle: University of Washington Press.

HAAG, WILLIAM G., 1962. "The Bering Strait Land Bridge," *Scientific American*, CCVI, 112–23.

HAILE, BERARD, 1938. *Origin Legend of the Navaho Enemy Way*. (Yale University Publications in Anthropology No. 17.) New Haven: Yale University Press.

——, 1943. *Origin Legend of the Navaho Flintway*. (University of Chicago Publications in Anthropology, Linguistic Series.) Chicago: University of Chicago Press.

HALLOWELL, A. IRVING, 1926. "Bear Ceremonialism in the Northern Hemisphere," *American Anthropologist* (New Series), XXVIII, 1–175.

——, 1934. "Some Empirical Aspects of Northern Salteaux Religion," *American Anthropologist* (New Series), XXXVI, 389–404.

HAMILTON, HENRY W., *et al.*, 1952. "The Spiro Mound," *The Missouri Archaeologist*, Vol. XIV.

HARRINGTON, M. R., 1921. *Religion and Ceremonies of the Lenape*. (Indian Notes and Monographs, Series 2, No. 19.) New York: Museum of the American Indian, Heye Foundation.

HASSRICK, ROYAL B., 1964. *The Sioux, Life and Customs of a Warrior Society*. Norman: University of Oklahoma Press.

HAURY, EMIL W., 1962. "The Greater American Southwest," in *Courses toward Urban Life*, eds. ROBERT J. BRAIDWOOD and GORDON R. WILLEY. (Viking Fund Publications in Anthropology No. 32.) New York: Wenner-Gren Foundation for Anthropological Research, Inc.

HAYNES, C. VANCE, JR., 1964. "Fluted Projectile Points: Their Age and Dispersion," *Science*, CXLV, 1408–13.

HEIZER, R. F., and WHIPPLE, M. A. (eds.), 1962. *The California Indians*. Berkeley and Los Angeles: University of California Press.

HERTZ, ROBERT, 1960. *Death and the Right Hand*. Translated by RODNEY and CLAUDIA NEEDHAM. Glencoe: The Free Press.

HEWITT, J. N. B., 1903. "Iroquoian Cosmology," *21st Annual Report of the Bureau of American Ethnology*. Washington, D.C.: Government Printing Office, pp. 127–339.

———, 1910. *Orenda*. (Bureau of American Ethnology Bull. 30.) Washington. D.C.: Government Printing Office.

———, 1928. "Iroquoian Cosmology, Second Part," *43rd Annual Report of the Bureau of American Ethnology*. Washington, D.C.: Government Printing Office, pp. 449–819.

HILL, W. W., 1936. *Navaho Warfare*. (Yale University Publications in Anthropology No. 5.) New Haven: Yale University Press.

———, 1938. *The Agricultural and Hunting Methods of the Navaho Indians*. (Yale University Publications in Anthropology No. 18.) New Haven: Yale University Press.

HODGE, FREDERICK WEBB (ed.), 1910. *Handbook of American Indians, Part II*. (Bureau of American Ethnology Bull. 30.) Washington, D.C.: Government Printing Office.

HOFFMAN, W. J., 1891. "The Midē'wiwin or 'Grand Medicine Society' of the Ojibwa," *7th Annual Report of the Bureau of Ethnology*. Washington, D.C.: Government Printing Office, pp. 143–300.

———, 1896. "The Menomini Indians," *14th Annual Report of the Bureau of Ethnology, Part I*. Washington, D.C.: Government Printing Office, pp. 3–328.

HOIJER, HARRY, 1938. *Chiricahua and Mescalero Apache Texts*. (University of Chicago Publications in Anthropology, Linguistic Series.) Chicago: University of Chicago Press.

HOLMBERG, UNO, 1964. *Finno-Ugric, Siberian*. (*The Mythology of All Races in Thirteen Volumes*, Vol. IV, eds. CANON JOHN A. MacCULLOCH and GEORGE F. MOORE.) New York: Cooper Square Publishers, Inc.

HONIGMANN, JOHN J., 1946. *Ethnography and Acculturation of the Fort Nelson Slave*. (Yale University Publications in Anthropology No. 33.) New Haven: Yale University Press.

———, 1949. *Culture and Ethos of Kaska Society*. (Yale University Publications in Anthropology No. 40.) New Haven: Yale University Press.

HSU, F. L. K., 1952. *Religion, Science and Human Crises*. London: Routledge & Kegan Paul Ltd.

HULTKRANTZ, ÅKE, 1953. *Conceptions of the Soul among North American Indians*. (The Ethnographical Museum of Sweden, Stockholm, Monograph Series, Publication No. 1.) Stockholm: Caslon Press.

———, 1957. *The North American Indian Orpheus Tradition*. Stockholm: Caslon Press.

——, 1961. Reprint from *The Supernatural Owners of Nature*. (Stockholm Studies in Comparative Religion No. 1.) Stockholm: Almqvist & Wiksell, pp. 53–64.

HUNT, GEORGE T., 1940. *The Wars of the Iroquois: A Study in Intertribal Trade Relations*. Madison: University of Wisconsin Press.

INVERARITY, ROBERT BRUCE, 1950. *Art of the Northwest Coast Indians*. Berkeley: University of California Press.

JENNESS, DIAMOND, 1935. *The Ojibwa Indians of Parry Island, Their Social and Religious Life*. (National Museum of Canada Bull. 78, Anthropological Series No. 17.) Ottawa.

——, 1955. *The Indians of Canada*. (National Museum of Canada Bull. 65, Anthropological Series No. 15.) Ottawa.

JENNINGS, JESSE D., 1952. "Prehistory of the Lower Mississippi Valley," in *Archeology of Eastern United States*, ed. JAMES B. GRIFFIN. Chicago: University of Chicago Press, pp. 256–71.

——, 1964. "The Desert West," in *Prehistoric Man in the New World*, eds. JESSE D. JENNINGS and EDWARD NORBECK. (Rice University Semicentennial Publications.) Chicago: University of Chicago Press.

JENNINGS, JESSE D., and NORBECK, EDWARD (eds.), 1964. *Prehistoric Man in the New World*. (Rice University Semicentennial Publications.) Chicago: University of Chicago Press.

JENSEN, ADOLF E., 1963. *Myth and Cult among Primitive Peoples*. Translated by MARIANNA TAX CHOLDIN and WOLFGANG WEISSLEDER. Chicago: University of Chicago Press.

JOCHELSON, W., 1908. "The Koryak," in *The Jesup North Pacific Expedition*, ed. FRANZ BOAS, Vol. VI. New York: G. E. Stechert.

——, 1926. "The Yukaghir and the Yukaghirized Tungus." (*The Jesup North Pacific Expedition*, ed. FRANK BOAS, Vol. IX.) New York: G. E. Stechert.

JOHNSON, FREDERICK (ed.), 1946. *Man in Northeastern North America*. (Papers of the Robert S. Peabody Foundation for Archaeology, Vol. III.) Andover: Phillips Academy.

JONES, WILLIAM, 1905. "The Algonkin Manitou," *Journal of American Folk-Lore*, XVIII, 183–90.

——, 1939. *Ethnography of the Fox Indians*. (Bureau of American Ethnology Bull. 125.) Washington, D.C.: Government Printing Office.

JOSEPH, ALICE, SPICER, ROSAMOND B., and CHESKY, JANE, 1949. *The Desert People*. Chicago: University of Chicago Press.

KARSTEN, RAFAEL, 1935. *The Origins of Religion*. London: Kegan Paul, Trench, Trubner & Co., Ltd.

KELLEY, J. CHARLES, 1952. "Some Geographic and Cultural Factors Involved in Mexican-Southeastern Contacts," in *Indian Tribes of Aborig-*

inal America, ed. Sol Tax. (Selected Papers of the XXIXth International Congress of Americanists.) Chicago: University of Chicago Press.

Kelly, Isabel T., 1939. *Southern Paiute Shamanism.* (Anthropological Records, Vol. II, No. 4.) Berkeley: University of California Press.

Kinietz, W. Vernon, 1940. *The Indians of the Western Great Lakes, 1615–1760.* (Occasional Contributions from the Museum of Anthropology of the University of Michigan No. 10.) Ann Arbor: University of Michigan Press.

Kluckhohn, Clyde, 1942. "Myths and Rituals: A General Theory," *The Harvard Theological Review,* 35, pp. 45–79.

———, 1944. *Navaho Witchcraft.* (Papers of the Peabody Museum of American Archaeology and Ethnology, Harvard University, Vol. XXII, No. 2.) Cambridge: Peabody Museum of American Archaeology and Ethnology.

Kluckhohn, Clyde, and Leighton, Dorothea, 1946. *The Navaho.* Cambridge: Harvard University Press.

Kramer, Samuel N. (ed.), 1961. *Mythologies of the Ancient World.* Chicago: Quadrangle Books, Inc.

Krause, Aurel, 1956. *The Tlingit Indians.* Translated by Erna Gunther. Seattle: University of Washington Press.

Krieger, Alex D., 1964. "Early Man in the New World," in *Prehistoric Man in the New World,* eds. Jesse D. Jennings and Edward Norbeck. (Rice University Semicentennial Publications.) Chicago: University of Chicago Press, pp. 28–81.

Kroeber, Alfred L., 1925. *Handbook of the Indians of California.* (Bureau of American Ethnology Bull. 78.) Washington, D.C.: Government Printing Office.

———, 1939. *Cultural and Natural Areas of Native North America.* Berkeley: University of California Press.

———, 1952. *The Nature of Culture.* Chicago: University of Chicago Press.

Kroeber, Alfred L., and Gifford, E. W., 1949. *World Renewal: A Cult System of Native Northwest California.* (Anthropological Records, Vol. XIII, No. 1.) Berkeley: University of California Press.

Kurath, Gertrude P., 1964. *Iroquois Music and Dance: Ceremonial Arts of Two Seneca Longhouses.* (Bureau of American Ethnology Bull. 187.) Washington, D.C.: Government Printing Office.

La Barre, Weston, 1960. "Twenty Years of Peyote Studies," *Current Anthropology,* I, 45–60.

La Flesche, Francis, 1921. "The Osage Tribe: Rite of the Chiefs; Sayings of the Ancient Men," *36th Annual Report of the Bureau of American Ethnology.* Washington, D.C.: Government Printing Office, pp. 37–597.

———, 1925. "The Osage Tribe: Rite of Vigil," *39th Annual Report of the*

Bureau of American Ethnology. Washington, D.C.: Government Printing Office, pp. 31–630.

——, 1930. "The Osage Tribe: Rite of the Wa-xó-be," *45th Annual Report of the Bureau of American Ethnology.* Washington, D.C.: Government Printing Office, pp. 523–833.

——, 1939. *War Ceremony and Peace Ceremony of the Osage Indians.* (Bureau of American Ethnology Bull. 101.) Washington, D.C.: Government Printing Office.

LANTIS, MARGARET, 1938. "The Alaskan Whale Cult and Its Affinities," *American Anthropologist,* XL, 438–64.

LASKI, VERA, 1959. *Seeking Life.* (Memoirs of the American Folklore Society, Vol. L.) Philadelphia.

LAUGHLIN, WILLIAM S., 1963. "Eskimos and Aleuts: Their Origins and Evolution," *Science,* CXLII, 633–45.

LÉVI-STRAUSS, CLAUDE, 1962. *Le totémisme aujourd'hui.* Presses Universitaires de France. (Paperback, *Totemism,* translated by RODNEY NEEDHAM. Boston: Beacon Press, 1963.)

LINTON, RALPH, 1922*a. The Thunder Ceremony of the Pawnee.* (Field Museum of Natural History Leaflet No. 5.) Chicago.

——, 1922*b. The Sacrifice to the Morning Star by the Skidi Pawnee.* (Field Museum of Natural History Leaflet No. 6.) Chicago.

——, 1923. *Annual Ceremony of the Pawnee Medicine Men.* (Field Museum of Natural History Leaflet No. 8.) Chicago.

——, 1936. *The Study of Man.* New York: D. Appleton-Century Company, Inc.

——, (ed.), 1940. *Acculturation in Seven American Indian Tribes.* New York: D. Appleton-Century Company, Inc.

——, 1943. "Nativistic Movements," *American Anthropologist,* XLV, 230–40.

LOEB, E. M., 1929. "Shaman and Seer," *American Anthropologist,* XXXI, 60–84.

——, 1932. *The Western Kuksu Cult.* (University of California Publications in American Archaeology and Ethnology, Vol. XXXIII, No. 1.) Berkeley: University of California Press.

LOWIE, ROBERT H., 1922. *The Religion of the Crow Indians.* (Anthropological Papers of the American Museum of Natural History, Vol. XXV, Part II.) New York, pp. 309–444.

——, 1924. *Primitive Religion.* New York: Boni and Liveright, Inc.

——, 1935. *The Crow Indians.* New York: Holt, Rinehart and Winston. (Paperback, 1956.)

——, 1947. *Primitive Society.* New York: Liveright Publishing Corp.

——, 1954. *Indians of the Plains.* (Anthropological Handbook No. 1 pub-

lished for the American Museum of Natural History.) New York: Mc-
Graw-Hill Book Company, Inc.

LUMHOLTZ, CARL, 1912. *New Trails in Mexico*. New York: Charles Scribner's Sons.

McALLESTER, DAVID P., 1954. *Enemy Way Music: A Study of Social and
Esthetic Values as Seen in Navaho Music*. (Papers of the Peabody
Museum of American Archaeology and Ethnology, Harvard Univer-
sity, Vol. XLI, No. 3.) Cambridge: Peabody Museum of American
Archaeology and Ethnology.

McKENNAN, ROBERT A., 1959. *The Upper Tanana Indians*. (Yale University Publications in Anthropology No. 55.) New Haven: Yale University Press.

MALINOWSKI, BRONISLAW, 1922. *Argonauts of the Western Pacific*. London. (Paperback, New York: E. P. Dutton and Co., Inc., 1961.)

———, 1948. *Magic, Science and Religion and Other Essays*. (Text edition.)
Glencoe: Free Press.

MANDELBAUM, DAVID G. (ed.), 1949. *Selected Writings of Edward Sapir
in Language, Culture and Personality*. Berkeley: University of California
Press.

MANGELSDORF, PAUL C., MacNEISH, RICHARD S., and GALINAT, WALTON C.,
1964. "Domestication of Corn," *Science*, CXLIII, 538–45.

MARTIN, PAUL S., QUIMBY, GEORGE I., and COLLIER, DONALD, 1947. *Indians
before Columbus*. Chicago: University of Chicago Press.

MASON, J. ALDEN, 1943. "Summary on the Cultural Relations between
Northern Mexico and Southeastern United States," in *El Norte de
Mexico y El Sur de Estados Unidos*. (Tercera Reunión de Mesa Redonda
sobre Problemas Antropológicos de México y Centro América.) Mexico,
D.F.: Castillo de Chapultepec, pp. 348–51.

MASON, RONALD J., 1962. "The Paleo-Indian Tradition in Eastern North
America," *Current Anthropology*, III, 227–78.

MATTHEWS, WASHINGTON, 1897. *Navaho Legends*. (Memoirs of the American Folk-Lore Society, Vol. V.) Philadelphia.

———, 1902. *The Night Chant*. (Memoirs of the American Museum of Natural History, Vol. VI.) New York.

MERRIAM, C. HART, 1955. *Studies of California Indians*. (Edited by the
staff of the Department of Anthropology of the University of California Press.) Berkeley and Los Angeles: University of California Press.

MICHELSON, TRUMAN, 1925. "Notes on Fox Mortuary Customs and Beliefs," *40th Annual Report of the Bureau of American Ethnology*.
Washington, D.C.: Government Printing Office, pp. 351–496.

———, 1927. *Contributions to Fox Ethnology*. (Bureau of American Ethnology Bull. 85.) Washington, D.C.: Government Printing Office.

——, 1929. *Observations on the Thunder Dance of the Bear Gens of the Fox Indians.* (Bureau of American Ethnology Bull. 89.) Washington, D.C.: Government Printing Office.

——, 1930. *Contributions to Fox Ethnology—II.* (Bureau of American Ethnology Bull. 95.) Washington, D.C.: Government Printing Office.

——, 1932. *Notes on the Fox Wâpanōwiweni.* (Bureau of American Ethnology Bull. 105.) Washington, D.C.: Government Printing Office.

MILLER, DAVID H., 1959. *Ghost Dance.* New York: Duell, Sloan and Pearce.

MISHKIN, BERNARD, 1940. *Rank and Warfare among the Plains Indians.* (Monographs of the American Ethnological Society, III.) New York: J. J. Augustin.

MOONEY, JAMES, 1891. "The Sacred Formulas of the Cherokees," *7th Annual Report of the Bureau of Ethnology.* Washington, D.C.: Government Printing Office, pp. 301–97.

——, 1896. "The Ghost-Dance Religion and the Sioux Outbreak of 1890," *14th Annual Report of the Bureau of Ethnology, Part II.* Washington, D.C.: Government Printing Office.

——, 1900. "Myths of the Cherokee," *19th Annual Report of the Bureau of American Ethnology, Part I.* Washington, D.C.: Government Printing Office, pp. 3–548.

——, 1932. *The Swimmer Manuscript: Cherokee Sacred Formulas and Medicinal Prescriptions.* Revised, completed, and edited by FRANS M. OLBRECHTS. (Bureau of American Ethnology Bull. 99.) Washington, D.C.: Government Printing Office.

MORENO, WIGBERTO J., 1943. "Relaciones Etnológicas entre Mesoamérica y el Sureste de Estados Unidos," in *El Norte de Mexico y El Sur de Estados Unidos.* (Tercera Reunión de Mesa Redonda sobre Problemas Antropológicos de México y Centro América.) Mexico, D.F.: Castillo de Chapultepec, pp. 286–95.

MORGAN, LEWIS H., 1901. *League of the Ho-De-No Sau-Nee or Iroquois.* (Edited and annotated by HEBERT M. LLOYD.) New York: Dodd, Mead and Co. (Reprinted in paperback by Human Relations Area Files Press, 1954.)

NELSON, EDWARD W., 1899. "The Eskimo about Bering Strait," *18th Annual Report of the Bureau of American Ethnology, Part I.* Washington, D.C.: Government Printing Office, pp. 3–518.

NETTL, BRUNO, 1956. *Music in Primitive Culture.* Cambridge: Harvard University Press.

NEWCOMB, FRANC J., and REICHARD, GLADYS A., no date. *Sandpaintings of the Navajo Shooting Chant.* New York: J. J. Augustin.

NORBECK, EDWARD, 1961. *Religion in Primitive Society.* New York: Harper & Brothers.

O'BRYAN, AILEEN, 1956. *The Dîné: Origin Myths of the Navaho Indians*. (Bureau of American Ethnology Bull. 163.) Washington, D.C.: Government Printing Office.

OLIVER, SYMMES C., 1962. *Ecology and Cultural Continuity as Contributing Factors in the Social Organization of the Plains Indians*. (University of California Publications in American Archaeology and Ethnology, Vol. XLVIII, No. 1.) Berkeley: University of California Press.

OPLER, MORRIS E., 1941. *An Apache Life-Way*. Chicago: University of Chicago Press.

———, 1944. "The Jicarilla Apache Ceremonial Relay Race," *American Anthropologist*, XLVI, 75–97.

———, 1945. "The Lipan Apache Death Complex and Its Extensions," *Southwestern Journal of Anthropology*, I, 122–41.

———, 1946. "The Creative Role of Shamanism in Mescalero Apache Mythology," *Journal of American Folklore*, LIX, 268–81.

OSGOOD, CORNELIUS, 1936. *Contributions to the Ethnography of the Kutchin*. (Yale University Publications in Anthropology No. 14.) New Haven: Yale University Press.

———, 1959. *Ingalik Mental Culture*. (Yale University Publications in Anthropology No. 56.) New Haven: Yale University Press.

PARK, WILLARD Z., 1938. *Shamanism in Western North America: A Study in Cultural Relationships*. (Northwestern University Studies in the Social Sciences, No. 2.) Evanston: Northwestern University Press.

PARSONS, ELSIE C., 1927. "Witchcraft among the Pueblos: Indian or Spanish," *Man*, XXVII, 106–12; 125–28.

———, 1932. "Isleta, New Mexico," *47th Annual Report of the Bureau of American Ethnology*. Washington, D.C.: Government Printing Office, pp. 193–466.

———, 1939. *Pueblo Indian Religion*. 2 vols. Chicago: University of Chicago Press.

PAULSON, IVAR, 1961. *Schutzgeister und Gottheiten des Wildes (der Jagdtiere und Fische) in Nordeurasien*. (Stockholm Studies in Comparative Religion, No. 2.) Uppsala: Almqvist & Wiksell.

———, 1964. *The Animal Guardian: A Critical and Synthetic Review*. (Reprinted for Private Circulation from *History of Religions*, Vol. III, No. 2.) Chicago: University of Chicago Press.

PETTAZZONI, RAFFAELE, 1954. *Essays on the History of Religions*. (Studies in the History of Religions, No. 1.) Leiden.

PRUFER, OLAF H., 1964. "The Hopewell Cult," *Scientific American*, CCXI, 90–102.

RADIN, PAUL, 1914. "Religion of the North American Indians," *Journal of American Folk-Lore*, XXVII, 335–73.

——, 1923. "The Winnebago Tribe," *37th Annual Report of the Bureau of American Ethnology*. Washington, D.C.: Government Printing Office, pp. 35–550.

——, 1926. *Crashing Thunder*. New York: D. Appleton-Century Company.

——, 1937. *Primitive Religion*. New York: Viking Press. (Paperback, New York: Dover Publications, Inc., 1957.)

——, 1948. *Winnebago Hero Cycles: A Study in Aboriginal Literature*. (Indiana University Publications in Anthropology and Linguistics, Memoir No. 1 of the International Journal of American Linguistics.) Baltimore: Waverly Press, Inc.

——, 1950. *The Origin Myth of the Medicine Rite: Three Versions. The Historical Origins of the Medicine Rite*. (Indiana University Publications in Anthropology and Linguistics, Memoir No. 3 of the International Journal of American Linguistics.) Baltimore: Waverly Press, Inc.

——, 1953. *The World of Primitive Man*. New York: Henry Schuman, Inc.

——, 1956. *The Trickster: A Study in American Indian Mythology*. New York: Philosophical Library.

RAPOPORT, ROBERT N., 1954. *Changing Navaho Religious Values*. (Papers of the Peabody Museum of American Archaeology and Ethnology, Vol. XLI, No. 2.) Cambridge: Peabody Museum of American Archaeology and Ethnology.

RAY, VERNE F. (ed.), 1957. *Cultural Stability and Cultural Change*. (Proceedings of the 1957 Annual Spring Meeting of the American Ethnological Society.) Seattle: University of Washington Press.

REICHARD, GLADYS A., 1921. "Literary Types and Dissemination of Myths," *Journal of American Folk-Lore*, XXXIV, 269–307.

——, 1934. *Spider Woman*. New York: The Macmillan Company.

——, 1939a. *Dezba, Woman of the Desert*. New York: J. J. Augustin.

——, 1939b. *Navajo Medicine Man*. New York: J. J. Augustin.

——, 1950. *Navaho Religion*. 2 vols. New York: Pantheon Books, Inc.

RÓHEIM, GÉZA, 1952. "Culture Hero and Trickster in North American Mythology," in *Indian Tribes in Aboriginal America*, ed. SOL TAX. (Selected Papers of the XXIXth International Congress of Americanists.) Chicago: University of Chicago Press.

RUSSELL, FRANK, 1908. "The Pima Indians," *26th Annual Report of the Bureau of American Ethnology*. Washington, D.C.: Government Printing Office, pp. 3–389.

SAHAGÚN, FRAY BERNARDINO DE, 1953. *The Florentine Codex, Book* 7. Translated by ARTHUR J. O. ANDERSON and CHARLES E. DIBBLE. (Monographs of the School of American Research, No. 14, Part 8.) Santa Fe.

SCHOOLCRAFT, HENRY R., 1851–57. *Historical and Statistical Information Respecting the History, Condition and Prospects of the Indian Tribes of the United States.* 6 vols. Philadelphia: Lippincott Gambo.

SCHUSTER, CARL, 1952. "A Survival of the Eurasiatic Animal Style in Modern Alaskan Eskimo Art," in *Indian Tribes of Aboriginal America*, ed. SOL TAX. (Selected Papers of the XXIXth International Congress of Americanists.) Chicago: University of Chicago Press, pp. 35–45.

SEARS, W. H., 1960. "The Gulf Coastal Plain in North American Prehistory," in *Selected Papers of the Fifth International Congress of Anthropological and Ethnological Sciences, September, 1956*, ed. ANTHONY F. C. WALLACE. Philadelphia: University of Pennsylvania Press, pp. 632–38.

——, 1964. "The Southeastern United States," in *Prehistoric Man in the New World*, eds. JESSE D. JENNINGS and EDWARD NORBECK. (Rice University Semicentennial Publications.) Chicago: University of Chicago Press, pp. 259–87.

SEBEOK, THOMAS A. (ed.), 1955. "Myth: A Symposium," *Journal of American Folklore*, Vol. LXVIII, No. 270.

SHIMONY, ANNEMARIE ANROD, 1961. *Conservatism among the Iroquois at the Six Nations Reserve.* (Yale University Publications in Anthropology, No. 65.) New Haven: Yale University Press.

SKINNER, A., 1924. *The Mascoutens or Prairie Potawatomi Indians.* (Bulletin of the Public Museum of the City of Milwaukee, Vol. VI, No. 1.) Milwaukee.

SKINNER, ALANSON, 1923. *Observations on the Ethnology of the Sauk Indians.* (Bulletin of the Public Museum of the City of Milwaukee, Vol. V, No. 1.) Milwaukee.

SLOTKIN, J. S., 1956. *The Peyote Religion: A Study in Indian-White Relations.* Glencoe: Free Press.

SMITH, C. EARLE, JR., and MacNEISH, RICHARD S., 1964. "Antiquity of American Polyploid Cotton," *Science*, 143, 675–76.

SPECK, FRANK G., 1919. *Penobscot Shamanism.* (Memoirs of the American Anthropological Association, Vol. VI, No. 4.) Menasha, Wis.

——, 1935. *Naskapi.* Norman: University of Oklahoma Press.

——, 1937. *Oklahoma Delaware Ceremonies, Dances and Feasts.* (Memoirs of the American Philosophical Society, VII.) Philadelphia.

——, 1940. *Penobscot Man.* Philadelphia: University of Pennsylvania Press.

——, 1949. *Midwinter Rites of the Cayuga Long House.* Philadelphia: University of Pennsylvania Press.

SPENCER, KATHERINE, 1957. *Mythology and Values: An Analysis of Navaho Chantway Myths.* Philadelphia: American Folklore Society.

SPENCER, ROBERT F., 1959. *The North Alaskan Eskimo: A Study in Ecol-*

ogy and Society. (Bureau of American Ethnology Bull. 171.) Washington, D.C.: Government Printing Office.

SPICER, EDWARD H. (ed.), 1961. *Perspectives in American Indian Culture Change*. Chicago: University of Chicago Press.

———, 1962. *Cycles of Conquest*. Tucson: University of Arizona Press.

SPIER, LESLIE, 1921. *The Sun Dance of the Plains Indians: Its Development and Diffusion*. (Anthropological Papers of the American Museum of Natural History, Vol. XVI, Part 7.) New York.

———, 1928. *Havasupai Ethnography*. (Anthropological Papers of the American Museum of Natural History, Vol. XXIX, Part 3.) New York.

STEFÁNSSON, V., 1913. *My Life with the Eskimo*. New York: The Macmillan Company.

STEVENSON, JAMES, 1891. "Ceremonial of Hasjelti Dailjis and Mythical Sand Painting of the Navajo Indians," *8th Annual Report of the Bureau of Ethnology*. Washington, D.C.: Government Printing Office, pp. 229–85.

STEVENSON, MATILDA C., 1894. "The Sia," *11th Annual Report of the Bureau of Ethnology*. Washington, D.C.: Government Printing Office, pp. 3–157.

———, 1904. "The Zuñi Indians: The Mythology, Esoteric Societies, and Ceremonies," *23rd Annual Report of the Bureau of American Ethnology*. Washington, D.C.: Government Printing Office.

STEWART, KENNETH M., 1946. "Spirit Possession in Native America," *Southwestern Journal of Anthropology*, II, 323–39.

STEWART, OMER C., 1948. *Ute Peyotism*. (University of Colorado Studies, Series in Anthropology No. 1.) Boulder.

STRONG, WILLIAM D., 1929. *Aboriginal Society in Southern California*. (University of California Publications in American Archaeology and Ethnology, Vol. XXVI.) Berkeley: University of California Press.

SWANTON, JOHN R., 1905. *Haida Texts and Myths*. (Bureau of American Ethnology Bull. 29.) Washington, D.C.: Government Printing Office.

———, 1911. *Indian Tribes of the Lower Mississippi Valley and Adjacent Coast of the Gulf of Mexico*. (Bureau of American Ethnology Bull. 43.) Washington, D.C.: Government Printing Office.

———, 1928a. "Religious Beliefs and Medical Practices of the Creek Indians," *42nd Annual Report of the Bureau of American Ethnology*. Washington, D.C.: Government Printing Office, pp. 473–672.

———, 1928b. "Social and Religious Beliefs and Usages of the Chickasaw Indians," *44th Annual Report of the Bureau of American Ethnology*. Washington, D.C.: Government Printing Office, pp. 169–273.

———, 1928c. "Social Organization and Social Usages of the Indians of the Creek Confederacy," *42nd Annual Report of the Bureau of American Ethnology*. Washington, D.C.: Government Printing Office, pp. 23–472.

SWANTON, JOHN R., 1931. *Source Material for the Social and Ceremonial Life of the Choctaw Indians.* (Bureau of American Ethnology Bull. 103.) Washington, D.C.: Government Printing Office.

———, 1946. *The Indians of the Southeastern United States.* (Bureau of American Ethnology Bull. 137.) Washington, D.C.: Government Printing Office.

TAX, SOL (ed.), 1952. *Indian Tribes of Aboriginal America.* (Selected Papers of the XXIXth International Congress of Americanists.) Chicago: University of Chicago Press.

TEICHER, MORTON I., 1960. *Windigo Psychosis: A Study of a Relationship between Belief and Behavior among the Indians of Northeastern Canada.* (Proceedings of the 1960 Annual Spring Meeting of the American Ethnological Society.) Seattle: University of Washington Press.

THOMPSON, J. ERIC, 1933. *Mexico before Cortez.* New York: Charles Scribner's Sons.

THOMPSON, LAURA, 1950. *Culture in Crisis: A Study of the Hopi Indians.* New York: Harper & Brothers.

THOMPSON, STITH, 1929. *Tales of the North American Indians.* Cambridge: Harvard University Press.

TOOKER, ELISABETH, 1964. *An Ethnography of the Huron Indians, 1615–1649.* (Bureau of American Ethnology Bull. 190.) Washington, D.C.: Government Printing Office.

TYLOR, SIR EDWARD B., 1889. *Primitive Culture.* 2 vols. 3d American edition. New York: Henry Holt and Company.

UNDERHILL, RUTH M., 1936. "The Battle at Spirit Mountain," in *The Masterkey,* Vol. X. Translated from the Mohave. Los Angeles: Southwest Museum, pp. 10–14.

———, 1938. *Singing for Power.* Berkeley: University of California Press.

———, 1939. *The Social Organization of the Papago Indians.* (Columbia University Contributions to Anthropology, Vol. XXX.) New York: Columbia University Press.

———, 1946. *Papago Indian Religion.* (Columbia University Contributions to Anthropology, Vol. XXXIII.) New York: Columbia University Press.

———, 1948. *Ceremonial Patterns in the Greater Southwest.* (American Ethnological Society Monographs, Vol. XIII.) New York: J. J. Augustin.

VAILLANT, GEORGE C., 1947. *Aztecs of Mexico.* Garden City: Doubleday & Company, Inc.

VOEGELIN, ERMINIE W., 1944. *Mortuary Customs of the Shawnee and Other Eastern Tribes.* (Prehistory Research Series, Vol. II, No. 4.) Indianapolis: Indiana Historical Society.

VOTH, H. R., 1903. *The Oraibi Summer Snake Ceremony*. (Field Columbian Museum Publications No. 83, Anthropological Series, Vol. III, No. 4.) Chicago.

——, 1912. *The Oraibi Marau Ceremony*. (Field Museum of Natural History Publications No. 156, Anthropological Series, Vol. XI, No. 1.) Chicago.

WALLACE, ANTHONY F. C., 1956. "Revitalization Movements," *American Anthropologist*, LVIII, 264–81.

WALLACE, ERNEST, and HOEBEL, E. ADAMSON, 1952. *The Comanches, Lords of the South Plains*. Norman: University of Oklahoma Press.

WATERMAN, T. T., 1930. "The Paraphernalia of the Duwamish 'Spirit-Canoe' Ceremony," *Indian Notes*, VII. New York: Heye Foundation, pp. 129–48; 295–312; 535–61.

WEBSTER, HUTTON, 1942. *Taboo: A Sociological Study*. Stanford: Stanford University Press.

——, 1948. *Magic: A Sociological Study*. Stanford: Stanford University Press.

WEYER, EDWARD M., JR., 1932. *The Eskimos: Their Environment and Folkways*. New Haven: Yale University Press.

WHITE, LESLIE A., 1932. "The Acoma Indians," *47th Annual Report of the Bureau of American Ethnology*. Washington, D.C.: Government Printing Office, pp. 17–192.

——, 1962. *The Pueblo of Sia, New Mexico*. (Bureau of American Ethnology Bull. 184.) Washington, D.C.: Government Printing Office.

WHITING, BEATRICE B., 1950. *Paiute Sorcery*. (Viking Fund Publications in Anthropology No. 15.) New York: The Viking Fund, Inc.

WILLEY, GORDON R., 1962. "Mesoamerica," in *Courses toward Urban Life*, eds. ROBERT J. BRAIDWOOD and GORDON R. WILLEY. (Viking Fund Publications in Anthropology No. 32.) New York: Wenner-Gren Foundation for Anthropological Research, Inc.

WILSON, EDMUND, 1959. *Apologies to the Iroquois*. (With a study of *The Mohawks in High Steel* by JOSEPH MITCHELL.) New York: Farrar, Straus, and Cudahy.

WITTHOFT, JOHN, 1949. *Green Corn Ceremonialism in the Eastern Woodlands*. (Occasional Contributions from the Museum of Anthropology of the University of Michigan No. 13.) Ann Arbor: University of Michigan Press.

WORMINGTON, H. M., 1962. "A Survey of Early American Prehistory," *American Scientist*, L, 230–42.

WYMAN, LELAND C., 1936. "Navaho Diagnosticians," *American Anthropologist*, XXXVIII, 236–46.

WYMAN, LELAND C., 1962. *The Windways of the Navaho*. Colorado Springs: The Taylor Museum of the Colorado Springs Fine Arts Center.

WYMAN, LELAND C., HILL, W. W., and OSANAI, IVA, 1942. *Navajo Eschatology*. (University of New Mexico Bulletin, Anthropological Series, Vol. IV, No. 1.) Albuquerque.

YINGER, J. M., 1957. *Religion, Society, and the Individual*. New York: The Macmillan Company.

INDEX